Maine Coast and Islands

Maine Coast and Islands

Key to a Great Destination

Christina Tree and
Nancy English

The Countryman Press   Woodstock, Vermont

To the residents of Maine,
who take good care of the most beautiful place we know.
—NE and CT

Maine Coast and Islands: Key to a Great Destination, 3rd edition
ISBN 978-1-58157-282-7

Interior photographs by the authors unless otherwise specified
Maps by Erin Greb Cartography, © The Countryman Press
Book design by Bodenweber Design
Composition by Eugenie S. Delaney

Published by The Countryman Press, P.O. Box 748, Woodstock, VT 05091
Distributed by W. W. Norton & Company, Inc., 500 Fifth Avenue,
New York, NY 10110
Printed in the United States of America

10 9 8 7 6 5 4 3 2

Contents

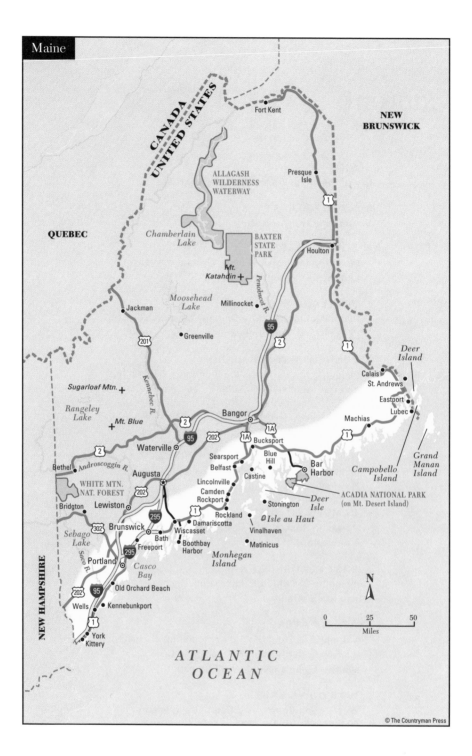

Maine

CANADA
UNITED STATES

NEW BRUNSWICK

Fort Kent

QUEBEC

ALLAGASH
WILDERNESS
WATERWAY

Presque Isle

1

Chamberlain
Lake

BAXTER
STATE
PARK

Houlton

Mt.
Katahdin

Penobscot R.

Moosehead
Lake

Millinocket

Jackman

95

Greenville

2

1

Deer
Island

201

Calais
St. Andrews

Kennebec R.

Sugarloaf Mtn.

Eastport
Lubec

Rangeley
Lake

Mt. Blue

Machias

Grand
Manan
Island

2

Bangor

1

95

202

1A

1A Bucksport

Waterville

Searsport

Blue
Hill

Bar
Harbor

Campobello
Island

2

Belfast

Castine

Bethel

Androscoggin R.

Augusta

Lincolnville

ACADIA NATIONAL PARK
(on Mt. Desert Island)

WHITE MTN.
NAT. FOREST

202

Camden
Rockport

Deer
Isle

Bridgton

Lewiston

1

Rockland

Stonington

295

Brunswick

Damariscotta

Isle au Haut

Sebago
Lake

Saco R.

Bath

Wiscasset

Vinalhaven

Freeport

Boothbay
Harbor

Matinicus

302

Portland

Casco
Bay

Monhegan
Island

N

NEW HAMPSHIRE

202

95

Old Orchard Beach

Wells

Kennebunkport

0   25   50
Miles

1

York
Kittery

ATLANTIC
OCEAN

© The Countryman Press

MAPS

Basics

LAY OF THE LAND: WATER, WATER EVERYWHERE

THE MAINE COAST IS LENGTHIER, more varied, and more accessible than most visitors assume. Kittery on Maine's southern border is officially just 211 driving miles southwest of Bar Harbor and 293 from Eastport, but the shoreline between Kittery and Eastport measures more than 4,500 miles—and some 7,000 miles if you count offshore islands.

That's more than the rest of the East Coast combined.

In contrast with much of this country's East Coast and most of the West Coast, Maine's shoreline rarely faces open ocean. With the exception of a sandy arc of land along the South Coast and a high, rocky stretch of Way Down East headlands known as the Bold Coast—both measuring less than 40 miles—the shore corkscrews in and out of coves and points, winding along bays and up wide, tidal rivers. More than a dozen ragged peninsulas extend like so many fingers south from Rt. 1,

Touring the rocky coast off Cape Elizabeth

separating the bays and rivers, notched in turn with numerous coves and harbors.

In many places islands are "hinged" to the mainland by bridges and causeways. Scientists tell us that the peninsulas and offshore islands are mountains drowned by the same glaciers that sculpted the area's many shallow (relatively)

There are plenty of places to sleep within earshot of the water; this is Coveside Bed & Breakfast.   Christina Tree

warm-water lakes. The tides shift from high to low roughly every 12 hours; these shifts are more extreme as you move northeast, measuring a difference of 9 feet in Kittery, 25 at Eastport.

Current offshore vessels tend to be leisure craft, fishing boats, and lobster boats, but for more than two centuries these waters were busy freight and passenger lanes. It's because visitors arrived primarily by water prior to the 1920s that summer resorts—from Popham Beach and Boothbay Harbor to Bar Harbor—are at the tips of peninsulas and hinged islands, miles from Rt. 1.

The Good News: This lengthy and convoluted shoreline harbors a wide choice of places to sleep as well as to walk and to eat within sound and sight of water. Access to coastal preserves has been dramatically increased in recent decades by both state and conservation groups.

The waters that splinter the coast ensure the distinctive character of the many relatively isolated communities. The feel as well as the shape of the coast changes as you travel northeast. The lightly settled and touristed region

Rock Gardens Inn   Christina Tree

Maine-Speak

Down East is a nautical term referring to the way the way the wind generally blows along the Maine coast: out of the southwest, ushering sailing vessels downwind and east. Moreover, the coast itself generally runs east more than north. This phenomenon is painfully obvious if you happen to be driving "south" on Rt. 1 at sunset. To further confuse the issue, coastal highways are labeled "north" and "south." Also: *Down* usually refers to traveling east. So instead of driving up north from Kittery to Bar Harbor, you are heading "Down East." In "Sense of Place" you discover that from the beginning of settlement the coast was divided into eastern and western Maine at the Kennebec River. However, Down East as a place is now equated only with the parts of Maine from Blue Hill Peninsula on "down."

beyond the turnoff for Bar Harbor is a very different Maine from the heavily populated and touristed South Coast. Still, the moment you cross the southern border, you know you're in Maine. Kittery and York both have their share of coves and rocky paths, and local accents are as strong as any to be found in Eastport.

The Bad News: You can't rush. The chief complaint among Maine visitors is "not enough time." The shape of the coast and the two-lane nature of Rt. 1, the coastal highway, hobble attempts to reach Acadia National Park from points south on a summer weekend, especially a long weekend.

The Key: Most visitors come to Maine for R&R. So turn off Rt. 1. Savor the salt air and the scenery in a lobster-boat-filled harbor. Slow down. Walk a shore path. Eat lobster in a real lobster pound. Talk to a local. Get out on the water ASAP.

View from the Cutty Sark Motel, York Beach
Christina Tree

REGIONS AT A GLANCE

South Coast

This 36-mile-stretch of coast accounts for 90 percent of Maine beaches. Many visitors get no farther. Family-geared lodging, from vintage motor courts to condo-style complexes, predominates. Dining options include some of the state's foremost restaurants as well as plenty of places to eat lobster, ice cream, and saltwater taffy. You'll find summer theater and a fine art museum in Ogunquit (ogunquit .org); a glimpse of colonial times in The Museums of Old York (oldyork.org); and

The Pier at Old Orchard Beach

Nancy English

Ram Island Lighthouse sits off the coast of Cape Elizabeth.

Nancy English

a sense of the shipbuilding era in the fine old sea captains' houses in Kennebunk-port (visitthekennebunks.com), as well as a fine Seashore Trolley Museum (trolley museum.org). There are brand-name outlets in Kittery (thekitteryoutlets.com), along with boardwalks in York Beach (gatewaytomaine.org) and Old Orchard Beach (oldorchardbeachmaine.com). Everywhere is the promise of endless sand. Luckily the lay of the land—salt marsh, estuarine reserves, and other wetlands—limits commercial clutter.

Portland and Casco Bay

Lively, walkable, sophisticated, Maine's largest city is also a working port facing an island-studded bay. Visitors head for the Portland Museum of Art (portland

Weatherbeaten, c. 1916, by Winslow Homer
Portland Museum of Art, bequest of Charles Shipman Payson

The Lobster Shack at Two Lights, Cape Elizabeth   Nancy English

museum.org) and then down Congress St. to the Old Port (visitportland.com), more than five square blocks built exuberantly during the city's peak shipping era and now laced with restaurants, cafés, shops, and galleries. From the waterfront Casco Bay Line (cascobay lines.com) ferries ply the bay, stopping at islands. Beyond the Old Port the two sights not to miss are Portland Head Light (portlandheadlight.com) in Fort Williams Park on Cape Elizabeth, and Portland Observatory (portlandland marks.org) on Munjoy Hill. Less than 20 miles north of Portland, Freeport (freeportusa.com) is Maine's premier shopping destination, anchored by L.L. Bean (llbean.com), open 24 hours, surrounded by 74 more upscale outlets.

Midcoast

The 100 miles of Rt. 1 between Brunswick and Bucksport are generally equated with Maine's Midcoast—but this region's depth is far greater. It extends south from Rt. 1 to the tips of roughly a dozen peninsulas and attached islands, 10 miles at Boothbay Harbor (boothbayharbor.com), a dozen to Pemaquid Point's famed lighthouse

New Harbor   Christina Tree

Rockland Harbor Trail

Christina Tree

(lighthousefoundation.org), as well as inland to river and lake towns. Inviting old communities, all with lodging, dining, and shopping, anchor Rt. 1. Brunswick (brunswickdowntown.org) offers summer theater, music, and the Bowdoin College (bowdoin.edu) museums. In Bath (visitbath.com) the Maine Maritime Museum (mainemaritimemuseum.org) is a must-see. Wiscasset (midcoastmaine .com) is known for antiques and Damariscotta (damariscottaregion.com), for oysters. Rockland (mainedreamvacation.com)—home to the Farnsworth Museum and Wyeth Center (farnsworthmuseum.org)—is also the departure point for most Windjammers (sailmainecoast.com) and Maine State Ferries (exploremaine.org). With its sea captains' houses and antiques shops Camden (visitcamden.com) is a justly famous resort, while Belfast (belfastmaine.org) and Searsport, home to the Penobscot Marine Museum (penobscotmarinemuseum.org), both evoke Maine's seafaring era.

East Penobscot

The dramatic new Penobscot Narrows Bridge (maine.gov/observatory) visually underscores the sense of turning a major coastal corner. From its observatory, 43 stories above the Penobscot River, you look off down Penobscot Bay and across the green shoreline curving eastward. What you see is the Blue Hill Peninsula (bluehillpeninsula.org) and a land finger with Castine (castine.me.us) at its tip. Deer Isle and Stonington (deerisle.com) straggle south from Blue Hill, off beyond the horizon. Here the intermingling of land and water creates a landscape that's exceptional, even in Maine. It's seasonal home to the state's largest concentration of artists and craftspeople, writers and musicians. While the major villages all offer fine galleries, studios are also salted along scenic roads, which lead to numerous preserves with water views.

Stonington Harbor

Christina Tree

Acadia Area

Mount Desert (pronounced *des-sert*) is New England's second largest island, one conveniently linked to the mainland south of Ellsworth (ellsworthchamber.org) by a causeway and bridge. Two-fifths of its 108 square miles are maintained as Acadia National Park (nps.gov/acad), laced with roads geared to touring by car; you'll also find more than 45 miles of "carriage roads" reserved for biking and skiing and 130 miles of hiking trails, with 12 miles reclaimed from neglect and newly opened. The beauty of "MDI" cannot be overstated. Twenty-six mountains rise abruptly from the sea and from the shores of four lakes. Mount Cadillac, at 1,532 feet, is the highest point on the U.S. Atlantic seaboard. Its broad summit, accessible by car, is said to offer the first view of sunrise in the United States, but it attracts a larger crowd at

View from The Claremont Hotel, Southwest Harbor

Christina Tree

The Bubbles at Jordan Pond

Nancy English

sunset. The island seems larger than it is because it's almost bisected by Somes Sound, a natural fjord dividing it nearly in two. On one side is the lively resort village of Bar Harbor (barharbormaine.com), gateway to Acadia; on the other are the more laid-back yachting villages of Northeast (mountdesertchamber.org) and Southwest Harbors (acadiachamber.com), along with the more workaday fishing village of Bass Harbor.

At the junction of Rts. 3 and 1 in Ellsworth, it's Rt. 3 that shoots straight ahead toward Bar Harbor and Rt. 1 that angles off, the road less taken. The 27 miles of Rt. 1 that begin at the Hancock/Sullivan Bridge and loop around Schoodic Peninsula (acadia-schoodic.org) to Winter Harbor are a National Scenic Byway, while the drive around Schoodic Point is a part of Acadia National Park. During summer months a passenger ferry links Winter and Bar Harbors, connecting on both ends with the free Island Explorer (exploreacadia.com) bus service.

View from Lubec

Christina Tree

Way Down East
Sadly, few tourists continue on down Rt. 1 into Washington County, a bleakly beautiful landscape of thick pine forests, blueberry barrens, and 700 miles of coast with dramatic cliffs and deep tidal bays carved by the highest tides on the eastern seaboard. Pickups outnumber cars, and lobster boats way outnumber pleasure craft. History

Town Dock, Eastport

Christina Tree

LEFT: Never know what you'll find at the 45th Parallel gift shop, Route 1 east of Eastport. RIGHT: Downtown Eastport   Christina Tree

is glimpsed in the graceful 1818 Ruggles House (ruggleshouse.org) in Columbia Falls, the 1770s Burnham Tavern (burnhamtavern.com) in Machias (machias chamber.org), and Roosevelt Campobello International Park (fdr.net), accessed from Lubec (westquoddy.com). Birders head out from Cutler (boldcoast.com) to Machias Seal Island for a close-up view of puffins. Eastport (eastportchamber .net), 82 miles northeast of Bar Harbor, draws artists with its northern light, fine architecture, and end-of-the-world feel.

Islands

There are 4,617 coastal Maine islands, but just 14 now support year-round communities, compared with 300 in the 19th century. Overnight lodging can be found on Chebeague Island (chebeague.org), Peaks Island (peaksisland.info), and Long Island (chestnuthillinn.com) in Casco Bay, accessible from Portland. The major island destinations are Monhegan, Vinalhaven, North Haven, Isle au Haut, Swan's Island, and Campobello. Each is different, but all share a community closeness and a way of welcoming visitors on their own terms. Monhegan, 11 miles out to sea, is barely a square mile, with less than 70 year-round residents. It attracts the largest number of day-trippers, thanks to excursion boats from Boothbay Harbor and New Harbor as well as ferries from Port Clyde. It also offers the widest choice of island lodging, including two vintage summer hotels. It has attracted prominent artists since the 1850s. Most of the island has been preserved as common space, laced by 17 miles of walking trails.

The islands with overnight lodging that are most easily accessed by frequent Maine State Ferry (exploremaine.org) service are Vinalhaven (vinalhaven.org) and North Haven (nebolodge.com). Both are roughly a dozen miles from Rockland but separated from each other by a narrow passage. Vinalhaven is Maine's largest offshore island and supports its largest year-round community and lobster fleet. Here visitors find food and lodging in Carver's Harbor, a quarter-mile walk from the ferry. Half the size, North Haven is summer home to some of the country's wealthiest families; the few shops and restaurants are within steps of the dock. On Mount Desert you can day-trip from Bass Harbor to Swan's Island (swansisland .com) and Frenchboro (bassharborcruises.com). Easily accessible from Northeast Harbor and Southwest Harbor, Little Cranberry Island (islesford.com) offers good food, a museum, and galleries as well as views.

Monhegan   Liam Davis

North Haven

MAKING PLANS

If You Have Just a Weekend
Pick a South Coast resort. Visit Portland.

If You Have a Week
The average initial visit to Maine is five days, just long enough to decide where you might want to spend more time on your next trip. More than 80 percent of first-time visitors return.

Putting your feet up on the balcony of a room at the Tidewater, Vinalhaven   Christina Tree

Maine's most popular resort towns—Ogunquit, Old Orchard Beach, Kennebunkport, Boothbay Harbor, and Camden—offer the lion's share of coastal lodging and are spaced like a giant's stepping-stones on the way to Bar Harbor. Spend a night or two on the South Coast, a day in Portland, and then a couple of nights along the Midcoast on your way to Acadia National Park. If you want to get off the beaten track (Rt. 1), pick a peninsula or two to explore on the way to or from Mount Desert. If you really want a sense of Maine, spend a night or two (don't just day-trip) on Monhegan or Vinalhaven, and/or continue beyond Mount Desert to Lubec and Eastport.

But everyone is different. For six suggested itineraries, see the end of this chapter.

Timing
High season along the Maine coast is short: July 4 through Labor Day. Please note that many of the places we list in this guide are seasonal. Many close on Labor

Morning fog at Rock Gardens Inn

Christina Tree

Day. Many more in summer resort areas close at the end of Columbus Day weekend. Call ahead if you are driving a distance to a weather-dependent destination or
in spring or fall.

Lodging is easier and sometimes cheaper midweek, even in August. If you do
want an August weekend at a modest price, reserve far ahead. June can be glorious
but weather is chancier, and many visitors book at the last minute. September days
are golden and generally clear; most seasonal businesses stay open through Columbus Day.

Portland attracts visitors year-round; in November they tend to stop en route
at outlets in Kittery and push on to those in Freeport. January through April is
off-season—and with reason—although there's a certain romance to a cozy inns
by the sea, especially popular around Valentine's Day. In May alewives return to
Damariscotta and beach-walkers, to the South Coast.

Weather and What to Bring

Weather is something you notice more in Maine than most places because it's
literally in your face. The sun can be shining brightly along Rt. 1 while a nearby
beach, peninsula point, or island is shrouded in fog. Even in August temperatures
can begin down along the frost line and soar by midday, only to plunge again at
night. It's the Labrador Current from Canada that cools the ocean here, chilling
the water to below comfort level for most of us but also bringing that refreshing
breeze. Tote a light backpack to shed or add clothing. Maine is all about comfort.
Wear a visor or baseball cap, even if you never do ordinarily. Don't be shy about
wearing a wool cap and gloves out on the water. Windbreakers, lightweight pants,
and comfortable shoes are acceptable dress in most restaurants. Don't forget to
pack your camera and binoculars.

If you plan to visit to visit Roosevelt Campobello International Park

Information Sources

The **Maine Office of Tourism** maintains visitmaine.com and a 24-hour information line (888-624-6345) that connects with a live call center. Request the thick, helpful, four-season guide *Maine Invites You* (accompanied by a Maine highway map). The guide is published by the **Maine Tourism Association** (207-623-0363; mainetourism.com). The MTA also maintains well-stocked and -staffed welcome centers with restrooms, most with WiFi. Its southern gateway center at **Kittery** (207-439-1319) on I-95 northbound (also accessible from Rt. 1) is a must place to stop. Others are found in **Yarmouth** on Rt. 1 just off-295, Exit 17 (207-846-0833); in **West Gardiner** at the I-95 service plaza, also accessible from I-295 (207-582-0160); in **Hampden** near Bangor on I-95 both northbound and southbound (207-862-6628/38); and in **Calais** (207-454-2211) at 39 Union St., geared to southbound visitors.

(fdr.net) on Campobello Island, you also need a passport or passport card (see getyouhome.gov).

TRANSPORTATION

Getting There

By Air

Portland International Jetport (207-774-7301; portlandjetport.org) is connected by major carriers to destinations throughout the country and Canada. Just off I-95, it offers all the major rental cars, also taxi and bus service into Portland.

U.S. Customs, Lubec   Christina Tree

Bangor International Airport (207-947-0384; flybangor.com) is the closest major airport to Bar Harbor with connections to East Coast destinations. Bar Harbor Airport (bhbairport.com) offers connections via Cape Air to Logan. Knox County Regional Airport (knoxcounty.midcoast.com/departments/airports) is in Rockland.

Logan International Airport in Boston (loganinternationalairport.com) offers the widest choice of both domestic and international flights, and Manchester /Boston Regional Airport (flymanchester.com) is also worth checking; both are linked by Mermaid Transport (gomermaid.com) and Concord Coach Lines (concordcoachlines.com) with Portland.

By Train

Amtrak's Downeaster (amtrakdowneaster.com) offers frequent daily roundtrips between Boston's North Station and Portland's rail-bus station just off I-95. It's 2½ hours each way and the way a train ride should be: comfortable and scenic.

The first Maine stop is in Wells; then Saco, just beyond the mighty falls; and Old Orchard Beach, within walking distance of the sand and the amusement park. Beyond Portland the line extends another 30 miles east, with stops in Freeport near L.L. Bean and steps from outlet shops, and in downtown Brunswick, within walking distance of Bowdoin College.

Amtrak's Downeaster links Portland with Boston.   Christina Tree

By Bus

Concord Coach Lines (800-639-3317; concordcoachlines.com) serves Portland (where its terminal adjoins Amtrak's), Brunswick, Bath, Wiscasset, Damariscotta, Waldoboro, Rockland, Camden, Belfast, and Searsport. It also offers a popular express from Boston's Logan Airport and South Station to Portland (where the terminal also serves Amtrak), and on to Bangor. Greyhound Bus Lines (800-231-2222; greyhound.com) also links Boston with Portland (where the terminal is old and grungy), Brunswick, and Bangor. The seasonal Bar Harbor Shuttle (207-479-5911; barharborbangorshuttle.com) links both Concord Coach and Greyhound terminals in Bangor with Bar Harbor. West's Coastal Connection (800-565-2823; westbusservice.com) offers a similar service to Machias and Perry (the Rt. 1 turn-off for Eastport) with flag-down stops in between.

By Car

Most Maine visitors come by car or pick up a rental as soon as they arrive. Check airport websites for rental options.

GETTING AROUND

Highways

The first thing you notice about I-95 in Maine is the way exits are numbered. Each represents mileage from the southern border at Kittery. I-95 becomes the Maine Turnpike (maineturnpike.com) in Kittery, site of a welcome center maintained by the Maine Tourism Association (mainetourism.com). It's stocked with handouts on everything to see and do in the state, operated by knowledgeable staffers, and offers restrooms, maps, pine-shaded picnic tables, and vending machines. Tollbooths begin in York (Exit 7). The first and only service area for coastal travelers is at Kennebunk. The turnpike extends 100 miles, turning inland beyond Portland. Exit 44 puts you on I-295, which takes you another 17 highway miles. Just the first 76 miles of Maine's coastal routes are multilane highway. At I-295, Exit 28, you hit Rt. 1, the mostly two-lane highway for the remaining 217 miles to Eastport. After several initial stoplights there are few traffic signals along its length.

For Traffic Updates

Check the Maine DOT website: 511.maine.gov. Or call 511 or 866-282-7578.

Maps

The state map is free but not great. The AAA map for Northern New England is a step up. Sooner or later Maine explorers pick up *The Maine Atlas and Gazetteer* (DeLorme), available throughout the state.

Are We There Yet?

Boston to Portland: 108 miles, average 2 hours.

    Portland to Bar Harbor: 175 miles, theoretically 31/2 hours but good luck!

Shortcuts

I-295, Exit 28 for Brunswick, puts you on Coastal Rt. 1. During peak travel times, you might want to avoid the backup in Brunswick and take I-295, Exit 32, instead. Follow signs for Rt. 1 and stick to middle lanes on Rt. 196.

    Around Rockland: Take Rt. 90 off Rt. 1 in West Warren to Rockport, just south of Camden.

    To Belfast East and Blue Hill/Deer Isle: I-295 to Augusta to I-95 to Exit 113 (Rt. 3) to Belfast, then Rt. 1 east to Rt. 15.

    Quickest way to Bar Harbor: Either the above route or Exit I-95 in Bangor to I-395 to Rt. 1A.

Car-Free

Check out the Maine Department of Transportation's website (exploremaine.org) for airport sites; train, private, and state ferry schedules; and local bus shuttles. *Suggestions:* Take Amtrak's Downeaster (amtrakdowneaster.com) to Wells and use Shoreline Explorer (shorelineexplorer.com) trolleys and buses to access lodging and beaches. The Downeaster also sets you within walking distance of lodging and beach in Old Orchard and at a station with frequent shuttle service to downtown Portland, from which Casco Bay Line Ferries (cascobaylines.com) tour the bay. Beyond Portland, the Downeaster also stops in Freeport—within walking distance of L.L. Bean and the outlets—and in downtown Brunswick, within walking distance of lodging and of Bowdoin museums. Concord Coach (concordcoachlines .com) drops you in Rockland at the ferry terminal; from there you'll find frequent service to Vinalhaven and North Haven (both navigable by bike). Fly or bus to Bar Harbor and use the peerless Island Explorer (exploreacadia.com) free bus to get around.

Excursion Trains

Maine Eastern Railroad (866-637-2457; maineeasternrailroad.com) is a seasonal, shoreline excursion train running 54 miles between Brunswick and Rockland, stopping regularly in Bath and Wiscasset, connecting in Brunswick with Amtrak's Downeaster from Boston. From Ellsworth, Downeast Scenic Rail (207-667-7819; downeastscenicrail.org) offers a tranquil excursion inland.

Amtrak and Maine Eastern both serve Brunswick.   Christina Tree

Ferries

Check exploremaine.org for state ferries (see *Islands*, above). The site also offers an overview of both public and private ferries. The major private companies include Casco Bay Lines (cascobaylines.com), based in Portland; Monhegan Boat Line (monheganboat .com) in Port Clyde; Isle au Haut Ferry Service (isleauhaut.com) in Stonington; and seasonal East Coast Ferries (eastcoastferries.nb.ca) linking Eastport with New Brunswick. The ferry to Nova Scotia resumed in 2014, during the summer only, now run by Nova Star Cruises (www.novastarcruises.com). The trip from Portland to Yarmouth, Nova Scotia, takes 11 hours and departs at 9 PM. The return trip from Canada departs at 10 AM.

By Schooner

Rockland and Camden (both served by bus) are departure points for Maine Windjammer cruises (sailmainecoast .com) throughout Penobscot Bay. The world's largest fleet of passenger-carrying coastal schooners, these Windjammers are graceful tall ships, most individually owned. Many are

Maine State Ferry at Vinalhaven   Christina Tree

East Coast Ferry from Eastport to Deer Island, NB   Christina Tree

The last fishing schooner built in New England—now a great way to sail.

Fred LeBlanc, courtesy Maine Windjammer Asssociation

19th-century vessels, some restored by their present captains. Most carry less than 30 passengers and offer sails ranging from overnight to nine days in Penobscot Bay and beyond, usually stopping to go ashore in small villages and on islands. The schedule is determined by wind and current. Vessels vary in size, ambience, policies, and price. Check the website. Inquire about special-event sailings.

Suggested Itinerary

FOR ART LOVERS

Artists lured Maine's early tourists, and both traditional landscape and contemporary art here continue to be outstanding. Portland and Rockland are home to the coast's two major art museums; both communities support numerous galleries and host Art Walks on the first Friday of each month. Check out artwalkmaine.org, a website detailing Art Walks in no less than 18 towns, including Bar Harbor, Bath,

Farnsworth Art Museum, Rockland
Courtesty, Farnsworth Art Museum

Monhegan Houses, c. 1916, by Edward Hopper   Portland Museum of Art, Bernstein Acquisition Fund

Belfast, Biddeford, Boothbay Harbor, Brunswick, Wiscasset, Stonington, and Eastport.

Portland First Friday Art Walks (firstfridayartwalk.com) fill the sidewalks of Congress St. with gallerygoers, and the Portland Museum of Art (portlandmuseum.org) is free. The event is the brainchild of Andres Verzosa of Aucocisco Galleries (aucocisco.com), always a worthwhile stop. Maine College of Art's own gallery, The Institute of Contemporary Art at the Maine College of Art (meca .edu), presents contemporary exhibits, with lectures and workshops. Salt Institute for Documentary Studies (salt.edu) depicts aspects of Maine life. Space Gallery (space538.org) presents unconventional art. Many more venues exhibit artwork, from coffee shops to shops with artisan and craftswork for sale.

Rockland Art Walks are supported by more than 20 galleries, anchored by

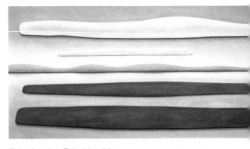

Painting by Eric Hopkins   Eric Hopkins Gallery, Rockland

View of Penobscot Bay from Caterpillar Hill, Sedgwick   Painting by Jill Hoy.

Evening sketch on Vinalhaven   Christina Tree

Stonington Harbor is a popular subject for artists.

Christina Tree

the Farnsworth Art Museum and Wyeth Center (farnsworthmuseum.org), which offers free admission every Wednesday evening as well as on first Fridays. The Farnsworth's permanent collection exhibits Maine's iconic artists from the 19th through 20th centuries and contemporary artists; changing exhibits vary. Rockland's leading galleries include Caldbeck Gallery (caldbeck.com); Harbor Square Gallery (harborsquaregallery.com), filling three floors of a 1912 building at 374 Main St.; and Archipelago Fine Arts (thearchipelago.net) at the Island Institute, representing some 300 artists and craftspeople on Maine islands.

Smaller and seasonal but significant gallery clusters are found in the villages of Blue Hill, Deer Isle, and Stonington, all spaced along Rt. 15 as it winds down the peninsula and linked islands that define eastern rim of Penobscot Bay. Standouts include Jud Hartmann Gallery (judhartmanngallery.com) in Blue Hill and the Turtle (turtlegallery.com) in Deer Isle. In Stonington—which also observes first Fridays with receptions at some dozen galleries July through October—look for the Jill Hoy (jillhoy.com), gWatson (gwatsongallery.com), and Isalos Fine Art (isalosfineart.com) galleries.

The island of Monhegan, the subject of many of Maine's most famous paintings, continues to draw summer artists from throughout the country. Their work is showcased in the Lupine Gallery (lupinegallerymonhegan.com) near the ferry landing. Pick up a map/guide to the studios of roughly 20 resident artists who welcome visitors.

Suggested Itinerary

Long Sands Beach, York Beach   Nancy English

FOR BEACHCOMBERS

The coastline of southern Maine offers some classic vistas of endless sand, a few beaches that stretch past the horizon, and several curved beaches that embrace ocean waves. Long Sands Beach in York Beach is a 2-mile arc of gray sand with good-sized ocean waves, bordered by sand that's wide at low tide and narrow at high, backed by parking spots along a street lined with summer rentals. Restaurants, shops, and old-style amusements cluster at the far end of the beach. A 7-mile stretch that draws a crowd is Old Orchard Beach, with its centerpiece Pier and its famous french fries, bars, and restaurants. The Amtrak Downeaster from Boston to Portland stops right in the middle of the beach. You might want to seach out B&Bs or rentals in the quiet stretch of this sand, backed by the historic summer community of Ocean Park (oceanpark.org).

Gooch's Beach in Kennebunk offers a view of Kennebunk River traffic at one end, and is a favorite spot for surfers. Buy a beach parking permit at the town offices or the police station, or at the chamber of commerce. Goose Rocks Beach,

A day at the beach at Reid State Park   Christina Tree

at the northern end of Kennebunkport's coastline (Kennebunk is south of the river, Kennebunkport north), is secluded and peaceful just off Rt. 9, but a parking permit is required from the Kennebunkport Police Station.

If you would just as soon skip Maine's prime beach resorts but still like to walk long beaches and are curious to test the waves, two neighboring Midcoast peninsulas offer inviting options. Check out Popham Beach State Park and Reid State Park on neighboring peninsulas south of Bath.

Suggested Itinerary

FOR BIRDERS

Warblers, chickadees, cardinals, starlings, and crows love the busy South Coast, and the northern thrush, vireo, boreal chickadee, and gray jay can be seen, with luck. Along the ocean the great blue heron can rise from a salt marsh anywhere from Peaks Island off Portland to Machias. Kingfishers dive for fish by Tenants Harbor near Pemaquid Point, bald eagles coast serene as the air itself on the Bagaduce River near Blue Hill, and ospreys bring dinner back to their nests off the docks at Robinhood Marina south of Bath.

Maine's destination birding season begins with a May Wings, Waves and Woods Festival in Deer Isle (deerisle .com), then a Spring Birding Festival (downeastbirdfest.org), celebrated Memorial Day weekend in the Lubec area with self-guided and guided hikes; the Acadia Birding Festival (acadia birdingfestival.com) takes place the following week. June and July are prime months for viewing puffins up close on Machias Seal Island (see *Puffin-Watching*), accessed from nearby Cutler. In September hawks circle lazily above Mount Agamenticus in York, and birders flock to Monhegan Island to record the fall migration. Throughout the year check with Maine Audubon (maineaudubon.org). It's based at Gisland Farm in Falmouth, with programs in Scarborough Marsh, Merrymeeting Bay, and weeklong summer programs at Hog Island Audubon Camp near New Harbor, which is also the departure point for Hardy Boat Cruises circling Egg Rock (again, see *Puffin-Watching*). View or download a superb free *Maine Birding Trail* map

Lesser yellowlegs — Karl Gerstenberger
kegerstenberger.zenfolio.com

Lesser yellowlegs — Karl Gerstenberger
kegerstenberger.zenfolio.com

Puffin-Watching

Maine's colorful Atlantic puffins lay just one egg a year. They were almost extinct at the turn of the 20th century, when the only surviving birds nested on either **Matinicus Rock** or **Machias Seal Island**. Since 1973 Audubon has helped reintroduce nesting on **Eastern Egg Rock** in Muscongus Bay, 6 miles off Pemaquid Point, and since 1984 there has been a similar puffin-restoration project on Seal Island in outer Penobscot Bay. The time to view puffins is June through early August. The only place you are allowed to view the birds up close on land is **Machias Seal Island**, and visitors are strictly limited. We recommend signing on with **Bold Coast Charters** (boldcoast.com) in Cutler. Puffins are smaller than generally realized, but with the help of binoculars you can also view the birds from the water on tours with **Hardy Boat Cruises** (hardyboat.com) from New Harbor, and the **Monhegan Boat**

Puffins on Machias Seal Island   Christina Tree

Line (monheganboat.com) from Port Clyde. The **Hog Island Audubon Camp** (maineaudubon.org) offers guided boat cruises to Eastern Egg Rock. **Project Puffin Visitor Center** (projectpuffin.org) in Rockland uses live-streaming mini cams and audio to provide a virtual visit with nesting puffins on Machias Seal Island.

/guide to 82 Maine birding sites at mainebirdingtrail.com; you can also request a glossy print version online or at one of the Maine Tourism Association welcome centers. Also see mainebirding.com for trip planning and tours, and the sidebar on birding in the "Monhegan Island" chapter.

Suggested Itinerary

FOR FOODIES

Portland offers the highest concentration of renowned dining spots (see that chapter). But on and near Mount Desert Island, there is another subset of excellence. In Southwest Harbor look for Red Sky (redskyrestaurant.com) and Xanthus at The Claremont Hotel (theclaremonthotel.com). Also outstanding: Burning Tree in Otter Creek, with its own organic gardens. All offer well-made meals and a track record in a region of restaurants that are open one summer and gone the next. On Main St. in Bar Harbor, Mache Bistro (machebistro.com)—run by well-known chef-owner Kyle

Beth's Farmstand is on Western Road in Warren.   Nancy English

Lobster roll at the Lobster Dock, Boothbay Harbor   Christina Tree

Yardborough—offers great dining. Most exciting of all is the fresh, local, and Mediterranean cuisine at Ellsworth's Cleonice (cleonice .com). Count on the season dictating the menu, and understand that "day-boat" next to the halibut means the fish was landed almost precisely yesterday. The terrific tapas show off chef-owner Rich Hanson's power to persuade the locals, who make this place hop year-round.

Along the Midcoast the standouts are Henry & Marty (henryand marty.com) and Trattoria Athena (trattoriaathena.com) in Brunswick, Solo Bistro (solobistro.com) in Bath, Ports of Italy (portsofitaly.com) in Boothbay Harbor, and Damariscotta River Grill (damariscottarivergrill .com) Damariscotta. In Rockland, the Midcoast's liveliest dining town, Melissa Kelly's Primo (primo restaurant.squarespace.com) is truly number one.

Gifts from the Sea

Cod and pollack are still found in Maine waters, along with Atlantic sturgeon, alewife and striped bass, yellowtail flounder, halibut, and haddock. Atlantic salmon are ever rarer, but farmed salmon are plentiful and local. Soft-shell clams remain abundant and oysters, especially in Damariscotta, are making a comeback. Locally raised mussels are also easily available, along with tasty crabmeat, painstakingly picked from hard-shell crabs. Lobsters are, however, what Maine is known for worldwide.

Salmon farms off Campobello Island
Christina Tree

Maine's clean, cold waters produce the planet's tastiest **lobster** (lobsterfrommaine.com). This hard-shell crustacean has a long body and five sets of legs, including two large front claws, one large, flat, and heavy and the other smaller, thinner. Lobsters don't like light, hiding by day and emerging at night to eat mussels, sea urchins, and crabs. Most are at least seven years old by the time they are caught because Maine regulates the minimum (also maximum) size of what can be sold. The state also prohibits catching pregnant females, and imposes trap limits and license controls. In the 1880s most lobster was canned. Lobster harvests have tripled in Maine since 1990. Prices have recently taken a

Lobster feast with all the fixings
Jim Dugan, courtesy Maine Windjammer Association

dramatic dip. Chief among the reasons, lobstermen will tell you, is the fact that about half the catch has been going to Canadian processors to sell as lobster tails and claws to mass markets. A recent change in Maine state law now permits Maine processors to do likewise. Linda Bean, granddaughter of L.L. Bean, has opened the first processing factory; more are in the offing. Even locally, however, lobstermen are frustrated by inflated lobster prices still on the menus at tourist restaurants. The best way to consume these tasty crustaceans remains in their entirety at a lobster shack by their home waters.

Crabcakes at Le Garage, Wiscasset

Christina Tree

FOR SHOPPERS

Outlet devotees head for Kittery (thekitteryoutlets.com) and Freeport (freeportusa.com). The two outlet centers repeat many of the name brands, but Freeport adds to the mix the flagship store of L.L. Bean (llbean.com), with a campus that includes stores devoted to hunting and fishing; to bike, boat, and ski; and more. There are also free workshops. L.L. Bean Discovery School (llbean.com/ods) is the best place of all to try out a new sport or take an hour to get a handle on kayaking. The company also sponsors free summer concerts (llbean.com/events). Freeport Village Station (onefreeportvillagestation.com), a complex across from the Bean campus, houses Coach, Nike, Brooks Brothers, and Calvin Klein, also the L.L. Bean Outlet. Thanks to Amtrak's Downeaster, it's possible to come by train from as far as Boston for an afternoon of shopping.

Kittery claims 120 outlets in a series of shopping centers strung along 1.3 miles of Rt. 1; these are less appealing because less walkable, but for shoppers from points south, they are more than an hour closer than Freeport. The anchor store here is the Kittery Trading Post (kitterytradingpost.com). Stonehill Kitchen (stonehillkitchen.com) in nearby York, just off I-95, Exit 7, is a major draw for fans of its products and Maine specialty foods, as well as for those who just want to sample them. Portland's Old Port is fun, and there's an intriguing stretch of shopping at the foot of Munjoy Hill, across from the Eastern Cemetery. Check out Ferdinand (ferdinandhomestore.com), with quirky motifs and inexpensive hipster trinkets, and Angela Adams (angelaadams.com), with high design, nationally recognized rugs, and women's purses.

The two Midcoast towns of Bath (visitbath.com) and Damariscotta (damariscottaregion.com) offer a particularly rewarding mix of small shops. Damariscotta is home base for Renys (renys.com), a family-owned Maine chain of 14 discount stores that fill the void and, as in Bath, the very spaces left by defunct department stores. Listing what Renys stocks is harder than listing what it doesn't.

Maine is famed for the quality of its potters; worth a detour are Georgetown Pottery (georgetownpottery.com) in its tiny namesake village south of Bath, Edgecomb Potters (edgecomb potters.com) on the way down Rt. 27 to the Boothbays, and Columbia Falls Pottery (columbiafallspottery.com) just off Rt. 1 way down east on your way to Eastport, where Raye's Mustard Mill (rayesmustard.com) is the place to stop.

Renys in Bath   Christina Tree

Sherman's Book & Stationery in Boothbay Harbor   Christina Tree

Suggested Itinerary

FOR LIGHTHOUSE BUFFS

Lighthouses, like lobsters, can be found up and down the East Coast and beyond. But it's Maine they symbolize.

More than 800 lighthouses still stand in the United States. Michigan counts 120 to Maine's 66—which include the Machias Seal Island Light maintained by the Canadian Coast Guard. Maine can, however, claim to lead the country in innovative ways of preserving and maintaining these landmarks.

No longer simply photogenic icons, more than a dozen lighthouse stations now invite visitors to clamber up into their tower and/or to explore their keepers'-houses-turned museums, welcome centers, or lodging.

The U.S. Coast Guard continues to service 56 Maine beacons but can no longer afford to preserve their supporting structures—the outmoded towers—as well as keepers' houses, outbuildings, and land. Some lighthouses were decommissioned as early as the 1920s; by the 1960s all beacons had been automated. Most are now solar-powered. By the 1980s nine lighthouses had been sold off, and several razed. Concern for the fate of the survivors was widespread and intense.

"Take away the lighthouses and you've taken away an essential part of Maine's identity, a part of who we are," Governor Angus King wrote in the introduction to the Maine Lights Program, a model for the National Historic Lighthouse Preservation Act of 2000. This legislation has enabled light stations to be acquired by nonprofits and—if there are no takers—auctioned off to private parties. With acquisition comes the mandate—but no funding—to preserve the historic real estate.

More than 42 Maine lighthouses have been transferred to nonprofits or sold since 2000. So it happens that each summer we see new adaptive uses and ways in which visitors can access and incidentally contribute to light station repair and maintenance. The American Lighthouse Foundation (lighthousefoundation.org), headquartered at Owls Head Light at the mouth of Rockland harbor, currently maintains 18 light stations, 9 of them in Maine. The 1825 tower is open on a regular schedule, weather and volunteers permitting. Just 25 feet high, it's an easy climb, and—given its site atop a high cliff—the view is a stunning 40-mile sweep from the Camden Hills up the bay and out across the islands.

Across the harbor Rockland Breakwater Light (rocklandharborlights.org) is open weekends—but weather can be a serious factor. Surrounded on three sides by water, the squat redbrick engine room (now a gift shop), tower, and adjoining clapboard keeper's house (under restoration) are sited at the end of an almost mile-long uneven granite breakwater, a 20-minute walk each way from shore. On a recent Saturday the tower's catwalk and deck were filled to capacity; according to volunteer Eric Davis, it's not unusual to log 600 visitors a day.

Pemaquid Point Lighthouse (lighthousefoundation.org) claims 100,000 visitors a year and may well be Maine's most photographed icon. Since 2003, the year this light was first pictured on Maine's quarter, volunteers have kept tower open daily all summer. The classic white 1824 tower looms high above smooth rocks that cascade invitingly down to the ocean, harboring tidal pools that delight kids of all ages. This was Maine's first light to be automated, and its keeper's house has long been the town-maintained Fisherman's Museum.

Monhegan Light

Christina Tree

Several other keepers' houses are now captivating small museums, open daily all summer. At Portland Head Light (portlandheadlight.com), the oldest (completed in 1790) and arguably the most handsome of all, exhibits describe, among other things, the history of lighthouses, beginning in Alexandria, Egypt, in 390 BC. At the Marshall Point Lighthouse Museum (marshallpoint.org) you can leaf through daily logs kept by its resident keepers from 1874 to 1970. The Monhegan Historical & Cultural Museum (monheganmuseum.org) includes striking works painted on the island by the likes of George Bellows and Rockwell Kent.

The ultimate destination for today's Maine lighthouse buffs is 2.5 miles off the mouth of the Kennebec River, maintained by the Friends of Seguin Island Light Station (seguinisland.org). Here the highest light above Maine waters retains the state's only still-active first-order Fresnel lens, visible from up to 40 miles. Weather permitting, a resident caretaker greets visitors, helping them off-load from a dinghy (there is no dock) and guiding them up the steep path into the museum and tower.

The Wood Island Lighthouse (woodislandlighthouse.org), marking the entrance to the Saco River, is far more visitor-friendly. Thanks to AFL and the local chapter of "Friends," the 42-foot-high tower and keeper's house are under restoration. Frequent guided tours begin with a boat ride from Biddeford Pool.

At Burnt Island Lighthouse (maine.gov/dmr/burntisland), built in 1821, visitors are greeted by docents in 1950s dress portraying the island's last lighthouse keeper and his family, guiding them around their '50s-furnished home and up into the light. Owned by Maine's Department of Marine Resources, the island is accessed by excursion boat tours from Boothbay Harbor.

Another Boothbay-area island light station is the newest to offer lodging: the Inn at Cuckolds Lighthouse (innatcuckoldslighthouse.com), on the rocky ledges off Southport Island. Here the keeper's house had already been razed and the distinctive lighthouse itself was under threat when a local couple applied to acquire it in 2004. They ultimately rallied local support to rebuild and are now open as a luxurious, two-suite bed & breakfast.

The privately owned Keeper's House Inn (keepershouse.com) on Isle au Haut, accessible by mail boat from Stonington, was Maine's first light-station-turned-inn. Recently reopened, it offers four guest rooms plus a "cozy" former oil house and a cottage.

Surprisingly little known, Whitehead Light Station (whiteheadlightstation .org) with its beautifully restored keeper's house welcomes visitors in seven guest rooms (private baths) and ample common space. Sited on a sizable island off Spruce Head, it's owned by century-old Pine Island (boys') Camp. Check out the openings for multiday summer workshops and September rental.

Goose Rocks Lighthouse (beaconpreservation.org) offers the most adventurous lighthouse lodging: a self-contained, three-story round channel marker at the outer end of the Fox Isles Thorofare. Privately owned, its ongoing restoration is financed largely through "Keepers Experiences." Guest "keepers" are met at the nearby North Haven ferry landing and eased up the ladders. BYO groceries.

The most economical lighthouse stay is way down east in the nicely restored Keeper's House at Little River Lighthouse (lighthousefriends.com/light.asp?ID =762), set on a small, trail-webbed island off the village of Cutler. Rates include transport, but it's BYO linens, towels, sleeping bag, food, beverages, and bottled water.

Cutler is also departure point for puffin-watching tours to Machias Seal Island (boldcoast.com), a bird sanctuary astride the boundary between the Gulf of Maine and Bay of Fundy. Nearby Quoddy Head State Park (stateparks.com /quoddy_head_state_park_in_maine.html), known for its clifftop hiking trails, is home to candy-striped West Quoddy Head Light, marking the easternmost point in the United States. The keeper's house serves as a welcome center for the Lubec area. On Campobello Island, accessed by bridge from Lubec, East Quoddy Head Lighthouse (campobello.com/lighthouse) is the pot of gold at the end of any East Coast lighthouse trail. Said to be the most photographed light in Canada, where it's known as Head Harbour Lighthouse, the white wooden tower is emblazoned with a red cross down its center. It's part of a full light station that fills a small island just offshore, accessible at low tide but a deadly crossing once the tide comes surging in through this narrow channel. Volunteers are on hand in-season to assist visitors. This is a great whale-watching spot.

So who needs to step inside a light or keeper's house? Perhaps the much-photographed Nubble Light (nubblelight.org) near the western extreme of Maine's 4,500-mile coastline is all the more appealing because it sits mysteriously aloof, just across a narrow channel from York's Sohier Park.

Increasingly, however, visitors are discovering lighthouses as live links to beautiful corners of Maine's coast and islands and a time in which everything and everyone moved by water. On Maine Lighthouse Day (lighthousefoundation .org/openlighthouseday.htm) in mid-September, more than a dozen lights hold open house. Lighthouse buffs may also want to check out the Maine Lighthouse Museum (mainelighthousemuseum.com) in the Gateway Visitors Center, 1 Park Dr., Rockland.

Sense of Place

NATURAL AND HUMAN HISTORY

NOTHING IS STILL where land meets water. In the course of a minute, grains of sand swirl, snails creep, a clam digs out of sight. In the course of an eon the whole landscape goes through revolutions.

THE DROWNED COAST

Look down in front of your feet when you stand on Cadillac Mountain, in Acadia National Park, and you can see grooves and indentations in the rock where a mile-thick layer of ice dragged itself and its load of stone and sand across the granite, heading south, until a shift in the climate melted it away. Little more than 10,000 years ago the glaciers made their final retreat, leaving behind enough sand and gravel to build Interstate 95 and thousands of other roads and buildings. They also dropped "erratic" boulders, stray giant rocks that you can see all over the coast: along Rt. 1 north of Machias, along hiking trails in the woods of Camden Hills, and on the side of South Bubble Rock, where a famous one is named Balance Rock.

Rivers created sand in front of the retreating glaciers, cut valleys out of the softer rock, and sorted the glacial till, carrying the fine sand down to the edge of the sea and sending the silt farther. Georges Bank, historically one of the finest fishing grounds in the world, sits on a bed of glacial silt and clay, and was itself once the extreme limit of the glacier that covered New England. The deep and enormous load of ice pushed the surface of the earth down underneath it. As the ice melted, the sea rose above the land, cresting 400 feet higher than it is today, and the coast was underwater. Then the earth moved upward, lifting itself out of the sea. Old deltas are now far from water, leaving curiosities like the Desert of Maine in Freeport, where overgrazing has exposed an old seashore, along with the vast, undulating blueberry barrens of Washington County.

The earth is now sinking slightly in the southern and northern tips of Maine,

An exhibit at Maine State Museum traces the history of man in Maine.   Christina Tree

and the sea has been rising, 6 feet in the last 3,000 years. The coastline changes all the time under the relentless action of the sea.

PEOPLE OF THE DAWN

The region's first men and women arrived even before the last glaciers had receded from northern Maine. They hunted woolly mammoths, bison, and caribou in a tundra-like landscape. An excellent exhibit, *12,000 Years in Maine*, in the Maine State Museum (mainestatemuseum.org) in Augusta depicts the distinct periods in this history and features the Red Paint People, named for the red pigments found sprinkled in their burial sites. They flourished between 5,000 and 3,800 years ago and are believed to have harpooned swordfish from large, seaworthy boats. Displays from this period in the Robert Abbe Museum (abbemuseum .org) on Mount Desert include awls, pear-shaped net weights, and weights for sophisticated "atlatl" spears. Dioramas depict 17th-century Penobscots skillfully adjusting to the vagaries of local climate: camping at waterfalls in autumn to catch migrating salmon, moving farther inland to their birch-covered lodges in winter, back down to sheltered coves in spring and to islands such as Mount Desert in summer. Sketches and notes from a 1604 expedition by Samuel de Champlain depict, by contrast, more settled Indian villages with cultivated gardens along Maine's southern coast, west of the Kennebec River.

Maine's coastal people had this continent's earliest dealings with Europeans, who, it seems, made a nasty impression from the start. A number of Natives were kidnapped and brought back to both France and England as trophies. Via the wide tribal trading network, word got around, engendering hostilities that contributed to the failure of the 1607 Popham Colony at the mouth of the Kennebec.

Early voyagers noted distinct tribes and estimated the total number of Native people living in present-day Maine at around 40,000. The French were unquestionably better at dealings with Maine tribes than the English, thanks in part to the work of Jesuits who established missions such as that at Mount Desert. These were, however, destroyed by the English. Tribes were soon caught up in hostilities between the European contenders for trade and territory, but it was sickness, especially smallpox and plague, carried by the intruders that decimated Native communities. Perhaps 75 percent of the Native population died by the year 1616. In 1701, faced with aggressive expansion by the English colonists, the Penobscot, Passamaquoddy, Maliseet, and Micmac tribes formalized a council known as the Wabenaki (People of the Dawn) Confederacy.

During the Revolution the Micmacs and Maliseets made the unlucky choice of siding with the Crown; after the war they fled to Canada. That left only the Penobscots and Passamaquoddies, who despite fighting with the colonists were made wards of the Commonwealth. The Penobscots were confined to a reservation at Old Town, near Bangor, and the Passamaquoddies to another at Perry, near Eastport. In 1786 the Penobscots deeded most of Maine to Massachusetts in exchange for 140 small islands in the Penobscot River, and in 1818 Massachusetts agreed to pay them an assortment of trinkets for the land. When Maine became a state in 1820, a trust fund was set up for the tribe, but ended up in the general treasury.

Fort Popham at the mouth of the Kennebec River   Christina Tree

In 1957 Native Americans in Maine were allowed to vote in national elections, and not until 1967 were they allowed to vote in state elections. Never mind that a 1928 bill made all Native Americans U.S. citizens. In 1977 the Penobscot, Passamaquoddy, and Maliseet Indians sued the state, claiming that all treaties granting land to Maine were null and void, because Congress never ratified them. They asked for $25 billion and 12.5 million acres of land. In 1980 they received a settlement of $81.5 million, but no land. The money has been invested in a variety of enterprises. The Abbe Museum (abbemuseum.org) in Bar Harbor showcases the cultures of Maine's present Wabenaki, the less than 7,000 members of the Penobscot, Passamaquoddy, Micmac, and Maliseet tribes who presently live in the state. The Passamaquoddy reservation (wabanaki.com) is the site of Indian Ceremonial Days in mid-August.

The Wabenaki are currently less involved in the state's flourishing tourism industry than they were in the 19th century, when they were sought-after hunting, fishing, and seagoing canoe guides and sold their stunning "fancy work" to summer tourists. The Maine Indian Basketmakers Alliance (maineindianbaskets.org) sponsors a July festival in Bar Harbor.

A LITTLE-KNOWN HISTORY

Maine's history is far too rich to begin to do it justice here. However, it's worth a try because so little of it is general knowledge—and because it's shaped so much of the Maine we see today.

By the 1500s European fishermen were harvesting cod from the abundant waters of Georges Bank, establishing fishing and trading stations including the one on Monhegan from which the Pilgrims secured food to see them through their first winters. Some of these outposts evolved into year-round trading centers such as Pemaquid (friendsofcolonialpemaquid.org), where excavations and a small museum suggest life circa 1630–50.The Pilgrims subsequently established their own Maine trading posts and, through the sale of beaver skins, were able to pay off their debt to the London merchants who financed their colony.

The first permanent European settlements in Maine were at Agamenticus (present-day York) in 1624. King Charles I of England, assuming it was his to give, gave all of Maine west of the Kennebec River to a British speculator from Plymouth, Sir Ferdinando Gorges, in 1639, directing that Gorges's portion of the mainland be named "Province or Country of Maine." Gorges chose Agamenticus, which he renamed "Georgeana," as the capital of his domain, but the ship on which he was to set sail was wrecked in the launching. This Don Quixote of Maine had to content himself with staying home and drawing up plans for an elaborate government. In 1640 the town boasted 43 officials, more than half its population.

Fort William Henry, originally built in 1692, reconstructed in 1908 at Popham Beach   Christina Tree

Through unlucky politics, Gorges wound up in prison, dying in 1647. In 1677 Massachusetts secured clear title to present-day Maine west of the Kennebec River.

Uneasy relations between the French and English continued for years before formal war was declared. The Maine coast, particularly east of the Penobscot River, was in fairly constant dispute. Maine was heavily involved in the series of raids and retaliations remembered as the French and Indian Wars (1675–1760), a period recalled at the reconstructed English Fort William Henry (friendsof colonialpemaquid.org) in Pemaquid. Following the defeat of the French at Quebec in 1759, English colonists began to settle on the coast in larger numbers. The Museums of York (oldyork.org) suggest life during Maine's brief, peaceful colonial period. Throughout the 18th century, Maine was part of Massachusetts, the only colony with an attached but noncontiguous "district."

THE REVOLUTION

While Bostonians threw tea into the harbor, a Falmouth (present-day Portland) mob seized the Imperial tax stamps in 1765. Zealous Maine patriots claimed the first naval victory of the war when colonists captured the British cutter *Margaretta* in Machias Bay in 1775, a battle James Fenimore Cooper called "the Lexington of the seas." The first colonial warship, *Ranger*, was built at Kittery in 1777.

During the Revolution, Mainers refused to ship their highly prized white pine masts to the British fleet. The Royal Navy bombarded Falmouth and burned much of it to the ground. The British established a naval base at Castine on Penobscot Bay with an eye to making eastern Maine into a Crown colony named New Hibernia. The area attracted hundreds of loyalist families. In 1779 the Commonwealth of Massachusetts sent a fleet of 18 armed vessels and 24 transports with 1,000 troops and 400 marines to capture Castine. There the unimpressive British Fort George was manned by just 750 soldiers, with two sloops as backup. The Massachusetts forces managed to disgrace themselves miserably, hanging around long enough for several British men-of-war to come along and attack them. The surviving patriots had to walk back to Boston, and many of their officers, Paul Revere included, were court-martialed for their part in the disgrace. No thanks to Massachusetts efforts, the 1783 Treaty of Paris established Maine's present easterly border at the St. Croix River.

The British didn't relinquish Castine until 1784, at which point loyalist families moved just across Passamaquoddy Bay from Eastport to New Brunswick. Some dismantled their Castine houses, reconstructing them in St. Andrews, where they stand today.

STATEHOOD

After the Revolution, Maine prospered and grew. It became a center for production of lumber for houses, barrels, and masts. Ships from safe harbors established trade routes around the world. At the same time, impoverished and land-hungry settlers flooded into the District of Maine, doubling and redoubling the population. In contrast with other parts of New England, where Revolutionary War veterans were rewarded for military service with land or otherwise encouraged to settle, here they found themselves treated as squatters and asked to pay rent to "proprietors" who claimed vast tracts of land, largely through titles still based on grants from King George.

Revolutionary War hero General Henry Knox became a notorious proprietor. He married the grand-daughter of Samuel Waldo, the Boston developer who owned most of the Midcoast area that's now Waldo County. In 1794 he built Montpelier (knoxmuseum.org), an elaborate, out-sized mansion, in Thomaston (it was reconstructed as make-work project during the Depression and welcomes visitors today). These land barons assumed that they could make a kill-ing off Maine's population surge, but their greedy plan backfired. As popu-lation grew, so did anger at the unfair demands of absentee landlords; their surveyors and rent collectors were increasingly harassed and driven off.

Maine state seal

Eventually, thanks to political pressure, an 1808 law enabled settlers to buy land on reasonable terms.

And still Massachusetts continued to treat Maine indifferently. Bay State Fed-eralists were strongly opposed to the War of 1812, which blockaded their lucrative maritime trade. They profited hugely from the war through privateering and sur-reptitiously cooperated with the enemy. The British again occupied eastern Maine in 1814, capturing Machias, burning Belfast, and reoccupying Castine. A few forts, notably Edgecomb at Wiscasset, were financed locally, but Massachusetts contrib-uted nothing. This fueled outrage against the mother state, which began to fear that Maine voters could rock the Federalist status quo.

On March 25, 1820, Maine became the 23rd state in the Union. The separa-tion papers from Massachusetts were signed at the Jamestown Tavern in Free-port (the tavern still operates today down the street from L.L. Bean). The new status, however, seemed to help little when its Canadian boundary was disputed in 1839. Ignored by Washington, the timber-rich new state took matters into its own hands by arming its northern forts. An 1842 treaty formally ended the war, but the new state went ahead and built massive Fort Knox at the mouth of the Penobscot anyway, just in case.

BOOM YEARS

At the center of the Maine State Seal stands a pine tree, signifying the tall white pines, unbroken by years of coastal wind and storms, that were coveted by the earliest explorers and subsequently turned into magnificent masts for generations of sailing ships. (A stand of century-old white pine graces the campus of Bowdoin College in Brunswick.)

By 1850 Maine was considered the shipbuilding capital of America. In Bath it's claimed that some 5,000 ships have been built along the long tidal reach of the Kennebec River. The state's golden age of shipbuilding and sail is dramatized here in the Maine Maritime Museum (mainemaritimemuseum.org).

Men of Searsport didn't just build ships, they built them to sail themselves. By 1845 the little town had constructed 99 vessels, including a full-rigged clipper; by 1860, 10 percent of the nation's deepwater shipmasters lived in Searsport. Their handsome homes still line Rt. 1 (some are now B&Bs), and their reunions in far-flung ports are chronicled in Searsport's Penobscot Marine Museum (penobscot marinemuseum.org). By 1860 one-fifth of the state's population were mariners, 759 of them masters of ships.

Although fishermen first discovered eastern Maine, they never settled there. Maine's first settlers were farmers; fishing didn't become a significant part of the economy until the 1830s, when the incoming human tide reached down east to present-day Hancock and Washington Counties. At the time Congress also granted fishermen a bounty for catching cod—which, when salted, was hugely popular with the burgeoning immigrant populations in coastal cities as well as southern and Caribbean plantations. As Colin Woodard notes in *The Lobster Coast*, the majority of these fishing schooners were owned by their captains, and crew members often held shares. Mackerel became another important catch, especially down east around Lubec and Eastport. By 1860 Maine claimed more full-time fishermen than any other state.

Maine's unlikeliest industry was ice. Massachusetts resident Frederick Tudor pioneered the concept of exporting ice from New England ponds to warmer climes but, as ski-area operators have since discovered, Maine temperatures fall below freezing more often than those in the Bay State. Tudor built vast icehouses on

The *Lewis R. French*, launched in 1871 in Christmas Cove, is the oldest windjammer in America.

Fred LeBlanc, courtesy Maine Windjammer Association

the Kennebec, creating another lucrative cargo for Maine schooners. (The small, commercial Thompson Ice House has been preserved as a museum on Rt. 129 in South Bristol.)

The Civil War had a profound effect on Maine, despite the absence of any shots fired on Maine soil. Confederate ships blocked and seized cargo vessels, and a large percentage of the seaworthy population marched off to war, many not to return. After the war, with the nation focused on westward and railroad expansion, Maine's once crucial sea-lanes were backroaded. New government policies, moreover, decimated the state's fishing fleet.

In the 1870s through the 1890s foreign stonecutters flocked to Stonington and offshore islands like Vinalhaven, supplying the granite to build many of our most famous buildings and bridges. During this period Bath shipyards turned out Down Easters, a compromise between the clipper ship and the old-style freighter that plied the globe, and numerous shipyards produced big multimasted schooners designed to ferry coal and lime. Canneries also proliferated, processing lobster and clams as well as herring and sardines. Eventually, however, refrigeration supplanted the need for ice, granite was replaced by cement, and canned fish were replaced by frozen. Life along Maine's once prosperous coast became increasingly challenging, and many of its more enterprising residents left.

Monument to Stonington stonecutters at Town Dock
Christina Tree

THE IMAGE

Tourism has always been driven by images. In the 1840s Thomas Cole and Frederic Church painted scenes of Mount Desert. Etchings and sketches in the era's many papers, magazines, and children's books by lesser-known artists began projecting coastal Maine as a romantic, remote destination. After the Civil War, Maine tourism boomed. Via railroad and steamboat, residents of cities throughout the East and Midwest streamed into the Pine Tree State, many toting guidebooks published by rail and steamboat lines to boost business. Developers were quick to claim that Mount Desert Island's thick fogs were "as healthy for the body as basking in the sun."

All along the coast and on dozens of islands from Passamaquoddy to Casco Bay, hotels of every size were built, some by Boston developers but most by Maine natives. As urban factories were forced to close due to heat, vacations became an option for more and more people, not just academics and the rich. Blue-collar workers came by trolley to religious camp meetings at Old Orchard Beach and York Beach along the South Coast, where previously ignored sands were backed by new developments.

It was during this period that "summer residents" reached numbers large enough to affect both the Maine economy and culture. A breed as much apart from the transient tourist as from the local resident, these folks built seasonal homes. Initially they were people with modest incomes who built modest shingled cottages. They were later joined by many of the era's wealthiest families, who built vast summer mansions, also usually shingled and "rustic" in decor. Summer colonies mushroomed from Kennebunkport to Hancock Point and on down to

Campobello Island. More than 200 lavish summer "cottages" were built in Bar Harbor, where a cadre of influential summer residents amassed 11,000 acres and persuaded the federal government to accept it in 1919 as the core of Acadia, the first national park east of the Mississippi.

World War I, coinciding with the proliferation of the Model A, brought an abrupt end to Maine's first tourism boom. The 1922 founding of the Maine Publicity Bureau (the present Maine Tourism Association), we suspect, reflects the panic of hoteliers. Then came the Depression. Over the next decades most of the island and coastal summer hotels went the way of coastal passenger boats and trains. "Motorists" stuck to motor courts and motels along Rt. 1, the tourist trail.

In 1947 much of Bar Harbor was destroyed in a forest fire. The French paper *Le Figaro* reported that the peasants of Maine had struck a blow against feudalism. The town's year-round residents did not like being called peasants. The fact is that Maine's wealthy summer residents prided themselves on their relationships with locals. Over pie and coffee, yachtsmen and lobstermen talked politics, weather, and boats. Summer residents embraced the romantic image of coastal Maine as a throwback to simpler times. The fact that "natives" came of sturdy European stock like themselves reinforced this image—which persists.

By the 1960s much of the coast had dropped off the tourist map. Gradually, over the next few decades, surviving summer hotels were restored as inns or condominiums. Bed & breakfasts began appearing in the 1980s, transforming former sea captains' homes and summer mansions into B&Bs, in the process reopening to visitors corners on the peninsulas, islands, and other off-the-beaten-track places.

For decades Acadia National Park was a public toehold in the mostly privately owned coast, but thanks to both state programs and private land trusts, coastal

State of Maine was one of many passenger steamers that ferried tourists from points south.

Courtesy Maine Maritime Museum

The Claremont Hotel in Southwest Harbor, painted in 1885 by Xanthus Smith

preserves are steadily increasing, largely through contributions of land and funds from third- and fourth-generation "summer residents," many of whom now live in Maine year-round.

It's also now easier than ever for casual visitors to get out on the water, the only way to really appreciate the beauty of this coast. The Maine Windjammer fleet (sailmaine.org), originally introduced in the '30s, has been reestablished and expanded, offering affordable multiday sailing cruises on traditional coastal schooners in Penobscot Bay. Kayaking outfitters introduce thousands each summer to the delights of paddling along quiet coves or out to islands, observing seals and waterfowl close up. Whale-watching expeditions also lure landlubbers, along with an ever-increasing number of excursion boats.

Maine coastal landscape has been shaped as much by tourism as by other forces in the state's history. In the 19th century summer visitors, including *Atlantic Monthly* editor William Dean Howells and Sam Clemens (Mark Twain), were responsible for restoring York's colonial buildings. Portland's Old Port, too, has been revitalized by catering to visitors—and where would L.L. Bean and all the Freeport outlets be without shoppers from away? On down the coast through Boothbay's busy waterfront, Rockland's galleries, and Camden's and Bar Harbor's teeming main street shops and restaurants, it's difficult to overstate the impact of tourism on this "Vacationland."

According to recent research, roughly 80 percent of Maine's visitors return after an initial visit. For many there is a longing to belong here. An incoming tide of commuters, telecommuters, and retirees is swelling and changing Maine's population, most dramatically along the South Coast. Up and down the coast there's

Summer-season garden party in York, 1884

Photograph by Frederick Quimby, courtesy Museums of Old York

talk of "WOOFs" (well-off older folks), who are becoming the volunteer engines of their adopted communities.

Visitors and transplants alike need to be aware of the special, increasingly fragile sense of place each community possesses, a compound of the many generations of people who have shaped it.

Tourism continues to be driven by images. Maine's icons include lighthouses and lobster boats, schooners and weathered wharves and fishermen. Whereas in other parts of the country natural beauty is the only draw, here human-built beauty is a big part of the picture.

1

South Coast

INCLUDING THE YORKS, KITTERY, OGUNQUIT, WELLS, AND THE KENNEBUNKS

MUCH OF SOUTHERN MAINE'S COASTLINE is flat, smoother than Maine's nickname the Rocky Coast might imply. Its estuaries and strands stretch out for miles along beaches and thin woods, presenting only a few stretches of the rocky outcroppings that mark most of the Maine beaches farther north. The water's edge in York Beach, Ogunquit, and the Kennebunks mostly soothes the eye and the mind with distant vistas of ocean surf and sand.

Long Sands Beach in York *Nancy English*

Yet enough variety marks the landscape that artists crowd into Ogunquit in good weather to paint its picturesque Perkins Cove and other harbors. City visitors have been frequenting the expanse of Long Sands Beach in York Beach for as long as cities have persuaded people to leave. And the heightened coastline in Kennebunkport, where rocks rise up out of the sea near Walker Point—the famous summer home of former president George H. W. Bush—endows the big summer houses there with drama and glamour that visitors to Cape Arundel Inn can take in on an overnight visit.

Every one of these communities is busy and sometimes jammed at the height of summer. Fall and late spring are preferable times for a visit, so long as the beach is not the only reason you come. And though the beaches are sublime,

LEFT: Perkins Cove is bordered by many gardens, including this elaborate one beside Barnacle Billy's. *Nancy English*

51

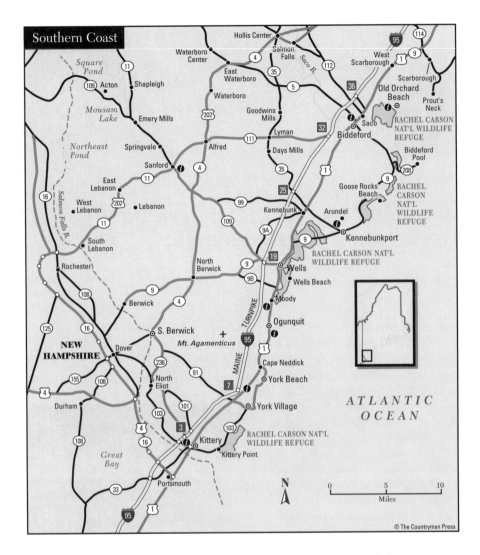

Southern Coast

hiking, biking, golfing, and surfing and kayaking in a wet suit extend the season. You certainly won't have to worry about finding a good meal, with restaurants open year-round that are renowned for the quality of their meals: Anneke Jans, Arrows, Joshua's, Angelina's, and 98 Provence.

The Yorks and Kittery

Check out these great attractions and activities . . .

For serious shoppers Maine's gateway is I-95, Exit 3, accessing a Rt. 1 lineup of familiar brand outlets. The homegrown anchor store here is The Kittery Trading Post (207-439-2700; kitterytradingpost.com; 301 Rt. 1), filled with sporting gear, shoes, and clothing, known for end-of-summer sales. Neighboring Bob's Clam Hut (201-439-4233; 315 Rt. 1) is the spot for fried clams;

York's most pleasant mile of shore is traversed by a footpath.

Christina Tree

Robert's Maine Grill (207-439-0300; 326 Rt. 1) across the road (same ownership) is an upscale version with an expanded menu, including a raw bar. Both places are known for the freshest seafood. A bit farther north you'll find When Pigs Fly Wood-Fired Pizzeria (207-438-7036; whenpigsflypizzeria.com and sendbread .com; 460 Rt. 1) next to this widely distributed bakery's company store, selling 25 kinds of bread, olive oil, and jams and jellies. Also up the road: Flight Adventures (207-439-8838; takeflightadv.com; 506 Rt. 1) provides a 20-minute training session before visitors take off on the high ropes courses. A guided zip-line tour lasts two hours.

The Kittery Historical and Naval Museum (207-439-3080; kitterymuseum .com), just north of the Rt. 236 rotary at I-95 Exit 2 (look for the 129-foot-high flagpole out front), is larger than it looks, with a film and displays dramatizing the amazing history of Maine's southernmost town.

This part of town is studded with restaurants. Loco Coco's Tacos (207-438-9322; locococos.com; 36 Walker St.) serves memorable poblano chilis stuffed with queso blanco. Just up Rt. 1, Beach Pea Baking Company (207-439-3555; beach peabaking.com; 53 State Rd.) is known for luscious cakes and chewy bread. Vegetarian dishes are excellent, and all the meat served in the sandwiches and salads is roasted here.

Wallingford Square is a good spot to wind up for dinner. Anneke Jans (207-439-0001; annekejans.net; 60 Wallingford Square, Kittery) serves fantastic bistro meals that might start with Bangs Island mussels finished with blue cheese and cream or fried olives; then go on to pan-roasted trout with potato chorizo hash.

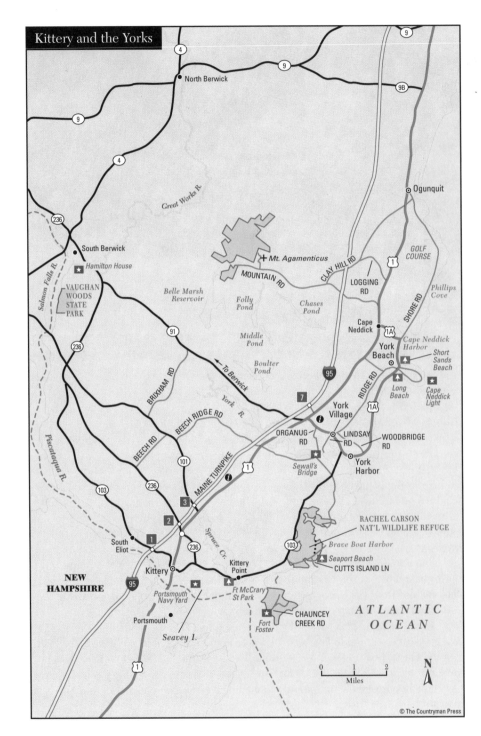

Kittery and the Yorks

Page contents labeled on map:

North Berwick

Ogunquit

Great Works R.

South Berwick
Hamilton House

VAUGHAN
WOODS
STATE
PARK

Mt. Agamenticus

MOUNTAIN RD

CLAY HILL RD

LOGGING RD

GOLF COURSE

Phillips Cove

SHORE RD

Belle Marsh Reservoir

Folly Pond

Chases Pond

Cape Neddick

Cape Neddick Harbor

Short Sands Beach

Salmon Falls R.

Middle Pond

York Beach

Cape Neddick Light

Boulter Pond

Long Beach

To Berwick

York R.

BRIXHAM RD

BEECH RIDGE RD

BEECH RD

RIDGE RD

York Village

WOODBRIDGE RD

ORGANUG RD

LINDSAY RD

Piscataqua R.

MAINE TURNPIKE

Sewall's Bridge

York Harbor

RACHEL CARSON NAT'L WILDLIFE REFUGE

Brave Boat Harbor

Seaport Beach
CUTTS ISLAND LN

South Eliot

Spruce Cr.

Kittery Point

NEW HAMPSHIRE

Kittery

Portsmouth Navy Yard

Ft McCrary St Park

Portsmouth

Seavey I.

Fort Foster

CHAUNCEY CREEK RD

ATLANTIC OCEAN

0   1   2
Miles

N

© The Countryman Press

Reserve. Next door AJ's Wood Grill Pizza (207-439-9700; ajswoodgrillpizza.com) serves organic, seven-grain dough that's grilled first on a wood-fired grill then topped with grilled vegetables and more and finished in the oven. Around the corner the Black Birch Restaurant (207-703-2294; theblackbirch.com), 2 Government St., pours a wide range of craft beer and makes scrumptious casual food like beer-battered haddock. Nearby Tulsi (207-451-9511; tulsiindianrestaurant.com), 20 Walker St) makes fabulous Indian food. The shrimp Balchow appetizer is fiery and aromatic.

Drive east on Rt. 103 to scenic Kittery Point, turn onto Gerrish Island Lane, and turn right at the end of Pocahontas Rd. to reach Fort Foster Park, a great place for a picnic and a walk on trails and beaches. Down Chauncey Creek Rd. in summer you are likely to encounter a traffic jam outside the Chauncey Creek Lobster Pound (207-439-1030; chaunceycreek.com; 16 Chauncey Creek Rd., Kittery Point). This is Maine's southernmost genuine source of of a good lobster dinner, which to our minds involves setting as much as steamed lobster. The outdoor seating here—some picnic tables sheltered from the rain but not heated—overlooks the tidal Chauncey Creek. BYOB. Scenic St. 103 continues to York Harbor.

The Stonewall Kitchen Store   Nancy English

A map is key to navigating the sprawl of the Yorks, four loosely connected villages that stretch many miles from the surf off York Beach inland to Cape Neddick and south to York Village and York Harbor. I-95 at Exit 7 leads to the handsome information center (with restrooms) maintained by the Greater York Region Chamber of Commerce (gatewaytomaine.org). It shares a driveway with Stonewall Kitchen (800-826-1752; stonewall kitchen.com/cafe.html), a delightful food and kitchen supply emporium and café, headquarters for a national business that began with some pots of homemade jam.

This is the oldest town in Maine. In 1642 it was Georgeana, America's first chartered city but quicky demoted to the town of York, part of Massachusetts. Fierce Native American raids followed, but by the middle of the 18th century a colonial village was established. In the late 19th century a group of summer residents, including William Dean Howells and Samuel Clemens (Mark Twain) along with local writer

Sarah Orne Jewett, became involved in an effort to preserve York's most hisoric buildings. Their legacy is The Museums of Old York (207-363-4974; oldyork.org), maintaining eight historic buildings. A visit starts with an orientation film in the visitors center, a reconstructed 1830s barn attached to Jeffers Tavern, built in 1754. The old Gaol was the only jail for the whole of the province of Maine until 1760, and parts of it date to 1719; female inmates' stories in the dismal cells make the visit memorable. A chandlery, a finely furnished 1730 house, a farm laborer's house, and a schoolhouse are other distinguished parts of this complex, open early June through the Columbus Day weekend, Monday through Saturday.

The George Marshall Store, the former chandlery that The Museums of Old York now maintain as an art gallery, is the starting point for the Cliff Path and Fisherman's Walk, a path along the town's most pleasant mile of shorefront. It leads east along the river, through shady Steadman Woods, across Wiggly Bridge (a 1930s suspension bridge), across Rt. 103, and on to York Harbor Beach. Continue east to the property line (this is our favorite part, but it's a bit rough). Returning the way you came is no hardship.

The rocky shore beyond York Village was Lower Town until a tony hotel opened there in 1871 and summer mansions were built at this more desirable address. A York Harbor corporation was formed to keep out unwanted development. The corporation's biggest fight, according to novelist Kenneth Roberts, was against Libby's Oceanside Camp, a tent-and-trailer campgound.

Libby's Oceanside Camp still sits on Roaring Rock Point, its trailers neatly

The Nubble Light, York Beach   Christina Tree

Brown's Ice Cream, York Beach

Nancy English

angled along the shore. Across form it is matching Camp Eaton, established in 1923. No other village boundary in New England remains as clearly defined as this between York Harbor and York Beach.

Beyond the campgrounds stretches 2-mile Long Sands Beach, lined with affordable cottage rentals. During its turn-of-the-20th-century "Trolley era," half a dozen big summer hotels and twice that many boardinghouses lined York Beach. Today this splendid beach remains accessible (metered parking).

Beyond Long Sands turn on Nubble Rd. to Nubble Light. The photogenic lighthouse is just offshore; there's parking in Sohier Park (seasonal information center/gift shop and restrooms). Follow the traffic flow back, stopping at Brown's Ice Cream (207-363-1277; 232 Nubble Rd.) on the way to Short Sands Beach, the lodging, dining, and shopping center of York Beach; the amuseument area and York's Wild Kingdom (207-363-4911; yorkzoo.com) are reminders of an earlier era. The heart of this village is The Goldenrod (207-363-2621; goldenrod.com), owned by the Talpey family since it opened in 1896—just in time to serve the first trolleys rolling in from Portsmouth, NH. Lunch and dinner specials are served up on time-polished tables. Goldenrod Kisses are made from saltwater taffy cooked and pulled in the windows, and the ice cream is house made.

Rt. 1A puts you back on Rt. 1 in Cape Neddick. If you would like to stretch your legs far from the popular places, head inland up Mountain Rd. to Mount Agamenticus, maintained by the Agamenticus Conservation Region (agamenticus .org). The trails can be used by bicyclists, hikers, and equestrians, but the summit is marred with cell phone antennas. Still, you can climb up to an open perch for a picnic with a splendid panorma. In fall this is also a prime hawk-viewing spot.

Checking In

Best places to stay in the
Yorks and Kittery

Dockside Guest Quarters (207-363-2868; docksidegq.com; 22 Harris Island Rd., York) is one of our favorite family-run inns, with a view of the harbor outlet from a handsome old house and four modern cottages. All 25 rooms and lodgings enjoy a water view. Fishing equipment, bicycles, and even Boston Whalers are available to guests. Breakfasts with egg dishes and homemade rolls and muffins are just the beginning.

York Harbor Inn (207-363-5119; yorkharborinn.com; 480 York St., York Harbor) includes 63 rooms in six buildings, four of them former mansions. The 22-room main inn offers some reasonably priced as well as luxurious units with ocean views. Given the popularity of the inn's two restaurants, we suggest opting for the privacy of another building.

If you're a tennis lover, The Stage Neck Inn (207-363-3850; stageneck.com; 8 Stage Neck Rd., York Harbor) offers tennis courts along with its outdoor pool, rooms with all the amenities, many with a water view, and a good restaurant. The bar downstairs might be even more congenial, with woodworking details that mimic the inside of a finely built sailing ship.

Smaller, more economical and intimate lodgings start with The Morning Glory Inn (207-363-2062; morninggloryinnmaine.com; 120 Seabury Rd., York), where Bonnie and Bill Alstrom provide a welcome, a flower garden, and an oasis of peace that visitors love. This is a bed & breakfast with three charming bedrooms, each with a patio or deck, perfect to enjoy the breakfast included in the rates.

In Kittery, The Portsmouth Harbor Inn and Spa (207-439-4040; innatportsmouth.com; 6 Water St., Kittery), an 1890s redbrick inn, stands just off the Kittery green and steps from a smaller bridge spanning the Piscataqua River, allowing guests to walk from this inn to New Hampshire's lively downtown Portsmouth for dinner or shopping, after enjoying some of the services offered at the spa. The seacoast lavender sugar scrub, exfoliation, and light massage, for example, sounds invigorating.

In York Beach the family-owned Cutty Sark Motel (207-363-5131; cuttysarkmotel.com; Long Sands Ave.) is the only lodging on the beach side of the road. All units have picture windows overlooking the ocean. The Anchorage Inn (207-363-5112; anchorageinn.com; 265 Long Beach Ave.) offers indoor as well as outdoor pools and facilities geared to families. The Union Bluff (207-363-1333; unionbluff.com; 8 Beach St.), dating from 1865 but thoroughly renovated and expanded, offers elevator-accessed rooms with ocean and Short Sands; its Union Grill is a popular dining spot.

Ogunquit and Wells

Check out these great attractions
and activities . . .

Ogunquit became famous as an artists' colony by the turn of the last century, and that legacy can be enjoyed in the excellent collection of more than 2,000 modern artworks owned by the

The sculpture garden at the Ogunquit Museum of American Art

Nancy English

Ogunquit Museum of American Art (207-646-4909; ogunquitmuseum.org; 543 Shore Rd., Ogunquit) May through October. Opened in 1953 just south of Perkins Cove and celebrating its 62nd year in 2015, the museum is set on a ledge overlooking the ocean, and its 3-acre garden is a fine spot to enjoy peace and quiet. Turning its gaze onto its immediate past, the museum's exhibits show off Ogunquit's art colony history and the roots of the Ogunquit Art Association. Works by Marsden Hartley, John Marin, Charles Burchfield, Wolf Kahn, and Marguerite and William Zorach, along with the large, forceful wooden sculptures standing outside by Bernard Langlais, are just a tiny few of the possibilities visitors will encounter.

Walking is the best way to get to know Ogunquit, and its lovely Marginal Way is the most scenic of its many walking trails. The trail hugs the shore and is set on rocky outcroppings south of Ogunquit Beach to Oarweed Cove, where walkers emerge into the lively (if not mobbed) area called Perkins Cove. It's cheaper to walk there than to pay for pricey parking, and you can climb into a trolley outside many of the area's motels and inns to reach one end or the other of the walk.

Walking right at water's edge is likely the most popular way to enjoy Ogunquit's 3.5-mile expanse of white sand, set in a long neck beside the Ogunquit River and running parallel to the town.

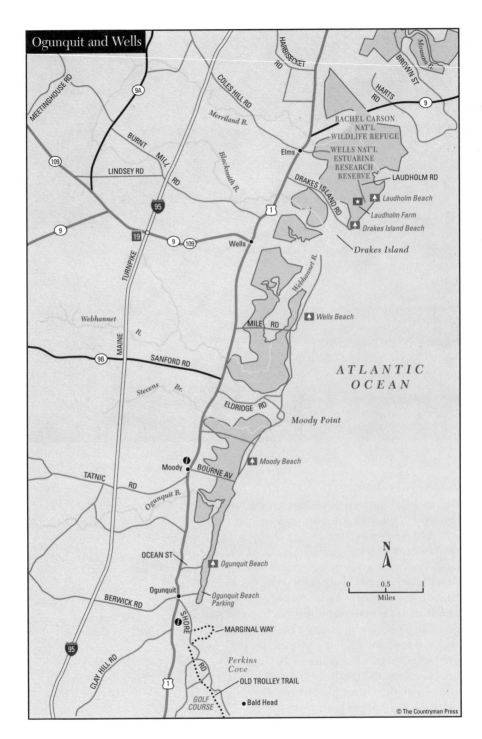

Ogunquit and Wells

MEETINGHOUSE RD
9A
COLES HILL RD
HARBISECKET RD
Mousam R.
BROWN ST
HARTS RD
9
Merriland R.
BURNT MILL RD
109
Blacksmith R.
RACHEL CARSON NAT'L WILDLIFE REFUGE
WELLS NAT'L ESTUARINE RESEARCH RESERVE
Elms
LINDSEY RD
95
DRAKES ISLAND RD
LAUDHOLM RD
Laudholm Beach
Laudholm Farm
Drakes Island Beach
19
1
Drakes Island
9
9 109
Wells
Webhannet R.
Webhannet
R.
MAINE
MILE RD
Wells Beach
9B
SANFORD RD
ATLANTIC OCEAN
Stevens Br.
ELDRIDGE RD
Moody Point
TATNIC RD
Moody
BOURNE AV
Moody Beach
Ogunquit R.
N

OCEAN ST
Ogunquit Beach
0   0.5   1
Miles
Ogunquit
Ogunquit Beach Parking
BERWICK RD
SHORE RD
MARGINAL WAY
95
Perkins Cove
CLAY HILL RD
1
OLD TROLLEY TRAIL
GOLF COURSE
Bald Head

© The Countryman Press

Carson Interpretive Trail, Wells

Nancy English

The Carson Interpretive Trail, 1 mile long, is part of the Rachel Carson National Wildlife Refuge, which has 10 different sites along the South Coast. It's open sunrise to sunset. Seats are provided at viewing stations along this level, short trail, located off Rt. 9 just south of the Kennebunk line in Wells.

Next door is the Wells National Estuarine Research Reserve at Laudholm Farm (207-646-1555; wellsreserve.org; just off Rt. 9). Comprising more than 2,000 acres of estuary, the reserve holds meadows and two barrier beaches once part of Laudholm Farm, a saltwater farm started in the 1640s and active until the 1980s. Now birders seek out the 7 miles of trails and protected coastline. Fiddle playing and pumpkin rolling are part of a popular festival called Punkinfiddle (punkinfiddle.org) held the last Saturday of September.

The Front Porch in Ogunquit has live performances in the second-floor piano bar

Nancy English

The last of former Hurricane Isaac blows out to sea off Ogunquit. Nancy English

Rt. 1 through Ogunquit and north to Wells and the Shore Rd. south to Perkins Cove are lined with lodgings and restaurants. Traffic often proceeds at a crawl. Some visitors like to stay close to the village of Ogunquit so they can walk to dinner, to the beach, and back to their rooms, with an assist from the free trolley. Nightlife in Ogunquit in summer is one the area's popular features, with entertainment like the Judy Show, a parody of Judy Garland, performed at Maine Street, a lively downtown bar, and the renovated Leavitt Theater, with first-run movies and a piano accompaniment for a series of silent movies put on in 2014. A cabaret performed at Café Amore (207-646-6661; amorebreakfast.com; 309 Shore Rd., Ogunquit) is another possiblity, with a fantastic singer named Mark Camacho—known as Marco—as well as cocktails and light snacks.

Musicians perform original numbers at Jonathans (207-646-4777; jonathans restaurant.com; 92 Bourne Lane, Ogunquit), which is also quite a good restaurant. Reserve tickets in advance for the often sold-out shows, perhaps presenting longtime stars John Mayall and Arlo Guthrie or the relative newcomer, singer-songwriter Melissa Ferrick.

Ogunquit Playhouse (207-646-5511; ogunquitplayhouse.org; 10 Main St., Ogunquit) has roots in the 1930s and the Little Theater Movement that planted theaters in small towns. The theater in Ogunquit was built in 1937 by Walter and Maude Hartwig, who started their own Manhattan Theatre colony in Ogunquit and hired stars like Ethel Barrymore to perform in summer. Sally Struthers plays leading roles every summer in this professional theater.

Checking In

Best places to stay in Ogunquit and Wells

Beachmere Inn (207-646-2231; beach mereinn.com; 62 Beachmere Place, Ogunquit) has been run by the women of the same family since 1937. It has undergone extensive renovation and rebuilding while continuing to enjoy a secluded location on the edge of the sea and proximity to the village of Ogunquit. Marginal Way is accessible through a gate in the lawn. Spacious accommodations emphasize function and beauty almost equally, with locally made, elegant furniture, kitchen-ettes, some gas fireplaces and a few wood-burning fireplaces, and of course wonderful views. A pub with a light-fare menu makes it possible to stay on the grounds, wandering from the oceanside to the green lawn and to the sauna, for days on end.

On one hot August Wednesday, owner and innkeeper Bruce Senecal—who runs Gazebo Inn (207-646-3733; gazeboinnogt.com; 572 Main St., Rt. 1, Ogunquit) with Scott Osgood—told us he'd already turned away 600 people, and it was only 1 PM! Make reservations early to be sure of a room at this well-run, affordable, and convenient bed & breakfast. The modern rooms have all the requisites, while the business retains a comfortable intimacy and welcome. Breakfast is stupendous, and a movie room with cushy couches along with a bar, outdoor pool, gym, sauna, and massage room keep the social scene lively. Footbridge Beach, away from the crowds and across the Ogunquit River, is a short hike away. Osgood and Senecal also own 2 Village Square Inn (207-646-5779; 2vsquare.com; 14 Village Square Lane,

Ogunquit) and Captain's Quarters (207-646-3733; captainogt.com; Rt. 1, Ogunquit), across from the Ogunquit Lobster Pound. Pets can visit the suites at Captain's Quarters, where rooms with kitchens and kitchenettes and lower weekly rates can make a visit economical.

The Dunes on the Waterfront (207-646-2612; dunesonthewaterfront .com; 518 Main St., Ogunquit) is an old favorite, with direct access to the mid-dle of the glorious Ogunquit Beach and comfortable rooms.

Just south of Perkins Cove, The Riverside Motel (207-646-2741; river sidemotel.com; 50 Riverside Lane, Ogunquit) offers basic, clean, and comfortable accommodations right in the heart of things. The rooms over-look the water, but the location keeps rates high in August. Another lodging with a primo location, a mile or two south of the Riverside Motel and near the border of York Beach, is Cliff House Resort & Spa (207-361-1000; cliffhousemaine.com; Shore Rd.), an elegant, historic resort with a new spa building and vanishing horizon pool that visitors can float in while staring at the vast ocean just beyond. A rocky

A comfortable, old-fashioned room at Clifftop at The Cliff House, Ogunquit, is filled by the sounds of the sea. Nancy English

The Riverside Motel sits opposite Perkins Cove

Nancy English

The Cliff House, Ogunquit

Nancy English

cliff under the main building gives the setting unusual drama; the dining room is set inside with panoramic views. Gas fireplaces in some of the new rooms and an indoor pool are improvements that came along after the U.S. military took over the place during World War II to use as a submarine lookout. Sleeping to the sound of crashing surf has been part of the night's stay since the beginning.

Listed last because it's out of town and one of our favorite places, The Beach Farm Inn (207-646-8493; beachfarminn.com; 97 Eldridge Rd., Wells) is far from the madding crowd and nicely appointed with fine furniture. The pool is in view of the breakfast porch, where blueberry pancakes might be served; the full breakfast is included in the rates. Modest rates reflect shared and private baths, and accommodations include two cottages.

Local Flavors

The taste of Ogunquit and Wells—local restaurants, cafés, and more

Joshua's (207-646-3355; joshuas.biz; 1637 Post Rd., Rt. 1, Wells) stands at the top of the list in this region, at least as far as we're concerned, because of its excellent, uncomplicated cuisine founded on fresh produce, much of it grown at the owners' own farm. Duck leg confit with port sauce and rack of lamb are two standards of excellence on the menu.

Owners Clark Frasier and Mark Gaier won the well-deserved Best Chef Northeast award from the James Beard Foundation in 2010, for their work at now-closed Arrows. Their MC Perkins Cove (207-646-6263; mcperkinscove.com; 111 Perkins Cove Rd., Ogunquit), might serve a lunch that starts with vibrant tomato soup, with perfect Bibb lettuce and a chicken salad. A bar menu lists a lobster roll and french fries, but raw oysters could start a more formal meal, with bacon-wrapped meat loaf or tea-smoked duck breast with apricot and star-anise-cured confit to follow. The ocean waves, crashing either near the building or down the rocky beach at low tide, make the view from the tables at the windows particularly wonderful.

Angelina's Ristorante and Wine Bar (207-646-0445; angelinasogunquit .com; 655 Main St., Rt. 1, Ogunquit) does Italian classics as good as they can be. Reservations are a must at this hopping restaurant named for owner David Giarusso's grandmother. His wonderful zuppa di pesce sings with bright basil, garlic, sweet tomatoes, and fresh seafood, and the high-quality veal and beef make just as good a dish of Piccata or pizzaiola. Risottos and fresh house pasta dishes are specialties. You'll wish you were staying long enough to try a lot more on the menu than you can sample in one night—but maybe you are.

Starting the day at Amore Breakfast and Café Amore (207-646-6661; amorebreakfast.com; 309 Shore Rd., Ogunquit), open 7 AM–1 PM, is a local tradition easy to observe when the menu offers bananas Foster French toast, coated with pecans and stuffed with cream cheese, or a lobster Benedict with two poached eggs and hollandaise around sautéed lobster; the café next door, open till 2, is the place for panini, salads, and sandwiches. Cove Café (207-646-2422; 20 Perkins Cove Rd., Ogunquit) makes good breakfasts too, though less elaborate, and if you

The Cove Café serves an excellent breakfast.

Nancy English

go early there just might be a parking place alongside.

Surf Point Grill at the Anchorage by the Sea (207-646-9384; anchorage bythesea.com; 125 Shore Rd., Ogunquit) serves all three meals in a dining room by the pool; locals like its burgers, ribs, steaks, and seafood.

For a boiled lobster, The Lobster Shack (207-646-2941; lobster-shack .com; 110 Perkins Cove Rd., Ogunquit) does it right, with a big sink to wash up at afterward in the dining room, and thick slab tables easy to get to work on. Lobsters, steamers, lobster stew, chowder and chili, some sandwiches, and beer round out the simple menu.

Kennebunk and Kennebunkport

Check out these great attractions and activities . . .

The Kennebunk River forms the boundary between Kennebunk and Kennebunkport, with the southern town, Kennebunk, the one you see first after exiting from the highway. The fine Main St. with brick buildings is quiet compared with the crowded sidewalks closer to the sea, where Kennebunk and Kennebunkport are connected by a little bridge over Rt. 9, with good casual restaurants like Federal Jacks—one of Maine's first brewpubs—on the Kennebunk side and Alisson's across the bridge in Kennebunkport.

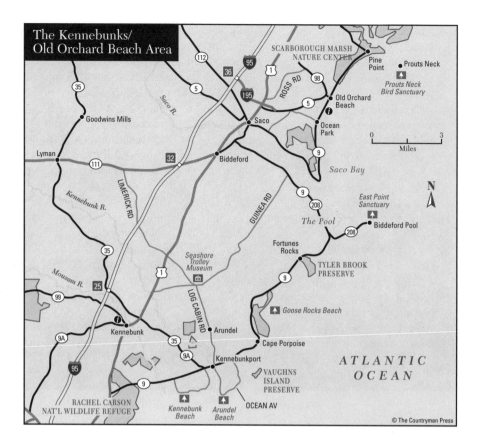

The Kennebunks/
Old Orchard Beach Area

SCARBOROUGH MARSH
NATURE CENTER

Pine Point • Prouts Neck

Prouts Neck
Bird Sanctuary

Old Orchard
Beach

Ocean
Park

Saco

Goodwins Mills

Lyman

Biddeford

Saco Bay

Saco R.

East Point
Sanctuary

The Pool • Biddeford Pool

Fortunes
Rocks

Seashore
Trolley
Museum

TYLER BROOK
PRESERVE

Goose Rocks Beach

Kennebunk R.

LIMERICK RD

Mousam R.

LOG CABIN RD

GUINEA RD

ROSS RD

Kennebunk

Arundel

Cape Porpoise

Kennebunkport

VAUGHNS
ISLAND
PRESERVE

ATLANTIC
OCEAN

RACHEL CARSON
NAT'L WILDLIFE REFUGE

Kennebunk
Beach

Arundel
Beach

OCEAN AV

© The Countryman Press

0   3
Miles

N

But back inland for another moment, The Brick Store Museum and Archives (207-985-4802; brickstoremuseum.org; 117 Main St., Kennebunk) holds exhibits about local history and artifacts in its own historic structure, an 1825 dry-goods store built by shipowner William Lord (whose home is the Captain Lord Mansion mentioned in *Checking In*). The museum has come to fill several buildings on the block as its work has grown over the years, with exhibits, lectures, and art shows among the offerings.

But one of its most popular is outside the walls and down the street, on the historic walking tours that guide visitors along a mile of flat sidewalks and streets to view the Colonial, Federal, Greek Revival, Queen Anne, and Colonial Revival architectural styles magnificently preserved in Kennebunk's historic district.

On the road to Kennebunkport, The Wedding Cake House pulls in all passing eyes. Though the house is privately owned, tours are sometimes offered as a special event. Its original owner, George W. Bourne, became enamored of Milan's Gothic cathedral on his journeys, and undertook similar ornamentation of his Federal-style house in 1852 using hand tools and with the assistance of a ship carpenter's apprentice.

The Kennebunkport Historical Society (207-967-2751; kporthistory.org; 8 Maine St., Kennebunkport) presents the Greek Revival Nott House with its Doric

The Wedding Cake House near Kennebunkport

Nancy English

colonnade for guided tours, showing off carpets, furniture, and wallpaper that are original to the house. A tasteful gift shop in the Carriage House sells souvenirs of gentility. Hours vary according to the season.

Christmas Prelude is a popular event in early December, opening up the Nott House for a champagne reception while the shops keep late hours and horse-drawn carriages pass in the streets. Tree lighting, a crafts fair, and a pancake breakfast offer more ways to get in the spirit.

The Seashore Trolley Museum (207-967-2712; trolleymuseum.org; 195 Log Cabin Rd., Kennebunkport) opened in 1939 when trolley cars were seeing their last days as basic mass transportation. Today more than 250 vehicles from all corners of the world are displayed, and buses are among them. A 3-mile excursion comes with the price of a ticket, with evening rides offered in summer. Locomotive engines like one from the Atlantic Shore Line Railway have been restored with thousands of hours of volunteer labor; in fact, everything you see here is a labor of love. Check out the fantastic museum store with the hard-to-find books for rail fans.

For a summer picnic, consider a visit to Black Rock Farm (207-967-5783; blackrockfarm.net; 293 Goose Rocks Rd., Kennebunkport), a nursery and farm that sells unusual and stunning plants and custom containers. The landscape, designed according to the owner's aesthetics, provides a taste of what a garden can be.

The conducter describes the Bowling Alley streetcar from New Haven, Connecticut, during the trolley ride at Seashore Trolley Museum.

Nancy English

Checking In

Best places to stay in Kennebunk and Kennebunkport

Three historic buildings standing around a small green in Kennebunkport offer luxurious rooms. The Captain Lord Mansion (207-967-3141; captainlord.com; 6 Pleasant St., Kennebunkport) is furnished with massive beds that might come equipped with steps; one over-the-top room has a bathroom with a gas fireplace. You won't lack for comfort in these plush surroundings, and the halls and parlors are just as elegant. A full breakfast in the country kitchen is part of the rates, but the spa services are extra.

Captain Fairfield Inn (800-322-1928; captainfairfield.com; 8 Pleasant St., Kennebunkport) is a little more restrained in its decor, perhaps show-ing off a more austere architectural style. The room called The Library has its own private porch. But visitors to any of the rooms enjoy the perks, from the excellent breakfast to the afternoon cookies.

The Captain Jefferds Inn (207-967-2311; captainjefferdsinn.com; 5 Pearl St., Kennebunkport) has a room called the Monticello with a lace-canopied queen-sized four-poster and a gas fireplace to keep the blue-and-white color scheme warm and friendly. The more rustic decor in the carriage house could be more to many's liking, and the amenities are just as fine. "Baxter" was inspired by Maine camps—but in this case everything works and nothing leaks.

Cape Arundel Inn (207-967-2125; capearundelinn.com; 208 Ocean Ave., Kennebunkport) is a local classic and the only inn on the open ocean. Rooms in the inn and in an addition all face the ocean, with big picture windows making the most of it. The fine restaurant is called Ocean, and the chef, Pierre Gignac, was once chef-owner at 98 Provence in Ogunquit, an excellent restaurant that closed in 2012.

The Colony Hotel (207-967-3331; thecolonyhotel.com; 140 Ocean Ave., Kennebunkport) is the real thing, an old resort still going strong, its strengths in its good, solid furniture, and its limitations in the old style that furniture maintains. If it's pleasing to your taste, it will satisfy—and an old-fashioned place is one of our favorite things. There's a heated saltwater pool, golf, and children's activities; breakfast is included in the rates.

Old Fort Inn (207-967-5353; oldfortinn.com; 8 Old Fort Ave., Kennebunkport) is off the main road in Kennebunkport with its own 15-acre site, worth the trouble of finding. The 16 guest rooms are handsomely lodged in a stone-and-brick carriage house, each holding its own wet bar and mini kitchen, and the tiled bathroom floors are heated. A pool, tennis court, and horseshoe pitch offer diversion, along with the fine antiques and gifts in the inn's shop (ownership and reservations chared with Cape Arundel Inn, above).

The Grand Hotel (877-455-1501; thegrandhotelmaine.com; 1 Chase Hill Rd., Kennebunk) overlooks the Kennebunk River, with modern rooms that have all the bells and whistles. The Tides Beach Club (207-967-3757; tidesbeachclubmaine.com; 252 Kings Hwy., Goose Rocks Beach) is inside an 1899 shingle-style summer hotel designed by John Calvin Stevens with windows open to the sound of waves. Visited by Sir Arthur Conan Doyle and Theodore Roosevelt in its early days, it's been renovated and updated. Across the street is glorious Goose Rocks Beach, constantly updated by

nature and always fresh. Fine dining in "TBC" might involve fish tacos, pulled pork or swordfish with wild mushroom ragout. Sister property Hidden Pond (207-967-6550; hiddenpondmaine.com; 354 Goose Rocks Rd., Kennebunkport) has luxurious "bungalows" and a fine-dining restaurant called Earth with an excellent reputation. Lamb chops with carrot marmalade and ricotta gnocchi with nasturtium butter appeared on the 2012 menu. Amenities in the cottages include custom snacks like six chocolate chip cookies and a bottle of milk ($18) or red velvet ice cream, berries, and champagne ($65); a fire pit; a six-seat golf cart that acts as a trolley between properties and goes to downtown at night; and yoga and paddleboard lessons.

Seaside Inn (207-967-4461; kennebunkbeach.com; 80 Beach Ave., Kennebunk) also enjoys a seaside location, this one south of the Kennebunk River on Kennebunk Beach. Nine generations of innkeepers have kept this property in the family, and although it has changed shape over the years the business lays claim to being the oldest inn in the country. Today the rooms are in a two-story modern building, while breakfast is served in an 1850 former boathouse. At this place you don't even have to cross the street to get to the beach, and off-season the rates are very attractive.

The Franciscan Guest House (207-967-4865; franciscanguesthouse. com; 26 Beach Ave., Kennebunk) is the most affordable lodging in this area, and if the rooms are Spartan, the Lithuanian breakfast with homemade farmer's cheese, raisin bread, carrot bread, and potato bread is not (and it's included in the rates). Shrines to the Virgin Mary and others dot the 66-acre grounds.

Down the road a bit and on the

other side from the Guest House is The White Barn Inn (207-967-2321; whitebarninn.com; 37 Beach St., Kennebunk), the *ne plus ultra* in elegance. Antiques-furnished rooms have every possible amenity and more, with fresh fruit on check-in just one small detail

and perhaps one small part of the 5.45 percent hospitality fee added to the steep bill. An elaborate tea is served in the afternoon to guests, and touring bikes are on offer, but spa services and the use of the yacht *True Blue* are extra.

Local Flavors

The taste of Kennebunk and Kennebunkport—local restaurants, cafés, and more

The White Barn Inn, described briefly above, is also a famous restaurant, rated 5 Diamonds by AAA and 5 Stars by *Forbes*. Set inside a barn that's filled with flowers, with tall windows inserted in handsome wood walls, this is an attractive place for a good meal and delivers extraordinary service. Pan-roasted quail and foie gras to start, followed by veal filet with lemon spaetzle and a mushroom and fontina tartlet, were on the menu in 2014 ($109 per person prix fixe).

The lobster roll at The Ramp, the downstairs bar at Pier 77 (207-967-8500; pier77restaurant.com; 77 Pier Rd., Cape Porpoise) is one of the

Outdoor seating at The Ramp in Cape Porpoise

Nancy English

best lobster rolls we've ever had, rich, slightly warm, utterly sensuous and fresh, and the seafood stew is fantastic. Cape Porpoise is north of the village of Kennebunkport, and Pier 77 is down Pier Rd. off Rt. 9, but the place is still part of Kennebunkport. The restaurant is more formal upstairs and lively and casual down, with a few seats outside to take in the sunset and the lobster boats unloading at the dock.

Also in Cape Porpoise, The Wayfarer (207-967-8961; wayfarercape porpoise.com; 9 Pier Rd., Kennebunkport) is a classic casual restaurant revered for its pies that has returned to life under the guidance of Brendan Levin, who has a mastery of dinner standards. BYOB.

Abbondante Trattoria & Bar (207-967-2211; abbondanteme.com; 27 Western Ave., Kennebunk) serves Italian dishes like rigatoni with sausage and peppers and papardelle Bolognese; 12-inch pizzas are baked in a wood-fired oven. The dishes are all available for takeout to create an easy and generous family dinner.

Nunan's Lobster Hut (207-967-4362; nunanslobsterhut.com; 9 Mills Rd.) is in Cape Porpoise village, and its series of rustic rooms have been sheltering hordes of lobster lovers since 1953. (Before that customers bought their lobsters in the front yard from an open kettle, $1.25 for the first one and 80 cents for a second!) Take a number and wait outside till a table is ready. Bring cash, because the business does not accept credit cards.

Local 50 (207-985-0850; localken nebunk.com; 50 Main St., Kennebunk) embraces local produce and meats and fish in all their glory, preparing them in Asian, French, or any other cuisine that makes sense, like a seviche of striped bass with pineapple salsa, pickled chili, and corn tortillas. There's a veggie noo-

dle bowl for vegetarians, and scallops, fish stew, steak frites, and lobster carbonara for the rest of us.

On the Marsh (207-967-2299; onthemarsh.com; 46 Western Ave., Lower Village, Kennebunkport) is a memorable restaurant overlooking a tidal marsh. Chef Jeffery Savage has perfected an elegant menu here, with local mushroom risotto and grilled asparagus or grilled venison "Denver leg" steak. The bar menu makes this place attractive with its half-pound Wagyu beef burger, too.

Nearby at Old Vines Wine Bar (207-967-2310; oldvineswinebar.com; 173 Port Rd., Lower Village, Kennebunk), owner Mike Farrell has put together a wine list that will keep you engaged and intrigued. Sipping the great wines, plates of Serrano ham or house-cured duck prosciutto, cheese plates or seasonal salads—perhaps an heirloom tomato tartine spread with basil pesto and covered with melted fresh mozzarella—could keep you from leaving for dinner anywhere else.

Port Lobster (800-486-7029; portlobster.com; 122 Ocean Ave., Kennebunkport) sells cooked lobsters and lobster rolls—and since it's the source of the picked lobster meat that fills lobster rolls at most local restaurants, you might as well get the stuff fresh from the source.

For the chance to enjoy a drink and a view, two places top the list. Tia's Topside (207-967-8821; tias topside.com; 12 Western Ave., Kennebunk) has a deck overlooking the river perfect for the cocktail hour; raw oysters, good steamers, and brunch too. David's KPT in The Boathouse Waterfront Hotel (207-967-8225; www.boathouseme.com; 21 Ocean Ave., Kennebunkport) is a posher place for that cocktail; the happy-hour wine is perfectly reasonable at $5 a glass, and the modern dining room soothing and calm on a quiet afternoon, off-season. The David's lobster roll, however, was $31 in 2014, and fish-and-chips on the dinner menu was $26.

For self-indulgence that won't wreck the budget, as so much on offer in Kennebunk and Kennebunkport can, try Rococo Artisan Ice Cream (207-251-6866; rococoicecream.com; 6 Spring St., Kennebunkport). You can get the Sunfish Wheat Ale flavor if you want to re-create happy hour on a cone; or try Nutella cranberry, molasses, gingersnap, or maple fig jalapeño. These will not necessarily be among the 14 on offer each day, but something amazing will be, we promise.

Portland Region

INCLUDING FREEPORT, OLD ORCHARD BEACH, PEAKS ISLAND, AND CHEBEAGUE

THE BIG CITY, MAINE-STYLE, is a place to explore on foot. In fact Portland's downtown is located on a foot-shaped peninsula with the Eastern Promenade, which looks out to sea, at its toe and the Western Promenade on the back of the heel. Congress St. runs down the length of it. At its intersection with Forest Avenue, the Arts District is in charge of filling the shop windows with art and artists' installations.

From Longfellow Square to Congress Square with the Portland Museum of Art; from City Hall and the top of Exchange St. down through the Old Port to Commercial St.—the main street of the waterfront Old Port— Portland teems with great restaurants, fine hotels, inns and B&Bs, excellent galleries, and extraordinary shops.

Easily accessible both north and south are beaches, amusement parks, and shopping destinations. Canadians have flocked to Old Orchard Beach for generations, and the beach community, now close to its own summertime train station, still thrives on visitors who love its diversions. Saco and Biddeford,

The mainmast of the USS *Portland*, a World War II battle cruiser, is part of a memorial on the Eastern Prom honoring the ship and its sailors. *Nancy English*

historic mill towns that flank opposite sides of the Saco River, have in common a revitalized mill district with its own brewpub and restaurant.

LEFT: Portland harbor *Nancy English*

One of the fine mansions overlooking the Eastern Promenade in Portland

Nancy English

North of Portland and just a 20-minute drive on I-295, Freeport sustains its shopping luster with a shopping complex, movie theater, and dozens of outlet stores. L.L. Bean's giant hunting boot, outside the door of its flagship store, isn't wearing out, of course, because the business fixes it when it does—just as it does anything a customer returns. Customers love the company's lifetime guarantee: Bring in worn-out boots—or anything else—for a replacement, no questions asked.

Saco, Biddeford, Old Orchard Beach, Scarborough, and Cape Elizabeth

Attractions, activities, accommodations, eateries, etc.

Saco Museum (207-283-3861; dyer librarysacomuseum.org; 371 Main St., Saco) has beefed up its exhibits, offering folk art and antiques among its permanent exhibits of paintings. A mill girl's bedroom makes vivid her long days with artifacts and racy letters. In Pepperell Square, Blue Elephant Café (207-281-3070; blueelephant catering.com; 12 Pepperell Square, Saco) serves well-made meals for breakfast and lunch.

Cross the river south for several good eating places. On Saco Island overlooking Saco River Falls is Run of the Mill Brew Pub (207-571-9648; 100 Main St., Saco), which serves its own excellent beer and decent pub food. A seat on the patio outside would be the ticket on a summer night, the air cooled by the river alongside.

Portland's Middle Street   Nancy English

Goldthwaite's, Biddeford Pool   Nancy English

The deck over the Saco River at Run of the Mill   Nancy English

Palace Diner (207-284-0015; www.palacedinerme.com; 18 Franklin St., Biddeford) brings culinary glory to a diner tucked among the (spruced-up) mills; everything on its breakfast and lunch menu is made with skill. Taste why it is cherished; dinners may be offered in the summer or for special events, and are not to be missed.

Jewel of India (207-282-5600; the jewelofindia.com; 26 Alfred St., Biddeford), which has a branch in South Portland (45 Western Ave., near The Maine Mall), presents the fine aromatics of freshly ground spices. In South Portland, the Bollywood DVDs that play on the weekend are delightfully energizing.

Of course, lobster and fried seafood aren't far from any spot on the coast. Biddeford's coastal community, called Biddeford Pool, has its own low-key place for seafood, Goldthwaite's (207-284-5000; poollobster.com; 3 Lester B. Orcutt Blvd., Biddeford Pool), where you order a lobster roll or something else at the counter, wait to be called, and enjoy your food at a picnic table in back near the water.

North of Saco's village on the commercial stretch of Rt. 1 an almost endless series of car sales lots is interrupted by a couple of amusement parks that have drawn local kids for decades. Funtown Splashtown USA (207-284-5139; funtownsplashtownusa.com; 774 Portland Rd., Rt. 1, Saco)—you can get a pass if it rains and return along with the sun—has waterslides, kiddy rides, and a wooden roller coaster called Excalibur, built in 1998 (you must be 48 inches or taller to ride). The water park has a family raft slide among its many waterslides.

Aquaboggan Water Park (207-282-3112; aquabogganwaterpark.com; 980 Portland Rd., Rt. 1, Saco) has really fast, really high, really steep waterslides that your kids will haul you up and down on for hours. Little ones will never be interested in leaving the wave pool. Lure them away to the mini golf course to dry out.

A visit to Old Orchard Beach puts many attractions within walking distance—if you don't mind considering the ocean the best water park of all. Palace Playland (207-934-2001; palaceplayland.com; Rt. 1, Old Orchard Beach) is the town's amusement park, with a Ferris wheel lighting the night sky and fireworks every Thursday night by the Pier. From the carousel for little people to Power Surge, for those 50 inches and taller, flinging your limbs in every direction, the rides are the attraction.

The Pier (oobpier.com) is its own world. First built in 1898, with concerts, a casino, and dancing, the tall structure stretched out over the waves until it was damaged by a storm. Repaired, it hosted crowds till a fire burned the entrance in 1907. Another storm chewed it up in 1909—and the repairs this time made the thing shorter. Frank Sinatra came to sing in the mid-1900s, the heyday. But in 1978 it seemed the thing was gone for good after a blizzard. Tradition proved too strong, however—it reopened in 1980. The Pier french fries are supposed to be terrific, and six restaurants and a variety of entertainment keep it hopping through the warm weather.

Motels line the main street. Those known to us as reliable include Billow-house (207-934-2333; billowhouse.com; 2 Temple Ave., Ocean Park) and, more casual, The Nautilus by the Sea (207-934-2021; nautilusbythesea.com; 2 Colby Ave., Ocean Park), both on the wide flat sandy beach that stretches for miles. Families will enjoy the sand south of Old Orchard Beach at Ocean Park, a 7-mile-

Crescent Beach is a quiet strand in Cape Elizabeth.   Christina Tree

An early-morning surfer at Higgins Beach
                                    Christina Tree

long beach beside a summer community with a long history of camp meetings and Sunday-morning services. A music program and tennis courts are more aspects of Ocean Park's offerings.

Dinner in Old Orchard Beach can be readily enjoyed at The Landmark (207-934-0156; landmarkfinedining.com; 28 East Grand St., Old Orchard Beach), a local institution that keeps getting better. More elegant, though not at all formal, and equally historic, Joseph's by the Sea (207-934-5044; josephsbythesea.com; 55 West Grand Ave., Old Orchard Beach) makes a dish called Pasta Maison, with angel-hair pasta, Maine shrimp, scallops, salmon, and mussels with cream that was a fine surprise—light, fresh, and delicate.

Following Rt. 9 north past Pine Point—part of the town of Scarborough—will bring you to Ken's Place (207-883-6611; 207 Pine Point Rd., Rt. 9, Scarborough), where the fried clams are terrific and the first Tuesday of the month you can count on fried oysters.

Along that same stretch of road is the Scarborough Marsh Audubon Center, open seasonally (207-883-5100 May through September, for year-round information call 207-781-2330; maineaudubon.org; Pine Point Rd., Rt. 9, Scarborough). Linda Woodard runs the center, offering self-guided walks and canoe tours—you can rent canoes here—as well as guided tours like a full-moon tour of the marsh or an edible and medicinal plant walk. The birding is extraordinary.

Another point of land in Scarborough rewards a visit. Black Point Rd.

Scarborough Marsh   Nancy English

Black Point Inn, Scarborough

Nancy English

stretches out into the sea on a point of land that ends at Prouts Neck. This gated community holds the Winslow Homer Studio, now owned by Portland Museum of Art (see the sidebar). Tours of the Homer Studio will not be offered in the summer, but you can walk around it, if you park at the Black Point Inn (207-883-2500; blackpointinn.com; 10 Black Point Rd.)—though you must also enjoy a drink or a meal at the inn. The inn deserves a visit in its own right, especially when the jazz combo plays on the glorious porch. It's a gracious old hostelry that has refocused on food and comfort. The 25 rooms are all top of the line in luxuriousness. This is reflected in the high prices, but remember that rates include a full breakfast and dinner, both likely to be worth your while. Golfing, tennis, beaches, and bikes are all at your disposal.

Another luxurious and tempting oceanfront inn on Rt. 77 in Cape Elizabeth is The Inn by the Sea (207-799-3134; innbythesea.com; 40 Bowery Beach Rd., Cape Elizabeth). Fifty-seven guest rooms range from enormous suites and two-bedroom cottages, all with a water view, to guest rooms with a gas fireplace. A pool, a spa, and a boardwalk to Crescent Beach State Park keep you entertained right where you are, and pet lovers love it here because they can bring their dogs, who come in for some high-end petting of their own. Sea Glass Restaurant is the inn's fine dining restaurant, earning high praise.

The Breakers (207-883-4820; www.thebreakersinn.com; 2 Bay View Ave., Higgins Beach) has the ocean view we are all seeking out, and comfortable rooms. Higgins Beach Inn (207-883-6684; higginsbeachinn.com; 34 Ocean Ave., Scarborough) has charming simple rooms that are attractive and affordable, especially if they share a bath. The inn's good restaurant, Garofalo's, features really delicious Italian dishes and many recipes from innkeeper Diane Garofalo's family. Higgins

Winslow Homer Studio, Scarborough

Nancy English

Winslow Homer Studio

The Portland Museum of Art bought the **Winslow Homer Studio** (portland museum.org/homer) in 2006 from the artist's great-grandnephew, who had enjoyed the building as a summer house and used to leave it unlocked for art lovers to visit. That informality is no more, but with a knowledgeable docent in charge, your visit will linger in memory as a glimpse of an irascible genius and his now protected vista of the Atlantic Ocean.

Visits require tickets and reservations ($55 for nonmembers, $30 for members, in 2014; tours offered in spring, summer, and fall, lasting 2½ hours). An upscale bus takes groups of no more than 10 to the studio from the museum.

The building has been restored to look much the way it did when Winslow Homer lived and painted here. The great American artist spent summers here from 1884—when the studio, a former carriage house, was embellished with a second-floor porch by local architect John Calvin Stevens—until Homer died at the studio in 1910 of natural causes. He was 74.

Portland Museum of Art docent Carol Patterson leading a tour at Cannon Rock, near the Winslow Homer Studio   Nancy English

And it was here that Homer painted his masterpieces, from *Fox Hunt* held by the Pennsylvania Academy of Fine Arts, to *Weatherbeaten*, part of the Portland Museum of Art Homer Collection. Homer steeped himself in the light and energy of the coast, once hiring a boy to row him offshore in a storm and often standing in observation of the heaving waves, absorbing the power of nature and imbuing his canvases with its majesty.

The iconic Portland Head Light is in Fort Williams Park, Cape Elizabeth. Nancy English

Beach is a short block down the quiet street, and surfers like it for its good waves. Families love the flat, wide, sandy beach too, where the surfers are kept off to the sides during prime beach hours.

Finally, but with the highest scenic importance, a visit to Portland Head Light in Fort Williams Park cannot be beat. The park holds decaying Goddard Mansion and Fort Williams, busiest during World War II, but Maine's oldest lighthouse, Portland Head Light (207-799-2661; portlandheadlight .com; 1000 Shore Rd., Cape Elizabeth) with its own museum in the keeper's

Fall apple picking at Snell Family Farm

Nancy English

quarters, is the main attraction. The lighthouse first warned mariners in 1791. It's a perfect setting for a picnic and for flying kites, while the rolling grassy hills and short oceanside path are other diversions. The Arboretum at Fort Williams Park (207-400-6706; arboretumatfortwilliams.org) opened its first landscaped garden here in 2012, Cliffside, which lies inland of a cliffwalk in the park. Within a few years the project will encompass 14 landscaped areas, with the resilience and beauty of native species showcased.

A beautiful drive out of town in the fall brings you to Snell Family Farm (207-929-6166; www.snellfamilyfarm.com; 1000 River Rd., Rt. 112, Buxton) for pick-your-own raspberries and apples, along with an overflowing farmstand.

The Arboretum at Fort Williams Park

Nancy English

Portland

Check out these great attractions and activities . . .

Walkable Portland holds several museums within a few blocks, starting with the biggest, the Portland Museum of Art (207-775-6148; portlandmuseum .org; 7 Congress Square). It's open daily 10–5, Memorial through Columbus Days, Fridays until 9; closed Mondays off-season; closed major holidays. The modern building that holds most of the exhibits was designed by Henry N. Cobb of I. M. Pei & Partners and built in 1983. Among its pleasures is the view from the inside out, across Congress Square. When you can turn away from the windows, the walls will reward you with art by Winslow Homer (see the sidebar about Homer Studio visits), Edward Hopper, Andrew Wyeth, some examples of the works of Picasso and Matisse, and many more. The 1801 McLellan House, where the museum was first opened, is a Federal-style mansion restored to its glory with bold, period wallpapers and carpets. In between are the L. D. M. Sweat Memorial Galleries, built in 1911 by John Calvin Stevens, which hold some of the museum's most loved 19th-century paintings and sculptures

The Children's Museum of

An old fountain marks Boothby Square in Portland.

Nancy English

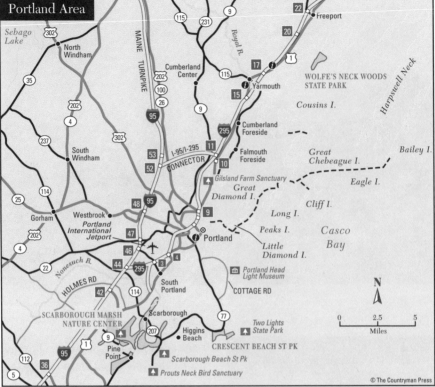

Portland Area

Sebago Lake

North Windham

Cumberland Center

Yarmouth

WOLFE'S NECK WOODS STATE PARK

Cousins I.

South Windham

I-95/I-295 CONNECTOR

Cumberland Foreside

Falmouth Foreside

Great Chebeague I.

Bailey I.

Gilsland Farm Sanctuary

Great Diamond I.

Eagle I.

Gorham

Westbrook

Portland International Jetport

Cliff I.

Long I.

Peaks I.

Casco Bay

Portland

Little Diamond I.

Nonesuch R.

HOLMES RD

South Portland

Portland Head Light Museum

COTTAGE RD

N

SCARBOROUGH MARSH NATURE CENTER

Scarborough

Two Lights State Park

Higgins Beach

CRESCENT BEACH ST PK

Pine Point

Scarborough Beach St Pk

0   2.5   5
Miles

Prouts Neck Bird Sanctuary

© The Countryman Press

Maine (207-828-1234; kitetails.org; 142 Free St.) is next door, a perfect spot to let the kids get rid of their energy after a tour of artwork, in the model lobster boat or the fire engine, the grocery store or the popular ATM—which gives out play money.

Down Congress St. a few blocks toward the sea is the Maine Historical Society (207-774-1822; mainehistory .org; 485 Congress St.), with a newly renovated library. The Longfellow Garden Society maintains the peaceful garden that borders the building. It's open to the public just past the buildings and is the perfect spot to eat the sandwich you bought for lunch. There are period furnishings in the Wadsworth-Longfellow House, built in 1785 by the grandfather of Henry Wadsworth Longfellow, the poet who was born in Portland and whose statue stands in Longfellow Square; tours are offered most days. The Maine Historical Society Museum holds changing exhibits.

Post Office Park at the beginning of fall

Nancy English

Looking into the second floor of Victoria Mansion from inside the Turkish Smoking Room   David Bohl

The Maine Jewish Museum (207-329-9854; mainejewishmuseum.org; 267 Congress St.) has permanent exhibits including one called *Jewish Voices of Maine* with recordings of religious music by cantors and oral history interviews. Art exhibits change with the seasons. The museum is housed in immigrant-era Etz Chaim Synagogue, built in the mid-1800s as a six-family apartment house and converted to a synagogue in 1921, with a (now restored) stained-glass window. Live broadcasts of 92nd Street Y programs, listed on the website, have free admission.

The Museum of African Art and Culture (207-871-7188; museumafricanculture.org; 13 Brown St.) is the creation of founder Oscar Mokeme, a descendant of Nigerian Igbo royal family healers. His collection of masks, bronzes, batiks, and wooden sculptures comes to life when he dons one for a ceremonial blessing.

Victoria Mansion (207-772-4841; victoriamansion.org; 109 Danforth St.) is a pleasant walk down Park St. past some of Portland's prettiest town houses. The mansion was built in 1858 by Ruggles Sylvester Morse, who made a fortune with New Orleans hotels; this was to be his summer home. The mansion was scheduled to be demolished in 1940 but was saved by a retired teacher, William Holmes, who used his own money to stave off decay. Room interiors created by Gustave Herter and 90 percent of the original furnishings make this mansion, the finest surviving Italian-villa-style house in America, remarkable. Its holiday decorations take the elaboration even higher. The resplendent Turkish Smoking Room benefits from refurbishing—and the absence of any smoke.

Greater Portland Landmarks Center for Architecture and Preservation (207-774-5561; portlandlandmarks.org; 93 High St.) is just down Danforth and up High, and its library is a fund of information about architecture in Portland. The center provides a variety of tours of Portland, including Homes of Portland's Golden Age, 1800–1860, which shows off the city's Federal, Greek Revival, and Italianate houses. The Portland Observatory gets its own tour. This maritime signal tower on the top of Munjoy Hill, a long walk across town, gives visitors who climb up its stairs a great view of Casco Bay and the White Mountains.

Portland Trails (207-775-2411; trails.org; 305 Commercial St.) has developed more than 50 miles of trails in and around Portland—the trail map is sold on the website. But from Casco Bay Lines on Commercial St. a wide paved path makes a

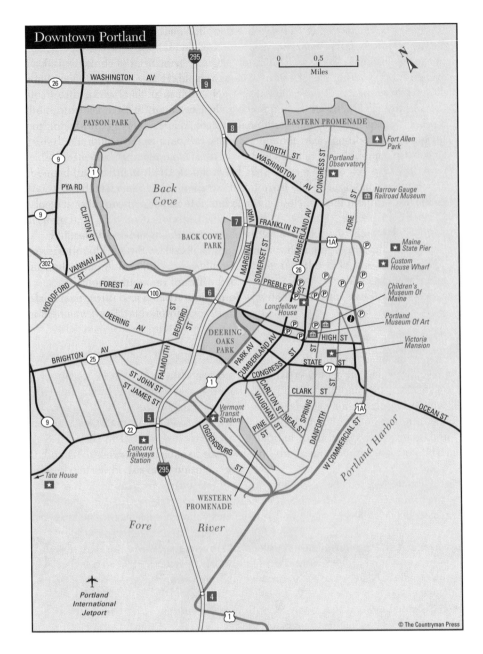

great hike around Eastern Promenade, and intrepid walkers will be able to circle the entire peninsula to reach Baxter Blvd., a charming path filled with Portlanders exercising every lovely day of the year. Guided walks offered on the website include moonrise tours.

Narrated tours can be enjoyed with Portland Discovery Land & Sea Tours (207-774-0808; portlanddiscovery.com; 3 Moulton St.) and Downeast Duck Tours (207-774-3825; downeastducktours.com; 94 Commercial St.). Spirits Alive (207-

A historic fire truck takes the curious around Portland, on Fire Truck Tours. *Nancy English*

In the Allagash Brewery Curieux aging area, the air is scented with caramel. *Nancy English*

Foodie Tours, Portland *Nancy English*

846-7753; spiritsalive.org) is a group dedicated to protecting the Eastern Cemetery (gates at 224 Congress St.), guiding visits to the graves through the summer on Sunday afternoons and describing the lives of the people buried here. Around Halloween, you might encounter the ghosts of those folks themselves—or perhaps they're actors—during the Walk Among the Shadows, a benefit for the organization held in early evening.

Wicked Walking Tours (wicked walkingtours.com; 72 Commercial St.) takes visitors around the Old Port to hear about the strange and horrible things that humans have done in the buildings and sidewalks of the port city. Buy tickets in advance online. Maine Foodie Tours (800-979-3370; maine foodietours.com) travel on foot or in a trolley to fish stores, cheese shops, bakeries, chocolate shops, and breweries, munching on samples. Fire Truck Tours (207-252-6358; Portland Fire Engine Company, 180 Commercial St.) offers tours in a historic fire engine. If beer appeals, Belgian-style Allagash Brewery (207-878-5385; allagash.com; 50 Industrial Way) starts you off with samples on your free tours, so you know exactly what's going on inside the whiskey barrels. Reserve a space online to take the tour and give yourself time for the drive to the brewery off outer Forest Ave. Sweetgrass Winery & Distillery (207-761-8446; www.sweet grasswinery.com; 324 Fore St.) is in the Old Port and offers tastings of its seasonal spirits, like an exquisite apple brandy, and wines made from fruits and grapes. And the best way to take in a range of beverages is The Maine Brew Bus (207-200-9111; www.themainebrewbus.com), which offers to drive you on several tours of the local breweries and distilleries, one price to sample concoctions from typically three places, with a snack included.

Checking In

Best places to stay in Portland

You visited the museums, took the tours—now where are you going to stay? The West End, Portland's wealthiest neighborhood and a modest walk from downtown, holds a few fine bed & breakfasts. The Morrill Mansion Bed & Breakfast (207-774-6900; morrillmansion.com; 249 Vaughan St.) has seven comfortably furnished rooms, each with private bath, with a feeling of luxury and fairly reasonable rates. Full breakfasts and afternoon treats keep guests happy, as they do at The Inn on Carleton (207-775-1910; www.innoncarleton.com; 46 Carleton St.), renovated and brought to a high polish by Buddy Marcom. The Chadwick (207-774-2137; thechadwick .com; 140 Chadwick St.), with its back garden, was Marcom's previous project, and new ownership is keeping up the good work.

Fancier rooms at The Pomegranate Inn (207-772-1006; pomegranate inn.com; 49 Neal St.) are decorated in a bold, colorful style by Heidi Gerquest, a Portland artist, but off-season rates are available. The Danforth (207-879-6557; danforthinn.com; 164 Danforth St.) is in an elegant building with refurbished rooms named for local places.

The Mercury Inn (207-965-6670; www.mercuryinn.com; 273 State St.) is green, comfortable, and contemporary. It's also close to downtown. Breakfast here is good yogurt and maybe strawberry muffins. A little farther away, The Inn at St. John (207-773-6481; innatstjohn.com; 939 Congress St.) is a favorite of budget-conscious travelers.

People who prefer hotels can find many of them, since several have opened in the last few years: the Press Hotel, under construction at our own presstime, will open in 2015.

Hyatt Place Portland (207-775-1000; www.portlandoldport.place .hyatt.com; 433 Fore St., Portland) zigzags its modern glass facade along Fore St., an area of that street locally reknowned for loud drunken weekend revelry. Ergo, book higher up for a view without a raucous serenade, but the earplugs offered at the front desk may not make much difference. Excellent amenities, otherwise.

Westin Portland Harborview (Eastland) (207-775-5411; www .westinportlandharborview.com; 157 High St., Portland) kept the big red EASTLAND sign on the roof and should have kept the name, since people assuming a harbor view are often out of luck (the top-floor cocktail lounge is the place with the view). To save the valet fee, you can park your own car in the garage just down High St.—but there's no avoiding the $9.95 WiFi fee. You can count on the gloss and lush comfort typical of the Westin chain inside the rooms.

Portland Regency (207-774-4200; theregency.com; 20 Milk St.), with its own health club and a good bar called The Armory Lounge. Free WiFi, and a great bar called the Armory Lounge. Guests in the Hampton Inn Portland Downtown—Waterfront (207-775-1454; 209 Fore St.) and Hilton Garden Inn (207-780-0780; hilton gardeninnportland.com; 65 Commercial St.) can see past buildings to the water, and both enjoy an indoor pool. The rooms in upscale Portland Harbor Hotel (207-775-9090; the portlandharborhotel.com; 468 Fore St.) might offer a marble bathroom, glassed-in shower, granite counters, and an oval spa tub.

Local Flavors

The taste of Portland—local restaurants, cafés, and more

not in the least speak to which is best. In fact, there is no easy answer to the question *Which is your favorite restaurant*, because there are so many places to love for so many different reasons.

Dinner

Remarkably, almost all of Portland's dining spots are sustaining themselves with enthusiastic crowds. It's been clear to the restaurateurs who cruise the streets and peer into the restaurant storefronts, wondering what the recession has done to dining out, that Portland is a town that invests heavily in dinner.

Customers do even better for themselves, with a variety of cuisines from Ethiopian and Cajun to haute French and down-home Down East. Visitors who plan their day around meals have some work to do to narrow down the choices. To make it easier for you, we've divided the spectrum into expensive, inexpensive, and cheap (prepared food and bakeries), which does

Expensive Dining

Back Bay Grill (207-772-8833; back baygrill.com; 65 Portland St.) rewards every visitor, whether you order a martini at the bar or go for a dish from every course on the menu. Hudson Valley foie gras with pickled bing cherries; the best crabcake in the state; the signature organic Scottish salmon, perhaps with chanterelles—all are brilliant proof this is the place you want to dine.

Fore Street (207-775-2717; fore street.biz; 288 Fore St.) opened in June 1996, bringing chef and part-owner Sam Hayward's obsession with local fresh ingredients into action amid a big, somewhat rustic, and often busy and noisy space. Almond butter on the wood-oven-roasted mussels makes them addictive, and spit-roasted pork

The dining room at Back Bay Grill

Courtesy of Back Bay Grill

loin and seared hanger steak have their own fan club. Best of all are seasonal items like summer lamb, fall squash, and winter scallops. Hayward was awarded the Best Chef Northeast medal from the James Beard Foundation in 2004.

Hugo's (207-774-8538; hugos.net; 88 Middle St.), elegant restaurant, serves dishes that combine fabulous flavor and beautiful looks. Vermont quail came almost boneless, juicy under the tang of an aromatic glaze; count on any dish to be perfectly made. Next door, a sister venture for a more casual crowd packs the bar and bench seating. Eventide Oyster Company (207-774-8538; eventideoysterco.com; 86 Middle St.) features an enviable drinks list, and its old-fashioned is the best in the city, but for some of us the oysters are the thing. John's River oysters from South Bristol were extraordinary, but there will be many others to try—perhaps with the whipped Tabasco. Fine cooked food too.

Petite Jacqueline (207-553-7044; www.bistropj.com; 190 State St.) might squeeze you in at the bar; call for a reservation for a table and dine on French classics like onion soup, choucroute garnie and rabbit, an always reliable fish meunière, and a plat du jour worth trying; the steak au poivre turns up on Sunday.

Miyake (207-871-9170; restaurant miyake.com; 468 Fore St.) serves the best sushi in town inside one of its most elegant dining rooms. Try the omakase, or chef's choice, because owner-chef Masa Miyake has a sure sense of flavors and puts together maki and sushi that will delight your taste buds: a touch of heat, the richness of a quail egg, perhaps silky wild salmon, and so many other things. If you're in luck, one of them will be fresh uni. Pai Men Miyake (207-541-9204; 188 State

St.) is a (less expensive) sister restaurant devoted to noodles and broths like elixirs, popular from the moment the doors opened.

Lolita Vinoteca and Asador (207-775-5652; www.lolita-portland.com; 90 Congress St.) is set on Munjoy Hill, serving its specialty, meat and more grilled in its central open-flame grill, along with lamb meatballs and green lentils, deft pasta dishes and fresh fish.

Piccolo (207-747-5307; www .piccolomaine.com; 111 Middle St.) has a knack for rustic Italian dishes full of earthy deep flavors, from a touch of anchovy with the roasted cauliflower to the savory depth of foraged fall mushrooms. The wine dinners, particularly with Devonish wines, are not to miss!

Caiola's (207-772-1110; caiolas .com; 58 Pine St.) is many people's favorite restaurant, relaxing, welcoming, and fun, with Abby Harmon's sure touch in the kitchen assuring that dinner will be wonderful. In late fall it might start with polenta fries with cheddar cheese and red pepper relish and go on to the terrific burger or house cannelloni. However you proceed, you won't go wrong.

Emilitsa (207-221-0245; emilitsa .com; 547 Congress St.) serves the owner's mother's Greek food, plates of lamb chops, a beautiful whole roast fish, and starters of tangy and richly flavored spreads. The bread will be crusty, the feta creamy and sharp, the wine acidic and strong; the vegetables are prepared with olive oil, lemon, garlic, and herbs in ways you will wish you could emulate every night at home.

Zapoteca (207-772-8242; www .zapotecarestaurant.com; 505 Fore St.) will park your car for you for free. Fresh lime juice makes the variety of magaritas refreshing; the guacamole, a humble thing, is made to order and better that way. Seviches, fine salsas,

Simple and perfect, Piccolo Cauliflower is a classic appetizer

Nancy English

enchiladas worth return trips, and excellent Mexican recipes with fish.

Vignola Cinque Terre (207-772-1330; vignolamaine.com; 10 Dana St.) offers thin-crust pizza, fine Italian wine lists, and a knack for Italian cured meats, zesty salads, and pasta, perhaps wrapped around lobster in ravioli or covered with house pancetta ragu. Much of the produce, fruit, and honey on the plates comes from the owners' farm.

five fifty-five (207-761-0555; fivefifty-five.com; 55 Congress St.) has a comfortable bar area and a bar menu for a quick introduction to Steve Corry's fine cooking. Hanger steak with a cloud of béarnaise, Sumner Valley chicken, Maine's most flavorful, with spaetzle and Madeira cream, or monkfish in a brandy wine reduction were for dinner in 2012. The spectacular ice creams are worth sampling, and this is a great place for brunch.

Brunch is more rustic at Local 188 (207-761-7909; local188.com; 685 Congress St.), a good place to meet for drinks that comes up with good specials and small plates too. House gnocchi, seared shrimp, and chorizo in Romesco sauce with penne and a house paella are specialties. Tapas ranging $4–14 make perfect snacks for a light appetite.

Sonny's (207-772-7774; sonnysportland.com; 83 Exchange St.) is owned by the same folks as Local 188. The historic space, a former bank, is remarkably attractive, and the bar area sleek and modern. Seviche, chiles rellenos, and Caribbean succotash capture the inflection of the menu. Arroz con pollo, mac and cheese with chorizo, and the house dry-aged rib eye are more honey for us bees.

Moderately priced, the Grill Room (207-774-2333; hardingleesmith.com; 84 Exchange St.) is one of three restaurants owned by Harding Lee Smith, who started his own entrepreneurial career after years of cooking for others on Munjoy Hill with his successful Front Room (207-773-3366; 73 Congress St.), with comfort food, generous portions, and lots of butter and salt. At the Grill Room, grilled steaks and fish are the center of the steak-house menu, but he keeps the prices low somehow or other, even when the chicken is organic.

The Corner Room (207-879-4747; 110 Exchange St.) is one block up the street from the Grill Room, but its menu centers on Italian specialties, and the fresh house pasta does a lot of the work of making dishes stand out.

Down on the waterfront is the fourth "room," Boone's Fish House & Oyster Room (207-774-5725; boones fishhouse.com; 86 Commercial St., on Custom House Wharf), where the upstairs space offers a more adventurous menu.

Paciarino (207-774-3500; pacia rino.com; 468 Fore St.) serves its own excellent fresh pasta in classic dishes you really cannot hope to taste except in Italy, or at least that's how it used to be. House goat cheese ravioli with caramelized onion, or seafood ravioli with sweet Maine shrimp, can be bought to cook at home as well as enjoyed in the restaurant.

Central Provisions (207-805-1085; www.central-provisions.com; 414 Fore St.) serves lunch and dinner daily on small plates; sea urchin noodles, fish with radishes, and lamb amazed one happy visitor. Suckling pig and white Peking duck are on the "hearty" list.

Inexpensive Dining

Empire Chinese Kitchen (207-747-5063; www.portlandempire.com; 575 Congress St.) makes perfect green beans, fabulous dumplings, jalapeño shrimp, and more—closed Tuesday, so the weekend is golden.

Duck Fat (207-774-8080; duck fat.com; 43 Middle St.) is owned by Rob Evans and Nancy Pugh, former owners of Hugo's. Their vision for a lunch place with crisp panini, extraordinary fries cooked up with duck fat, soup, salad, and specials, has kept folks coming back. The milk shakes will intoxicate you with their richness; the Original is made with double Tahitian vanilla bean crème anglaise gelato.

Oh No Café (207-774-0773; ohno cafe.com; 87 Brackett St.) is a neighborhood place you'll want to drive to for a fantastic sandwich, fine soups, and wonderful breakfast specials. The roast chicken with avocado, tomato, and red onion is one favorite, but we always go for the grilled hanger steak salad with cucumbers and blue cheese.

El Rayo Taqueria (207-780-8226; www.elrayotaqueria.com; 101 York St. and also 245 Rt. 1 in Scarborough) makes perfect margaritas, fish tacos with chipotle mayo, and burritos and quesadillas; the summer scene includes live music and waves of happiness.

158 Picket Street Café (207-799-8998; 158 Benjamin Pickett St., South Portland) makes soups with heat and depth, and sandwiches that resound with pesto and fresh mozzarella or chutney and cured meat, and chewy fresh bagels too.

Otto and Enzo (207-773-7099; ottoportland.com; 576 Congress St.) prove that cheap food can provide as exalted an experience as the expensive kind. Pizza by the slice, thin crust and marvelous, is sold on the left in Otto, to be eaten at a stool in the tiny customer area, on the sidewalk at a seat in good weather, or on your walk home. The mashed potato, scallion, and bacon is perfection, and the mushroom and cauliflower does just as well. Next door you can sit at a table and eat the great pizza, order a whole pie and share it, and drink some inexpensive plonk or beer and have a salad. No dessert, no other things on the menu. No one minds.

Order outside at the Flatbread Company, Portland

Nancy English

Boda (207-347-7557; bodamaine .com; 671 Congress St.) serves Thai street food, and again a taste of what the real stuff is like makes you wish all the Thai places in town would attempt to be equally authentic. Pomelo fruit salad on betel leaves, with coconut, peanut, lime, ginger, and shrimp, is an example, and the beef Thai curry is far beefier and less sweet than you might be used to.

Bonobo (207-347-8267; bonobo pizza.com; 46 Pine St.) has excellent pizza, cooked in a wood-fired oven, and the namesake version with mushrooms, prosciutto, spinach, leeks, Fontina, and cream can't be beat. Good wine, several salads, and soups round out the menu.

Flatbread Company (207-772-8777; flatbreadcompany.com; 72 Commercial St.) is a chain of high-quality, wood-fired pizza places, and Portland's is right on the water. Enjoy your flatbread overlooking Casco Bay Lines, and order from the outdoor window.

Nosh Kitchen Bar (207-553-2227; 551 Congress St.) does the city's favorite burger and crunchy fries—with bacon dust! Late nights and lunches along with dinner hours keep the door open, as do plates of house-cured meat and an exceptional beer list. Across the street, even-more-reasonable Taco Escobarr (207-541-9097; tacoescobarr .com; 548 Congress St.) serves juicy little tacos anointed with your choice of salsa.

Slab (207-245-3088; www.slab portland.com; 25 Preble St.) presents Stephen Lanzalotta's locally adored Sicilian slab pizza, a poufy chewy thick-dough pizza with savory tomato and a restrained amount of cheese on top.

Veranda Thai Cuisine (207-874-0045; verandathaicuisine.com; 9 Veranda St.) and its sibling business across the street, Veranda Noodle Bar (207-874-9090; verandanoodlebar .com; 14 Veranda St.) with pho and vermicelli dishes, are fine examples of conventional Thai restaurants.

Casco Bay Lines

Nancy English

Asmara (207-253-5122; 51 Oak St.) should not be missed. This Eritrean restaurant is run by Asmeret Teklu, who makes fresh injera, a soft, delicious bread you use to scoop up the cooked greens, meat, and beans. Springy and resilient, the ancient bread has a refreshing sour flavor that makes a fine contrast with the long-cooked, savory dishes—perhaps collards or red lentils, or lamb stew with okra—served for both lunch and dinner.

Prepared Food and Bakeries

Standard Baking Company sells bread from the bakery downstairs (207-773-2112; 75 Commercial St., Portland), a resource for scones and luscious morning buns. The business shares ownership with Fore Street.

Rosemont Markets (207-774-8129 at 580 Brighton Ave., and 207-773-7888 at 88 Congress St., Portland; rosemontmarket.com) make wonderful pies with seasonal fruit, cakes and quiche,

meat loaf, and their own pastrami, sandwiches, soups, spreads, and sauces. They also stock local vegetables, fruits, and berries, fine cheeses from Maine and far afield, good and low-priced wines, and provisions of all kinds. In 2015, a new location will open at Pine St. and Brackett in the West End.

Holy Donut (207-874-7774 at 194 Park Ave., and 207-775-7776 at 7 Exchange St., Portland; theholydonut .com) is the place for Maine potato doughnuts in scrumptious flavors like pomegranate, fresh lemon, and dark chocolate sea salt.

Scratch Baking Company (207-799-0668; scratchbakingco.com; 416 Preble St.) is worth a trip to South Portland to taste the slow rise, chewy levain, country white, and sour rye. Bagels are a specialty, and the pastries exceptional.

Aurora Provisions (207-871-9060; auroraprovisions.com; 64 Pine St.) makes a fine dinner; the dolmathes

Standard Baking Company, Portland

Nancy English

among its prepared foods and lemon bars among the delectable baked goods are both excellent examples. You can get everything you need here, from soup to nuts, wine to coffee.

Speaking of coffee, Arabica (207-899-1833; 2 Free St.) roasts its own beans and sells them, as well as brewing them for fine cappuccinos, lattes, and espressos in their airy coffeehouse. Crisp, fresh toast with butter is a specialty, unusually fine because of the chewy fresh bread they stock from a local baker. Bard Coffee (207-899-4788; bardcoffee.net; 185 Middle St.) has a fine location and even better cup of coffee. Free WiFi. Speckled Ax Espresso (207-660-3333; 567 Congress St.) teamed up with Allagash to make an Ethiopian coffee Belgian ale called James Bean. Count on extreme attention to the predilections of the beans, which are all wood-fire roasted.

The Portland Farmers Markets, on Saturday morning in Deering Oaks

The best bagels in town and an array of baked goods at Scratch Baking Co. in South Portland's Willard Square

Nancy English

Park and on Wednesday through the lunch hour at Monument Square, attract crowds who come to gaze in adoration at the result of farmers' labors. The produce gets better and better.

At the Portland Farmers Markets   Nancy English

Arabica in Portland   Nancy English

Portland Farmers Markets produce   Nancy English

Peaks Island and Chebeague Island

Attractions, activities, accommodations, eateries, etc.

Casco Bay Lines (207-774-7871; casco baylines.com; 56 Commercial St., Portland) is the starting point for an excursion out to the islands of Casco Bay. Its red-and-yellow ferries make several trips daily year-round to commuter-filled Peaks Island, where a meal and a walk or a bicycle ride make up an excellent day trip. Down Front is the name of the part of the island near the ferry dock, reached after a mere 20 minutes on the ferry, and it's also the location of the island's store, post office, two inns, and a few restaurants.

The Inn on Peaks Island (207-766-5100; innonpeaks.com; 33 Island Ave., Peaks Island) sits at the top of the little hill you climb after getting off the ferry. Its handsome rooms provide excellent retreats, with cottage furniture and views, while the dining room with outdoor seating in good weather makes terrific fried clams, fried Maine shrimp, and burgers as well as more serious entrées like prime rib on Friday and Saturday nights.

Cockeyed Gull (207-766-2800; cockeyedgull.com; 78 Island Ave., Peaks Island) is an institution on the island with a twist—the Korean owner, whose grilled salmon and rack of lamb are second to none out here, can also make some fine Korean dishes. The deck has an incredible view of Portland's harbor glimmering in the distance, and the sunset.

Brad's Island Bike Rental (207-766-5631; 115 Island Ave., Peaks Island) rents bikes, often on the honor system, with a box to put your money in and a selection of well-maintained bikes to choose from. A bike trip around the island takes a leisurely 45 minutes, but a few stops and explorations of the rocky coves fill the day up quickly. When you park your bike back at Brad's and head to the ferry, there's always time for an ice cream cone at Down Front, at the top of the hill by the ferry dock.

Chebeague Island is an hour and a half away from Portland, when you ride the ferry from Casco Bay Lines. Anyone interested in staying awhile will prefer to park at the Rt. 1, Yarmouth, parking lot of Chebeague Transportation Company (207-846-3700; chebeaguetrans.com; Chebeague Island). After you pay a parking fee you climb into a bus for a ride (included in the parking charge) to the dock on Cousins Island, where the ferry picks up passengers to Chebeague. The Chebeague Island Inn (207-846-5155; chebeagueislandinn.com; 61 South Rd., Chebeague Island) has an upscale menu that makes dinner an event, most of it completely satisfying. The long, wide porch filled with wicker chairs will always be a lovely place to take in the sunset and enjoy a drink at the end of a day exploring the island, and the golf course between that porch and the water is open to visitors. Your island explorations will also be assisted by the generosity of Mac Passano, the Bike Man of Chebeague, who provides bicycles for free.

Freeport and Yarmouth
Attractions, activities, accommodations, eateries, etc.

L.L. Bean (877-755-2326; llbean.com; 95 Main St., Freeport) is open, as many of you know, 24 hours a day, 365 days of the year. That's lucky for the warehouse workers on the third shift who want to go Christmas shopping at 3 AM when work lets out (the warehouses that fulfill phone orders are down Desert Rd.) and just as lucky for the tourists driving through Freeport anytime of the day or night. Believe us, the buildings are peaceful and quiet late at night. Although the round-the-clock hours pertain only to the Flagship Store, the L.L. Bean Hunting & Fishing Store, the L.L. Bean Bike, Boat & Ski Store, the L.L. Bean Home Store, and the L.L. Bean Outlet are certainly open late into the night as the Christmas holidays approach. The L.L. Bean complex is decked out with its own tall holiday tree flashing light, and the town does the holiday right too.

Sparkle Weekend (freeportusa.com has the full event listing) in Freeport includes tree lighting next to L.L. Bean, carolers, free hot cocoa, and free horse-drawn carriage rides on one weekend in early December. L.L. Bean's Northern Lights offers its own free horse-drawn carriage rides every afternoon and into the early evening on Saturday and Sunday from late November to late December.

In almost any weather the company hosts its Outdoor Discovery Schools, in which anyone can enjoy an introduction to a variety of sports, depending the season, by calling 888-552-3261 for a $20 "discovery course" or signing up at the Outdoor Discovery School kiosk in the Flagship Store. Scenic kayak tours, a four-hour trip, are sometimes offered just for women and cost $75 in 2012. Target skills and

L.L. Bean's big boot   Bill Davis

sporting clays—a clay target game similar to shooting skeet—are other possibilities. All equipment is provided.

In 2012 there were more than 200 shops to check out in Freeport. Coffee shops like Isabella's Sticky Buns (207-865-6635; 2 School St., just off Rt. 1 one block north of L.L. Bean) provides the necessary coffee and cinnamon bun to get you through the day, as well as terrific sandwiches and soup. A customer who really wishes to unwind will find all exquisite at Jacqueline's Tea Room (207-865-2123; 201 Main St.), by reservation only 11 AM–3 PM, where tea is a ceremony and the busy world is worlds away.

But maybe you don't think about eating as soon as the subject of shopping comes up, like us. In that case, consider the intersection of Bow and Main Streets in Freeport the center of your world. On the western side of the street are all the L.L. Bean stores except the Outlet, which is now located in the Freeport Village Station (207-552-7772; onefreeportvillagestation.com), just a few steps down Bow St. and to your right. Also in Freeport Village Station are outlets for Nike, Calvin Klein, Coach, Brooks Brothers, and Famous Footwear. Parking lots are located just off Main St. on both sides, including inside the parking garage of Freeport Village Station (enter from Depot or Mill St.).

Along Main St. you'll see Burberry, Cole Haan, Jones New York, and Polo Ralph Lauren. Down Bow St. look for J. Crew and The North Face.

Thos. Moser Cabinetmakers (207-865-4519; thosmoser.com; 149 Main St.) is at the north end of the village, and shows off wooden handcrafted furniture with lines as graceful as the flight of a migrating seabird.

Cold River Vodka (207-865-4828; coldrivervodka.com; 437 Rt. 1) is south of the village on a stretch of Rt. 1 worth driving to, not only to tour the distillery of this award-winning business—one of the first of Maine's boutique distilleries—but also to visit Cuddledown's Outlet (207-865-1713; cuddledown.com; 554 Rt. 1) and discover your own best deal among the many storefronts in this busy section of the coast.

For both shopping and dining, Harraseeket Inn (207-865-9377; harraseeket inn.com; 162 Main St.) cannot be beat. The elegant inn has an indoor pool, a formal and exceptional fine dining restaurant, The Maine Dining Room, and a more casual but very good breakfast, lunch, and dinner place called The Broad Arrow Tavern. Both emphasize local and wild food sources, and The Broad Arrow is decorated like a Maine camp.

If you wish to decorate your home that way, The Mangy Moose (207-865-6414; themangymoose.com; 112 Main St.) has everything you need, from moose antlers to a taxidermied bobcat—but more typical of this fun store are the Maine embroidered pillows, great books, and maple syrup.

Brewster House Bed & Breakfast (207-865-4121; brewsterhouse.com; 180 Main St.), James Place Inn (207-865-4486; jamesplaceinn.com; 11 Holbrook St.), and White Cedar Inn (207-865-9099; whitecedarinn.com; 178 Main St.) are all well-run B&Bs, serving good breakfasts to their guests and providing the personal touch and local knowledge so helpful to visitors.

At any of those inns, you're likely to hear a recommendation for Azure Café (207-865-1237; azurecafe.com; 123 Main St.) for its well-made Italian specialties. The Mediterranean Grill (207-865-1688; mediterraneangrill.biz; 10 School St.) makes good kebabs, spanakopita, and moussaka. Of course, you might not have yet satisfied your taste for lobster, and a scenic spot to crack open a freshly steamed lobster is close at hand: Harraseeket Lunch & Lobster (207-865-4888; harraseeket lunchandlobster.com; Main St., South Freeport). Order lobster and steamers at one window in the back, on a deck overlooking the water, and fried seafood at another by the picnic tables and awning.

Harraseeket Lunch & Lobster, South Freeport   Nancy English

Brunswick/Bath Region

INCLUDING THE HARPSWELLS, PHIPPSBURG PENINSULA, AND GEORGETOWN PENINSULA

COASTAL RT. 1 OFFERS EASY ACCESS but no views of Brunswick, Maine's premier college town, or of Bath, the handsome old shipbuilding city that's home to the Maine Maritime Museum. The highway double-barrels past both communities, shortchanging them along with the Midcoast's most convenient—yet surprisingly peaceful—peninsulas and bridge-linked islands.

Between its Brunswick and Bath exits, Rt. 1 shadows the Androscoggin River for a way, giving motorists a glimpse of the area's many hundreds of miles of waterfront. Two of Maine's longest and mightiest rivers—the Kennebec and the Androscoggin—meet in Merrymeeting Bay above Bath. Cove-notched peninsulas stretch south from both communities.

Harpswell, south of Brunswick, is known for its seafood restaurants but also offers some of the coast's best kayaking. Phippsburg and Georgetown, south of Bath, are home to the Midcoast's biggest and best beaches.

Brunswick

Check out these great attractions and activities . . .

If you want to continue along the coast, you have to leave I-295 and switch to Rt. 1 at Brunswick (brunswickdown town.org). Exit 28 puts you abruptly on a commercial strip; at a particularly long light, Rt. 1 angles off to the left. Continue straight instead, up leafy Pleasant St. to Maine St. Turn right and right again at Brunswick Station and the Brunswick Visitors Center (207-721-0999; 16 Station Ave.) with WiFi and restrooms. Here you can board Amtrak's Downeaster (amtrakdowneaster.com), a Concord Coach (concordcoachlines.com), or the local

LEFT: Front Sreet, Bath

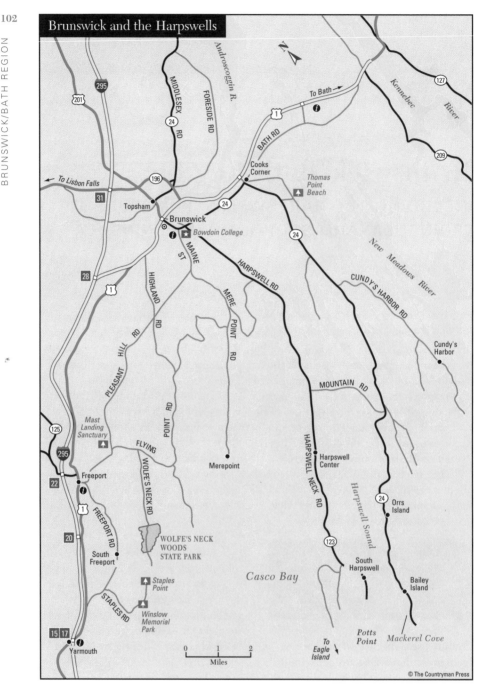

Brunswick and the Harpswells

© The Countryman Press

Brunswick Farmer's Market on the Mall

Christina Tree

Brunswick Explorer. It's also the seasonal departure point for the Maine Eastern Railroad (see the sidebar). Park here and stroll, either up Maine St. to the Bowdoin College (bowdoin.edu) campus, or down to shops and restaurants.

Brunswick's Maine St. is the widest main street in the state, laid out in 1717 with a grassy "mall" near the upper end, the scene of farmer's markets and summer band concerts. Its long lower blocks are lined with shops, galleries, and restaurants. This is a true college town with reasonably priced restaurants, an outstanding bookstore (Gulf of Maine Books, 134 Maine St.), and frequent alternative films at Eveningstar Cinema (149 Maine St.) and the Frontier Café & Cinema Gallery (14 Maine St.). Galleries cluster at the lower end of the street. Second Friday Art Walks (artwalkmaine.org/brunswick) reveal many more studios and other art venues along the way.

Founded in 1794, Bowdoin is not only the pride but also very much a part of Brunswick. Its visitor-friendly campus is the July and August venue for the Bowdoin International Music

Poet Gary Lawless presides over the Gulf of Maine Bookstore in Brunswick.   Christina Tree

The Pickard Theater at Bowdoin College

Christina Tree

Eagle Island State Historical Site

Christina Tree

Festival (bowdoinfestival.org) and for the Maine State Music Theater (msmt.org), Maine's most popular summer stage. The nearby Bowdoin College Museum of Art (bowdoin.edu/artmuseum) has been recently renovated and expanded, the better to display its varied collection and changing exhibits, which include contemporary artists. Don't miss the Peary-MacMillan Arctic Museum, hidden away in Hubbard Hall. It's a trove of trophy Arctic wildlife and gear from the

Maine RR Excursion Meets Amtrak

The **Maine Eastern Railroad** (866-637-2457; maineeasternrailroad.com) runs on weekends July until late October. The 56-mile run from Brunswick to

Rockland—with stops in Bath, Wiscasset, and Newcastle—takes just over two hours, traveling along the coast in plush, streamlined 1940s and '50s coaches and dining car, pulled by a 1950s diesel electric engine. Check the website for current schedule and fares, also special events. Note that the **Amtrak Downeaster** (amtrakdowneaster.com) from Boston also serves Brunswick. Tickets for both the Downeaster and Maine Eastern are available at the visitors center/station (brunswick-station.com).

Maine Eastern Railroad

Christina Tree

pioneer attempts by Bowdoin graduates Robert Peary and Donald Baxter MacMillan to reach the North Pole. For more about the colorful and controversial Admiral Peary—and his role in the 1890s equivalent to the 1960s race to the moon—visit his ship-shaped home on Eagle Island (pearyeagleisland.org), now a state historic site.

Tip: Brunswick's museums are closed Monday; seasonal concerts are Wednesday evening on the mall, and farmer's markts are held there Tuesday and Friday.

The Harpswells

Check out these great attractions and activities . . .

Famed for its seafood restaurants, and generally known as "the Harpswells" because it's so ragged, cut by water and stitched by bridges, this is a great place to stay. Harpswell (harpswell maine.org) claims hundreds of islands and more shoreline than any other town in Maine. Harpswell Sound is a particularly appealing, sheltered place for kayaking—and H_2Outfitters (h2outfitters.com), sited at the Cribstone Bridge on Orrs Island, is in a great spot to access it. They offer tours ranging from a few hours to several days.

From Maine St. at the edge of the Bowdoin campus, Rt. 123 runs south, past farm stands and gallery signs. In Harpswell Center the 1775 white-clapboard Elijah Kellogg Church, named for a former pastor who was a popular 19th-century children's book author, faces the matching Harpswell Town Meeting House across the road. Admittedly, most people who come this far are on their way to two of the area's popular seafood restaurants (see *Local Flavors*).

Most tourists actually turn off Rt. 123 six miles below Brunswick, onto Mountain Rd., which crosses Harpswell Sound on its way to Sebascodegan Island. The road ends at Rt. 24, where a right takes you through scenic Orrs Island and across

Joshua Chamberlain

Local historians argue that the Civil War began and ended in Brunswick—and a case can be made. It was here that Harriet Beecher Stowe penned *Uncle Tom's Cabin*, a book credited with starting the war; and Joshua Chamberlain—the Bowdoin College professor (and later president) considered Maine's greatest Civil War hero—was the Union general chosen to accept the South's surrender at Appomattox. Thanks to the Ken Burns PBS *Civil War* series and a spate of Civil War films and books, Chamberlain's popularity has surged in recent years. The **Joshua Chamberlain Home and Museum**, 226 Maine St., has been rescued from demolition and largely restored by the **Pejepscot Historical Society** (207-729-6606). Chamberlain (1828–1914) is best remembered for his valor and leadership defending Little Round Top during the Battle of Gettysburg. He ended the war as a major general and was chosen by General Grant to meet with General Robert E. Lee at Appomattox. As the Confederate regiments marched into the Union camp to lay down their arms, Chamberlain had his troops salute them, a gesture of respect that infuriated some Northerners but helped reconcile many Southerners to defeat. After the war Chamberlain served four one-year terms as governor of Maine, and served 1881–83 as president of Bowdoin College. The house itself evokes the sense of this intriguing man—as well as of a young Henry Wordsworth Longfellow, who lived here in 1832–33 while a student at Bowdoin, three decades before Chamberlain moved in.

Joshua Lawrence Chamberlain

Penobscot Historical Society

the recently rebuilt Cribstone Bridge. Built with granite blocks, laid honeycomb-fashion to allow tidal flows, the bridge puts you on Bailey Island. Continue past picturesque Mackerel Cove and keep an eye out for Washington Ave. on the left. Park at the small shingled building here that's an Episcopal church and follow the signs and path along the water to the Giant Staircase. The staircase itself is a series a clefts in the cliffs with a flight of smooth boulders rising through the surf. The rocks all along this path look deceptively soft, like petrified driftwood.

Back on Rt. 24 continue to Land's End, where a large gift store and small statue by Casco Bay honor Maine fishermen. Return up Rt. 24 to Rt. 1. There are plenty of photo and shopping ops along the way. Cundy's Harbor, a well-marked 7-mile roundtrip detour, is another place to savor seafood with a view of lobster and sailboats in another quiet inlet.

Checking In

Best places to stay in Brunswick and the Harpswells

Brunswick Inn (207-729-4914; the brunswickinn.com; 165 Park Row, Brunswick), the best place to stay in town, is a gracious, 1840s Greek Revival mansion with long windows and a pillared porch. It's buffered from Maine St. traffic by the grassy "mall," but is within walking distance of both the Bowdoin College campus and downtown shops and restaurants. The 15 guest rooms and suites are divided between the original house and a contemporary carriage house; ample common space includes a hearthside bar. The Brunswick Hotel and Tavern (207-837-6565; thebrunswickhoteland tavern.com; 4 Noble St., Brunswick) is a 48-room, four-suite facility with a restaurant near the campus. The

Daniel (207-373-1824; thedanielhotel .com; 10 Water St., Brunswick), renovated in 2013, offers 24 elevator-accessed guest rooms and suites, a fitness center, and The Coast Bar + Bistro near the Androscoggin. The Black Lantern (207-725-6165; black lanternbandb.com; 57 Elm St., Topsham) is a comfortable, moderately priced B&B on the Androscoggin River, across the bridge in Topsham.

Harpswell Inn (207-853-5509; harpswellinn.com; 108 Lookout Point Rd., Harpswell) was once an annex to one of the 52 now vanished hotels and boardinghouses in Harpswell during the steamboating era. With lawns sloping to the water near a quiet point, this three-story, white-clapboard B&B offers peace, all the comforts, and easy access to kayaking and lobster pounds. Middle Bay Farm Bed & Breakfast (207-373-1375; middlebayfarm.com; 287 Pennellville Rd., Brunswick), sited on a quiet cove, is a particularly

Harpswell Inn

Christina Tree

Driftwood Inn, Bailey Island

Christina Tree

beautiful spot. There are four guest rooms in the gracious 1830s main house; the neighboring Sail Loft houses two suites, each with cooking facilities and two small bedrooms. Grounds include a dock, ideal for launching kayaks. Open seasonally, The Captain's Watch B&B (207-725-0979; 916 Cundy's Harbor Rd., Harpswell) is a cupola-topped former Civil War–era hotel that now offers four spacious water-view rooms, as well as access to sailing with the innkeeper's

38-foot *Symbion II*. Open seasonally and facing Casco Bay from Bailey Island, Driftwood Inn and Cottages (207-833-5461; thedriftwoodinn maine.com) is a vintage-1905 compound of rustic cottages and a central lodge with a pine-walled dining room, serving breakfast and dinner. A small, saltwater swimming pool is set in the rocks. The 16 rooms vary in price, comfort, and view; reasonably priced housekeeping cottages are available by the week.

Local Flavors

The taste of Brunswick and the Harpswells—local restaurants, cafés, and more

Brunswick

As you might expect of Maine's premier college town, Brunswick offers widely varied and affordable dining options.

Open for Dinner Only

Henry & Marty (207-721-9141; henry andmarty.com; 61 Maine St.) offers a welcoming atmosphere and varied menu. Trattoria Athena (207-721-0700; trattoriaathena.wordpress.com; 25 Mill St.) serves tender goat chops, braised rabbit, and fine seafood; wild boar ragu makes a savory, brilliant sauce on zigzag-edged tender house pasta. El Camino (207-725-8228; 15 Cushing St.) is also open for dinner only but in a class of its own: funky, friendly, and widely beloved for inventive Mexican food, utilizing chemical-free seafood and meat, organic and largely local produce. There are vegan and vegetarian options, memorable margaritas, and a wide choice of beers.

Open for Both Lunch and Dinner

Tao Restaurant (207-725-9002; tao-yuan.me; 22 Pleasant St.) is an attractive upscale Asian fusion oasis with a wide choice of well-seasoned small plates, and Lemongrass (207-725-9008; lemongrassme.com; 212 Maine St.) serves reasonably priced Vietnamese specialties, tasty noodle soups, fresh spring rolls, and "Goi" salads. Wild Oats Bakery and Cafe in Tontine Mall (207-725-6287; wild oatsbakery.com; 149 Maine St.) is the town gathering place, a find for from-scratch pastries and breads, healthy build-your-own sandwiches and salads. Whatever you do, don't pass up Gelato Fiasco (207-607-4002 gelato fiasco.com; 74 Main St.), the source for offbeat flavors of irresistible ice cream, made from scratch daily, open until 11 PM. The Great Impasta (207-729-5858; thegreatimpasta.com; 42 Maine St.), just off Rt. 1, is a favorite stop for motorists as well as for local pasta lovers; plaques on booths honor regulars.

Scarlet Begonias (207-721-0403; 16 Station Ave.) is another reasonably priced source of pastas and pizzas, also salads and overflowing sandwiches.

A shade off the beaten path, Libby's Market (207-729-7277; 42 Jordan Ave.) is a small variety store that's well worth finding for truly amazing lobster rolls. Nearby the Fat Boy Drive Inn (207-729-9431; 111 Bath Rd.) is a must for nostalgia buffs: no 1950s reconstruct but a real drive-in with carhops that's survived because it's good and reasonably priced.

Spacious and informal with seasonal deck dining overlooking the Androscoggin, Sea Dog Brewing (207-725-0162; seadogbrewing.com) is a good bet for families. It's housed in the vintage-1868 (former) mill, 1 Main St. in Topsham, just across the bridge, the other side of Rt. 1 from Brunswick's Maine St. Also good for families and for solo travelers in search of a comfortable place with WiFi is Frontier Café & Cinema (207-725-5222; explorefrontier.com). Housed at the back of the big brick (former) mill known as Fort Andross (14 Maine St.), it features long windows overlooking a dam and falls on the Androscoggin. The reasonably priced menu evokes different parts of the world frequented in his previous work by owner Gil Gilroy; check the website for frequent films, lectures, and events in the adjoining small theater.

The Harpswells

The Harpswells harbor numerous seasonal places to eat lobster and fresh fish by the water. Locals head for Morse's Cribstone Grill (207-833-7775) across Rt. 24 at the Cribstone Bridge, a glass-walled tavern right on the water, owned by local lobster dealers. The Dolphin Marina & Restaurant (207-833-6000; dolphin marinaandrestaurant.com) is 2.5 miles off Rt. 123 at Basin Point in South Harpswell—but that doesn't seem to prevent everyone from finding it. The Saxton family's long-established, recently expanded restaurant, overlooking Casco Bay, is known for its chowders and lobster stew, but options include everything from sandwiches to sirloin, and everything comes with

Morse's is the place for seafood on Bailey's Island.

Christina Tree

blueberry muffins. On a warm summer day Holbrooks (207-729-9050) in Cundy's Harbor is another great waterside spot to feast at picnic tables on local seafood. On Bailey Island Cook's Lobster House (207-833-2818; cooks lobster.com) is a large, long-established tourist landmark.

Bath

Check out these great attractions, activities, and accommodations . . .

Most communities retain the best of what they build, but all the biggest and most magnificent structures built in Bath have sailed away. Over the years some 5,000 vessels were built here.

Most would have towered high above the present mellow, brick downtown and striking Italianate, Greek, and Georgian Revival mansions lining Washington and High Streets.

Still towering above the city, the one landmark visible from Rt. 1 is Bath Iron Works' 400-foot-high red-and-white construction crane, proclaiming the city's ongoing shipbuilding status.

American shipbuilding began downriver from Bath in 1607, with the launch of the Popham Colony's 30-ton pinnace *Virginia*. It peaked during the post–Civil War era during which 80 percent of this country's full-rigged ships were built in Maine, almost half in Bath. Obviously this is the place for a museum about ships and shipbuilding, and the Maine Maritime Museum (mainemaritimemuseum.org) fills the bill magnificently (see the sidebar). Allow at least an hour—or an entire day if you take a cruise downriver to view lighthouses or a guided paddle into

Merrymeeting Bay to view seals and eagles. Check the current activities and events calendar for this lively, family-friendly museum.

From Rt. 1 the exit ramp to downtown Bath slants steeply down to the Kennebec River, just before the wide, soaring Sagadahoc Bridge. The rehabbed, brick Bath Railway Station (207-442-7291; visitbath.com) here houses a friendly, well-stocked visitors center with restrooms. Continue on under the bridge to Commerical St. You are welcome to stop by Bath Freight Shed to watch volunteers recontructing the *Virginia*, the ship built downriver at the Popham Colony in 1607 (mfship.org). Just beyond, the inviting Waterfront Park offers interpretive panels, benches, and parking. Nearby Front St. is the city's lively heart, its 19th-century brick buildings chockablock with restaurants and shops. Check out both floors of Renys (renys.com), carrying a wide selection of discounted wares, from lawn chairs to stationery, toys, and Maine specialty foods. Markings Gallery (207-443-1499; markingsgallery.com; 50 Front St.) blends locally made, quality clay, glass, jewelry, art, woodworking, and mixed media—and Now You're Cooking (207-443-1402; acooksemporium.com). Around the corner Halcyon Yarn (207-442-7909; halcyon yarn.com; 12 School St.) is a mecca for knitters, spinners, and rug hookers, with yarns distributed worldwide. The Maine Maritime Museum, set in extensive riverside grounds, is a few minutes' drive south along Washington St.

Given its choice of dining and central location, Bath makes a good base. The Inn at Bath (207-443-4294; innatbath.com; 969 Washington St.), a restored 1830s mansion in the historic district, is the city's best B&B. A new four-story, 94-room Hampton Inn (207-386-1310; 140 Commercial St.) offers water views and easy access to shops and restaurants.

Bath Waterfront Park is a great place to sit, stroll, and picnic.   Christina Tree

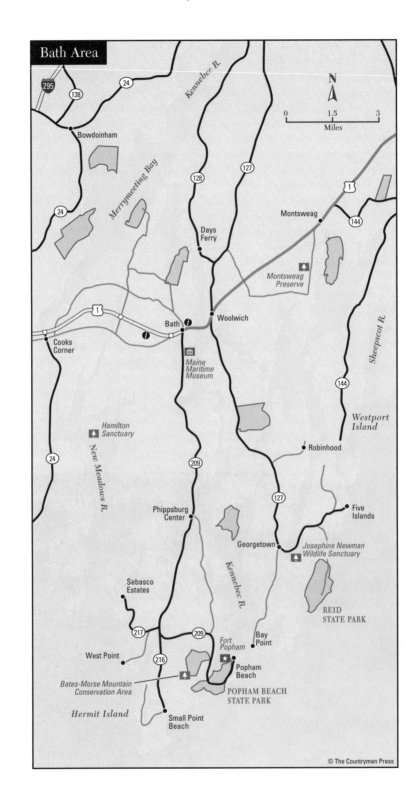

Bath Area

N

0   1.5   3
Miles

Kennebec R.

295
138
24

Bowdoinham

Merrymeeting Bay

24

128

127

Days
Ferry

Montsweag

1

144

Montsweag
Preserve

Bath

Woolwich

Cooks
Corner

Maine
Maritime
Museum

Hamilton
Sanctuary

New Meadows R.

24

209

Sheepscot R.

Westport
Island

144

Robinhood

Phippsburg
Center

127

Five
Islands

Georgetown

Josephine Newman
Wildlife Sanctuary

Kennebec R.

Sebasco
Estates

REID
STATE PARK

West Point

217

209

216

Bay
Point

Fort
Popham

Popham
Beach

Bates-Morse Mountain
Conservation Area

POPHAM BEACH
STATE PARK

Hermit Island

Small Point
Beach

© The Countryman Press

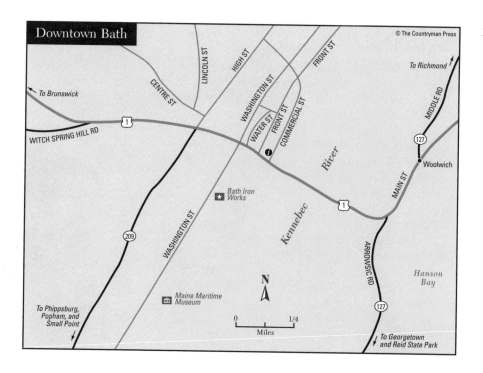

© The Countryman Press

To Richmond

To Brunswick

WITCH SPRING HILL RD

LINCOLN ST

HIGH ST

WASHINGTON ST

WATER ST

FRONT ST

COMMERCIAL ST

FRONT ST

CENTRE ST

MIDDLE RD

Woolwich

River

Kennebec

MAIN ST

WASHINGTON ST

Bath Iron Works

ARROWSIC RD

Hanson Bay

To Phippsburg, Popham, and Small Point

Maine Maritime Museum

N

0   1/4

Miles

To Georgetown and Reid State Park

The Chocolate Church Arts Center (207-442-8455; chocolatechurcharts.org; 804 Washington St.) offers frequent entertainment. The big event here is Bath Heritage Days, a multiday extravaganza surrounding the Fourth of July. Highlights: an old-time parade, guided tours, live entertainment, fun competitions, and fireworks over the Kennebec.

Note: It's possible to be car-free in Bath. Arrive via the Maine Eastern Railroad and take advantage of the Bath Trolley, which circulates around town, stopping frequently at the station and the Maine Maritime Museum.

Local Flavors

The taste of Bath—local restaurants, cafés, and more

The best retauarant is Solo Bistro (207-443-3373; solobistro.com; 128 Front St.), open year-round for lunch and dinner. The decor is Scandinavian, simple and sleek, and the chef's way with locally sourced ingredients is inspired. There's always a wide choice and a reasonably piced three-course, prix fixe special. Wednesday dinner is a standout value, and Friday nights feature live jazz. Beale Street Barbeque and Grill (207-442-9514; mainebbq.com; 215 Water St.), open for lunch and dinner, is known far and wide for its Tennessee-style pulled pork, ribs, and Reubens. Kennebec Tavern and Marina (207-442-9636; kennebectavern.com; 119 Commercial St.), open for lunch and dinner, is a spacious oasis with booths and tables overlooking the Kennebec River, plus a seasonal waterside deck. The menu is large, reasonably priced, and can hit the spot after a day of driving. At

Maine Maritime Museum

Both the **Maine Maritime Museum** (207-443-1316; mainemaritimemuseum.org; 243 Washington St.) and **Bath Iron Works** (gdbiw.com) are sited on a 4-mile-long reach of the tidal Kennebec River, with banks sloping at precisely the right gradient for laying keels. Open 9:30–5 daily, the museum's extensive, 20-acre-plus campus includes the brick-and-glass Maritime History Building and the Percy & Small Shipyard, the country's only surviving wooden shipbuilding yard. The permanent collection of artwork, artifacts, and documents totals more than 21,500 pieces. The pride of Bath, you learn, were the Down Easters, a compromise between the clipper ship and old-style freighter that plied the globe between the 1870s and 1890s, and the mammoth multimasted schooners designed to ferry coal and local exports like ice, granite, and lime. Two sleek sculptures depict the hull and stern of the six-masted *Wyoming*, the largest wooden sailing vessel ever built in the United States. Both are built to scale and spaced as far apart as they would have been on the actual ship, which was built on this spot. Permanent exhibits include *Distant Lands of Palm and Spice*, a fascinating and occasionally horrifying glimpse of where and why Maine ships sailed. Exhibits aside, the museum involves visitors in the significance of its surroundings. You can choose from a dozen cruises and other tours. There is plenty here for children, including a hands-on pilothouse and pirate-boat climbing structure. Check the website for frequent workshops and special events.

Figurehead
Sam Skofield
Courtesy, Maine Maritime Museum

Maine Maritime Museum,
Bath   Courtesy, Maine Maritime Museum

The size of a six-masted vessel built on this spot is suggested by the sculpture.   Christina Tree

Mae's Café (207-442-8577; maescafe andbakery.com; 160 Center St.) breakfast omelets are available all day and the luncheon salads and specials have a loyal following. For a quick lunch, pick up a sandwich (good soup too) at the Starlight Café (122 Front St.; closed weekends) and carry it the short block to Waterfront Park. Café Crème (56 Front St.) offers espresso, snacks, and WiFi. The Cabin (552 Washington Ave.) is a justly popular local gathering spot for first-rate pizza in the evening; lunchtime tends to be crowded with workers from the Bath Iron Works across the road. Byrnes Irish Pub (207-443-6776; byrnesirishpub.com; 38 Centre St.) and the Admiral Steakhouse (207-443-2555; admiralsteak house.com; 768 Washington St.), both under the same ownership, round out dining and drinking choices.

Phippsburg Peninsula and Popham Beach

Attractions, activities, accommodations, eateries, etc.

From the Maine Maritime Museum drive south on Rt. 209, down the narrow peninsula that's the town of Phippsburg (phippsburg.com). You cross Winnegance Creek, an ancient shortcut between Casco Bay and the Kennebec River. At Bisson's Center Store (a picnic source) be sure to turn left onto Parker Hill Rd., which puts you almost instantly in Phippsburg Center. On your left is one of Maine's oldest and most imposing mansions, while beyond lies a classic white-clapboard church shaded by a giant, ancient linden tree. The cupola-topped four-square mansion, onetime home of Maine's first U.S. congressman, is now the 1774 Inn at Phippsburg

A newly launched naval vessel sails away down the Kennebec by the Maine Maritime Museum.

Christina Tree

1774 Inn at Phippsburg

Christina Tree

(207-389-1774; 1774inn.com). Its original woodwork and airy feel have been gracefully, unstuffily restored, and the grounds slope to the river. Follow this road down the east side of the peninsula and at the junction with Rt. 209 turn left. Note the entrance to Popham Beach State Park (hotline: 207-389-9125) with 3 miles of sand. The beach width varies with the tide, but there is plenty of room here to walk: 519 acres and full facilities. Rt. 209 ends shortly beyond the state park, roughly 15 miles south of Bath, at Fort Popham, a granite Civil War–era fort (with picnic benches) at the mouth of the Kennebec River. A wooded road, walking only, leads to 20th-century fortifications in Fort Baldwin Memorial Park; a six-story tower offers views upriver and out to sea.

Popham Beach actually extends right to Fort Popham; access is free, but parking is limited. Spinney's Restaurant (207-389-1122) here is currently up for sale but we refuse to believe that this waterside landmark won't survive. The local secret is Percy's General Store (207-289-2010) around the corner. Its back room offers water-view booths, good from breakfast on through lobster dinners. Check out the steamers.

There are two roads less taken in Phippsburg. From Rt. 209, Sebasco Rd. accesses the western side of the peninsula. Near this junction North Creek Farm (northcreekfarm.org) is an extensive nursery and perennial garden specializing in roses, also a great spot for lunch. Sebasco Harbor Resort (sebasco.com) down the

ABOVE: Locals head for the water-view booths in the back of Percy's General Store. Christina Tree

BELOW: A cottage at Rock Gardens Inn   Christina Tree

road offers golf and more than 130 rooms, divided among its main lodge, annexes, and 22 cottages on scattered on 550 acres. Weddings and reunions are specialties. Facilities include tennis courts, a large swimming pool, a full children's program, adult activities, and a spa. Hidden away on a point within but beyond this resort, albeit with access to all its facilities, is Rock Gardens Inn (rockgardensinn.com), the century-old core of the entire Sebasco compound. Its 10 artfully furnished and positioned cottages and a small lodge with a dining and common space are also geared to families, but in June, July, and September many guests are here for the widely respected Sebasco Art Workshops. Still another gem hidden away down the road (turn off onto Black Landing Rd.) is Anna's Water's Edge (207-389-1803). Sited on a commercial wharf, with informal dining inside and out, this is a local favorite for steamed lobster and clams as well as a full menu (reservations accepted).

Phippsburg's other road less taken leads to Small Point, which defines the eastern rim of Casco Bay. The legendary beaches here are mostly private, but unspoiled Sewall Beach is accessible by foot through the Morse Mountain Preserve (morseriver.com) from Rt. 216. Hermit Island Campground (hermit island.com), with beach and a number of waterside tent sites, is a beloved phenomenon with a loyal following.

Arrowsic/Georgetown

Attractions, activities, accommodations, eateries, etc.

Just east of the Sagadahoc Bridge, at the Dairy Queen that's been there forever, turn south onto Rt. 127. Cross a shorter bridge and you are on Arrowsic Island. Half a dozen miles south another short bridge puts you both in and on Georgetown, the name of the town and the island, one that's generally considered part of the larger peninsula.

The Osprey Restaurant, Robinhood Marine Center   Christina Tree

Reid State Park, Georgetown

Christina Tree

Robinhood Rd., named—if you believe it—for a local Indian chief, leads to the Robinhood Marine Center (robinhoodmarinecenter.com), site of The Osprey Restaurant (207-371-2530), another local dining destination with a varied menu and water views.

The big shopping destination on Rt. 127, some 9 miles south of Rt. 1, is Georgetown Pottery (georgetownpottery.com). While there are branches else-where, this showroom is worth a drive, with an extensive selection of practical, hand-painted pottery that's created right here.

Rt. 127 curves east across the island and then splits. Seguinland Rd. leads to Reid State Park (207-371-2303), with nearly 2 miles of beach, dunes, marsh, ledges, and ocean, also a saltwater lagoon, good for small children. There's plenty of room here for everyone; parking areas and facilities are widely spaced among Half Mile, Mile, and East Beaches. Guests at local lodgings can take advantage of free passes and their hosts' advice on where to find the least frigid water. Neigh-boring Grey Havens (207-371-2616; greyhavens.com), a vintage-1904 summer hotel built by the park's donor, has recently received a thorough and tasteful over-haul. Its classic "Blue" dining room is once more an attractive dining spot.

Fifteen miles from Rt. 1, Rt. 127 ends at a commercial lobster wharf and Five Islands Lobster and Grill (207-371-2990; fiveislandslobster.com). It's all outdoors

Coveside B&B, Five Islands

Five Islands Farm

and all about steamed lobsters and clams with corn and potatoes, lobster rolls, and fried seafood (BYOB). Just up the road look for Five Islands Farm (fiveislandsfarm.com), a small shingled emporium selling wines, local produce, and one of the region's largest selections of Maine artisanal cheeses. The gold at the end of this rainbow is, however, Coveside Bed and Breakfast (207-371-2807; coveside bandb.com). Tucked into a corner of quiet Gotts Cove, this is an exceptional hideaway with seven bright, comfortable rooms with water views. Sumptuous breakfasts are served, weather permitting, on a flower-filled patio above a lawn that slopes invitingly to shaded Adirondack chairs on the shore. You won't want to leave.

Macintosh apples

Nancy English

4

Boothbay/Damariscotta Region

INCLUDING WISCASSET
AND THE PEMAQUID PENINSULA

THE 7 MILES OF RT. 1 between Wiscasset and Damariscotta access some of the most varied and rewarding stretches of shoreline along the entire coast. In summer months, to the annoyance of motorists bent on making time, the stretch is also a major speed bump. Wiscasset is the first coastal town (heading northeast) that Rt. 1 runs right through. It looks like a great place to stop, and many do. That turns them into pedestrians, who cross back and forth among the village's antiques shops and restaurants, which in turn annoys other motorists. Traffic can back up in both directions, for miles.

Once across the Sheepscot River on Wiscasset's wide new bridge—which was supposed to have solved the traffic snarl—many cars turn down Rt. 27, following it 12 miles south, down the spine of a peninsula to Boothbay Harbor. This is the area's liveliest resort, with the lion's share of lodging options. Often, however, these can be booked more solidly in August than nearby, less-touristed communities.

Rt. 1 bypasses downtown Damariscotta, but nobody should. The brick main street is a gem with great shopping and dining. It's the gateway to a small region with a large, quiet lake and long tidal rivers. Stretching south from Damariscotta, the Pemaquid Peninsula is known for the famous lighthouse at its tip. There's much more there, however: busy working lobstering harbors at Round Pond and New Harbor, boatbuilding in Bristol, and yachting at Christmas Cove.

Wiscasset	This historic, visitor-friendly village is an obvious way stop. The places to eat are varied and good, antiques stores abound, and the historic buildings are beautiful. We usually avoid the worst of
Attractions, activities, accommodations, eateries, etc.	

LEFT: Topside Inn, Boothbay Harbor

Christina Tree

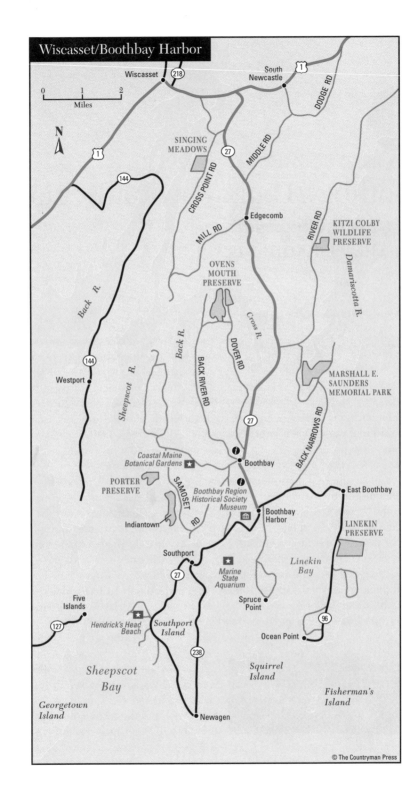

Wiscasset/Boothbay Harbor

© The Countryman Press

Lunch at Le Garage, Wiscasset   Christina Tree

the seasonal traffic by ducking off Rt. 1 before it becomes Main St. Turn down Lee St. and follow it down to Fore St. and Water St. Here Waterfront Park offers parking and restrooms.

Since food is usually the first point of interest here, let's begin with the obvious: Red's Eats. The line at this legendary snack bar (just before the bridge) is frequently long, and the seating at its picnic tables is limited, but Red's lobster rolls pack an entire lobster and consistently get raves, as do the fried clams and hot dogs. There's no legend and usually no line at Sprague's Lobster (207-882-7814) across the road. Never mind that its deck is right on the river and the lobster rolls are generous and fresh; there are also crab rolls and really good clam fritters. The weatherproof, year-round place to eat here is Sarah's (207-822-7504; sarahscafe.com), corner of Main and Water, with seasonal outdoor seating. The menu is extensive, featuring pizza, chowders, salads, and lobster more than 15 different ways. Down Water St., Le Garage (207-882-5409; legarage.com) is frequently less crowded at lunch (try a seafood crêpe) than restaurants on the main drag, and it's the preferred choice for dinner. Specialties include traditional creamed finnan haddie, cider-glazed chicken breast, and delicious crabcakes. Reserve a table on the porch. South of town on Rt. 1 The Sea Basket (207-882-6581) is also a dependable stop, known for its lobster stew. If you just want to pick up a picnic and push on, then Treats (207-882-9192; 80 Main St.) fills your bill with terrific sandwiches you can take along to the Sherman Lake Rest Area, 4 miles up Rt. 1. There picnic tables overlook a tidal river (it was a lake until the dam broke), and there are restrooms. But we suggest you linger longer in Wiscasset.

Still the shire town of Lincoln County, Wiscasset is only half as populous as it was in its shipping heyday—which, judging from the town's clapboard mansions, began after the Revolution and ended around the time of the Civil War. Lincoln County Courthouse, built in 1824 on the town common, is the oldest functioning courthouse in New England. At one point, it's claimed, Wiscasset was the busiest international port north of Boston.

The town's early-19th-century mansions certainly reflect great wealth. Two of these, Castle Tucker at Lee and High Streets and the Nickels-Sortwell House, 122 Main St., are both open for tours seasonally on weekends (historicnewengland .org). The 32-room Musical Wonder House (207-882-7163; musicalwonderhouse .com; 18 High St.) houses some 5,000 music boxes as well as a collection of player grand pianos and organs, spring-wound phonographs, music birds, and much more. By contrast the town's other attraction, the Old Lincoln Country Jail and

Wiscasset, Waterville & Farmington RR

Christina Tree

Museum (207-882-6317; 133 Federal St., Rt. 218), is a chilling vintage-1813 model, in use until 1930.

From Wiscasset, Rt. 27 runs northwest to Dresden Mills. From there it's just a few miles to the haunting Pownalborough Court House (207-882-6817), a three-story throwback to 1761. Rt. 218 veers northeast, paralleling the Sheepscot River through backcountry to Head Tide Village and Alna, home of the Wiscasset, Waterville & Farmington Railway (207-882-4193; wwfry.org) with its narrow-gauge excursion train.

West of Wiscasset, Rt. 144 heads from Rt. 1 down quiet Westport Island. It's 8 miles to the Squire Tarbox Inn (207-882-7693; squiretarboxinn.com; 1181 Main Rd., Westport), a Federal-era farmhouse offering destination dining. Dining is in a former summer kitchen with a large colonial fireplace and ceiling timbers that were once part of a ship; in summer there's also a screened deck. The menu is classic Continental but with signature Swiss specialties and, always, delicious roesti potatoes. Ingredients are local, with strawberries, greens, and many vegetables from the inn's own organic farm. The parlor and four largest guest rooms in the "new" (1825) part of the house all have working fireplaces; seven more rustic rooms are in a converted 1820s carriage barn. The extensive grounds include a walking path and farm (with goats and chickens); amenities include mountain bikes and a rowboat.

The place to stay in middle of the village of Wiscasset itself is Marston House (207-882-6010; marstonhouse.com) at the corner of Main and Middle Streets.

Its two guest rooms, each with private entrance and working fireplace, are in the carriage barn, back behind an antiques shop specializing in early American textiles and furnishings. Snow Squall Inn (207-882-6892; snowsquallinn.com; 5 Bradford Rd.) is south of town, set back from Rt. 1. It's a comfortably elegant 1850s house named for a clipper ship. There's an unusual amount of common space as well as four air-conditioned guest rooms in the main house, and three 2-room suites in the Carriage House. Highnote (207-882-9628; wiscasset.net/highnote; 26 Lee St.) is a high-Victorian mansion with a shared bath, reasonable rates, and European-style breakfasts.

The Boothbays

Check out these great attractions and activities . . .

In the village of Boothbay Harbor water is more than a view. You cross it—via a footbridge—to get from one side of town to the other, and you can explore it on a wide choice of excursion boats and in sea kayaks. It is obvious from the very lay of this old fishing village that its people have always gotten around on foot or in boats. Though parking has increased in recent years, it's still a challenge. Cars feel like an intrusion.

Boats are what all three of the Boothbays have traditionally been about. Boats are built, repaired, and sold in East Boothbay and Southport. Boat excursions range from an hour-long sail around the outer harbor to a 90-minute crossing (each way) to Monhegan Island. Fishermen can pursue giant tuna, stripers, and blues, and nature lovers can cruise out to see seals, whales, and puffins.

Boothbay Harbor   Christina Tree

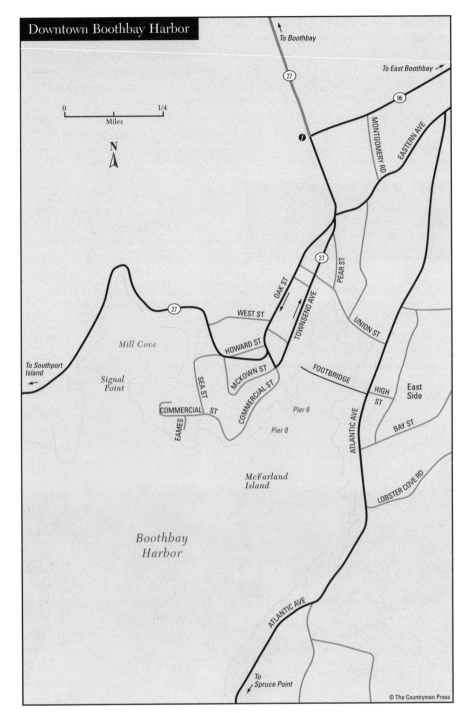

Downtown Boothbay Harbor

To Boothbay

To East Boothbay

27

96

MONTGOMERY RD

EASTERN AVE

0   1/4
Miles

N

27

PEAR ST

OAK ST

WEST ST

TOWNSEND AVE

UNION ST

Mill Cove

HOWARD ST

To Southport
Island

MCKOWN ST

FOOTBRIDGE

HIGH
ST

East
Side

Signal
Point

SEA ST

COMMERCIAL ST

BAY ST

COMMERCIAL   ST

Pier 6

ATLANTIC AVE

EAMES

Pier 8

LOBSTER COVE RD

McFarland
Island

Boothbay
Harbor

ATLANTIC AVE

To
Spruce Point

© The Countryman Press

Shopping on the library lawn

Christina Tree

In the middle of summer Boothbay Harbor itself is full of tourists licking ice cream cones, chewing freshly made taffy and fudge, browsing in shops, looking into art galleries, listening to band concerts on the library lawn, and, of course, eating lobster. You get the feeling it's been like this every summer since the 1870s.

On your way into town stop by the Boothbay Harbor Chamber of Commerce (207-633-2353; boothbayharbor.com) information center just before the lights at the junction of Rt. 27 with Rt. 96. Pick up a map. East Boothbay is a left onto Rt. 96 at the lights and the harbor is straight ahead, but Boothbay Harbor is complicated. Turn on Union St. to reach the lodging places and restaurants along Atlantic Ave. on the east side of the harbor (connected to downtown by the footbridge). Otherwise follow the one-way streets to the harborfront and/or out the other end of the village toward Southport Island.

Thanks to the fervor of developers from the 1870s on, this coastline is distinguished by the quantity of its summer cottages, many of which can be rented by the week, even in old summer compounds like Capitol and Squirrel Islands. Many quite large "Maine rustic cottages" line Shore Dr. along Ocean Point at the end of Rt. 96. With so many families on board in summer you'll find a wide choice of drop-in activities for kids. The obvious family attractions are Boothbay Railway Village (207-633-4727; railwayvillage.com) on Rt. 27, 3 miles north of the harbor, and the Maine State Aquarium (207-633-9559; maine.gov/dmr/rm/aquarium), at the end of McKown Point Rd., where tanks are filled with sea creatures from Maine waters, from alewives to a 17-pound lobster.

The area's single biggest attraction these days is the Coastal Maine Botanical

Coastal Maine Botanical Gardens

Christina Tree

Gardens (207-633-4333; mainegardens.org), back up Rt. 27 to the common in Boothbay, then out Barter's Island Rd. This 270-acre spread includes a visitors center with a gift shop and café, surrounded by a kitchen garden, a children's garden inspired by children's books, a rose garden, and an amazing Garden of the Five Senses. Native species, more than 350, represent the majority of plantings. Wooded paths lead down through a series of gardens to a the Shoreline Trail; here too you can get out onto the water in either an excursion boat or a rental kayak. It's not difficult to spend the better part of a day here.

Thanks to the Boothbay Region Land Trust (207-63-4818; bbrlt.org; 137 Townsend Ave.), there are now also easily accessible waterside preserves with many miles of trails meandering through hundreds of acres of spruce and pine, down to smooth rocks and tidal pools. Pick up a brochure and map (showing 30 miles of pet-friendly trails) to the easily accessible properties. The 1,700 acres of land under the trust's protection include Porter Preserve, with 23 wooded acres, including a beach, on Barter's Island not far beyond the botanical gardens.

Sooner rather than later we suggest that you get out on the water. Check out the lineup of boat excursion companies along the piers in Boothbay Harbor and reserve seats on those that appeal to you. At least visit the Burnt Island Light Station; in July and August guides portray the family who lived there in the 1950s. It's a 15-minute boat ride from Pier 8. Balmy Days Cruises (207-633-2284; balmydaycruises.com/lighthouse) also offers harbor and coastal tours, mackerel fishing, day sails, and—the biggie—a day trip to Monhegan Island. At Pier 1, Cap'n Fish Boat Cruises (207-633-3244; mainewhales.com) specializes in whale-watching trips, but they also offer a wide variety of cruises including a puffin-watching cruise around Egg Rock off Pemaquid and trap-pulling from a lobster boat. Schooner Lazy Jack (207-633-3444; schoonerlazyjackcruises.com) also offers two-hour sails, departing Pier 1. Friendship sloop Sarah Mead (pets welcome) sails from the Spruce Point Inn (207-380-5460; sailmuscongus.com).If you'd rather paddle your way along the shoreline, sign on for a tour with Tidal Transit Company (207-633-7140; kayakboothbay.com; 18 Granary Way). A number of deep-sea charters are also based here.

Boothbay Harbor offers its share of quality shops. Long-standing landmarks include House of Logan (207-633-2293; 20 Townsend Ave.), with traditional men's and women's clothing, and its companion store, Abacus Gallery (207-633-2166; abacusgallery.com; 12 McKown St.). Since its 1971 opening Abacus has spawned shops in several more towns, but this remains our favorite, especially for jewelry, whimsical sculptures, and well-crafted gifts. Sherman's Book & Stationery Store (800-371-8128; shermans.com; 5 Commercial St.) is a two-story emporium filled with souvenirs, kitchenware, games, and art supplies as well as books, specializing in nautical titles. Check out the variety of olive oils and vinegars (great house presents) at Eventide Epicurean Specialties (207-350-4244). Back up on Rt. 27 Edgecomb Potters (207-882-9493; edgecombpotters.com; 727 Boothbay Rd.) is a two-tiered gallery filled with deeply colored pots, vases, lamps, bowls, cookware, and jewelry. There's a small seconds corner and a sculpture garden.

The peninsula is home to upward of a dozen art galleries, anchored by Gleason Fine Art (207-633-6849; gleasonfineart.com; 31 Townsend Ave.), representing some of Maine's foremost artists. Another dozen-plus are scattered along the shore from Ocean Point to Southport Island, all holding open studio on first Fridays, June through October.

Boothbay Harbor offers plenty of ways to get out on the water.   Christina Tree

Whether they're looking for art shops, galleries, beaches, or shore paths, visitors sooner or later find their way out Rt. 96 to East Boothbay, a small village that's home to big boatyards. The East Boothbay General Store (207-633-7800) is a source of morning doughnuts, unusual pizzas, and sandwiches to take on down to Ocean Point for a picnic on the beach or shore path. It's also a must to cross the Townsend Gut swing bridge to

Boothbay Harbor is a good shopping town.
Christina Tree

The Shore Path at Ocean Point is a great place to picnic Christina Tree

Hendricks Head Beach, Southport Island Christina Tree

Southport Island. Head down Beach Rd. to Hendrick's Head Beach or all the way down Rt. 27 to Newagen with its smooth rocks overlooking the entrance to Sheepscot Bay. It was this landscape that inspired Rachel Carson, who first summered on the peninsula in 1946, to write much of *The Edge of the Sea* (1955) and then *Silent Spring* (1962), the book that changed global thinking about human beings' relation to basic laws of nature.

When the sun sets, everyone from every corner of this region seems to converge on Boothbay Harbor's boardwalk and the many restaurants that are never enough in high season. Don't miss out on the Down East Ice Cream Factory (207-633-3016), with great flavors like Perry's Nut House. Nearby entertainment options include dinner and musical revues at the Carousel Music Theater (207-633-5297), as well as live performances at the Opera House (207-633-5159; operahouse.com) and Boothbay Playhouse (207-633-3379; boothbayplayhouse.com).

Checking In
Best places to stay in the Boothbays

For anyone who wants to stay within walking distance of the Boothbay Harbor village action, Topside Inn (207-633-5404; topsideinn.com; 60 McKown St.) is the pick. It's sited atop McKown Hill, a quiet island above the hubbub, with views west to the sunset over the water and islands. Rooms are divided between the handsome 1876 mansion with its common space and breakfast room, and a pair of two-story motel-style annexes with back balconies facing the water. Another great location is the Five Gables Inn (207-633-4551; fivegablesinn.com; 107 Murray Hill Rd.) in East Boothbay. Sited across from a quiet waterside byway, it's not far from Ocean Point on one hand and the harbor on the other. Its 16 rooms (15 with a bay view) are imaginatively, comfortably furnished; 5 have a working fireplace, and the smaller third-floor gable rooms offer some of the best views of the water. Guests meet and mingle in the spacious, cheerful common room with its large hearth, and along the veranda.

The Boothbays are also home to several seasonal, full-service, long-established resorts. The largest and toniest is Spruce Point Inn Resort & Spa (207-633-4152; sprucepointinn.com;

On the veranda at Five Gables

Christina Tree

Swim or sail at Linekin Bay.

Christina Tree

88 Grandview Ave.), set in 57 land-scaped acres on a peninsula separating Boothbay Harbor from Linekin Bay. Rooms are divided among the handsome 1890s Main Inn and several recently renovated contemporary lodges and vintage cottages, all with splendid views. Lodging options also include family-geared multibedroom town houses with full kitchens and wood-burning fireplaces. Amenities include a choice of pools (one harborside), tennis courts, a full-service spa, a children's program, and frequent boat shuttle service across the harbor to downtown. At the tip of Southport Island, Newagen Seaside Inn (207-633-5242; newagenseasideinn.com) has a more remote feel, and a loyal following. The original inn houses traditional guest rooms and suites as well as common space; there are also junior suites with cooking facilities and the Little Inn, plus a scattering of classic cottages. Facilities include a heated freshwater pool and tennis courts. Best of all is the

shore path along the rocks, beneath the pines. Ocean Point Inn (207-633-4200 or 800-552-5554; oceanpointinn .com; 191 Shore Rd., East Boothbay) is an informal, moderately priced complex of 61 rooms, suites, cottages, and apartments with a heated pool and Adirondack chairs overlooking the ocean. Ocean Point's shore path and beach are close by. Last but not least is Linekin Bay Resort (207-633-2494; linekinbayresort.com; 92 Wall Point Rd.), a century-old, family-geared compound tucked into a quiet cove, with a focus on sailing. The "lodges" and rustic cabins are set along the shore, backed by pines on 20 acres. In high season reasonable rates include three meals as well as use of sailboats (lessons are available), kayaks, tennis, and more.

Boothbay Harbor has more than its share of large waterside motor inns, but for these we defer to the AAA and Mobil guides. In the harbor we do recommend the Flagship Inn

(207-633-5094; boothbaylodging .com; 200 Townsend Ave.). It's open year-round and affordable, with air-conditioning and a swimming pool. A reasonably priced, seasonal, unabash-edly 1950s alternative is the Mid-Town Motel (207-633-2751; 96 McKown St.) in Boothbay Harbor. Check with the chamber of commerce for several prime local sources for vacation rentals.

Local Flavors

The taste of the Boothbays—local restaurants, cafés, and more

The seasonal Ports of Italy (207-633-1011; portsofitaly.com; 47 Commercial St.) is the high-end preferred dining spot on the harbor. The pasta is home-made, the Italian flavors are genuine, and the upstairs dining room is bright, with a lovely outside area, weather permitting. What The Thistle Inn (207-633-3541; thistleinn.com; 55 Oak St.) lacks in water views, it offers in the quality of locally sourced entrées, both high-end and casual fare. At The Boat House Bistro (207-633-0400; the boathousebistro.com; 12 The By-Way) it's the same extensive, largely tapas-style menu for both lunch and dinner, served in any of the dining rooms on three floors; the open rooftop deck offers the best water views. Lunch on wild mushroom ragu simmered in cognac cream and dine on a choice of seafood paellas. The offshoot Mine Oyster (207-633-6616; mineoyster.net) on Pier 1 is more of a nightspot with a seafood menu and a raw bar featuring local Glidden Point oysters. The Rock-tide Inn (207-633-4455; rocktideinn .com; 35 Atlantic Ave.) is worth a visit, if just to see its ships' models; the main dining room decor and menu are traditional.

The fact is that it's lobster most folks are here to eat, and the simpler, the better. The Lobster Dock (207-633-7120; thelobsterdock.com; 49 Atlantic Ave.) at the east end of the

Get a table on the deck at the Lobster Dock.   Christina Tree

footbridge gets top rating for lobster rolls, either hot with drawn butter or cold with a dab of mayo, as well as lobster and shore dinners or prime rib. Crabcakes are a specialty. Robinson's Wharf (207-633-3830; robinsonswharf .net) on Southport Island, just across Townsend Gut from Boothbay Harbor, is the other sure winner. On a sunny day sit on the dock at one of the picnic tables and watch the boats unload their catch. Choices include lobsters and lobster rolls, fried shrimp, clams, scallops, fish chowder, lobster stew, sandwiches, and homemade desserts. There is also the Clambake at Cabbage Island (207-633-7200; cabbageisland clambakes.com), a long-standing tradition. The clambake includes lobsters, clams, corn, and potatoes steamed in seaweed then served on picnic tables. In bad weather a circa-1900 lodge seats up to 100 people by a huge fireplace. The charge includes the boat ride to the harbor island from Fisherman's Wharf.

Boothbay Harbor offers a number of places for a satisfying lunch or reasonably priced dinner. Blue Moon Café (207-633-2220; bluemoonbooth bayharbor.com; 54 Commercial St.) is a little café with a seaside deck, good for crabcakes and fresh greens. Chowder House (207-633-5761; chowderhouse inc.com; Granary Way beside the footbridge) has a waterfront deck and a menu that includes chowders, crab rolls, grilled ribs, and a full bar. Baker's Way (207-633-1119; 89 Townsend Ave.) is just the place for fried apple dumpling, you think, and then you smell lemongrass cooking and wonder where you are. There are two worlds here: a full bakery, and a restaurant that serves traditional, reasonably priced Vietnamese foods. McSeagulls (207-633-5900; mcseagullsonline.com; 14 Wharf St.) offers wharfside dining and can get crazy packed in high season. It's a local gathering place off-season because it's good. Try the lobster with northern white beans.

Location alone—on Cozy Harbor Wharf, Southport Island (near Hendrick's Head Beach)—would make Oliver's (207-633-8888; call to check hours) worth finding. The deck is a great spot to feast on mussels steamed in wine, leeks, and garlic; fish tacos; or salads. In East Boothbay, Lobsterman's Wharf (207-633-3443; lobster manswharf.com; 224 Ocean Point Rd.) offers plenty of inside seating, but the prime spots are on the deck with a view of yachts and tugboats at the neighboring boatyard. Get there early.

Damariscotta/ Pemaquid Peninsula

Check out these great attractions and activities . . .

Damariscotta's musical name means "meeting place of the alewives," and in spring spawning alewives can indeed be seen climbing more than 40 feet up a fish ladder from Great Salt Bay to the fresh water in Damariscotta Lake.

The area's first residents also found an abundance of oysters here, judging from the shells they heaped over the course of 2,400 years on opposite banks of the river just below Salt Bay. Native Americans also had a name for the peninsula jutting 10 miles seaward from this spot: *Pemaquid* means "long finger." At one tip of this finger stands Pemaquid Light (lighthousefoundation.org), pictured on Maine's quarter as well as on countless calendars because it looks just like a lighthouse should look. It stands atop

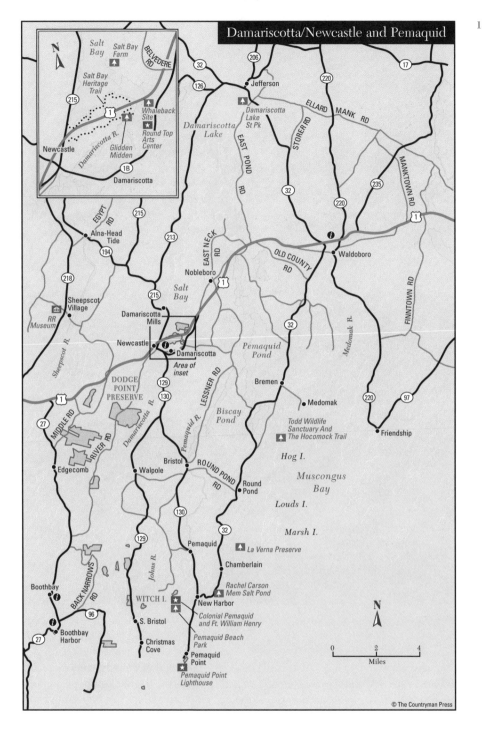

© The Countryman Press

Pemaquid Light stands atop rocks, great for clambering.   Christina Tree

dramatic but clamber-friendly rocks. These are composed of varied seams of granite schist and softer volcanic rock, ridged in ways that invite climbing, and pocked with tidal pools that demand stopping. The former keeper's house is now The Fisherman's Museum (207-677-2492); visitors are welcome to climb the 39 steps inside the light itself. There are also picnic tables here above the rocks, under the pines.

Pemaquid Light has never been more famous, but the surrounding area is a

Frank Waltz counts alewives as they make their annual climb up the fish ladder in Damariscotta Mills. Damariscott Water Association

Recycle Art sculpture Garden, Bremen

Christina Tree

shadow of the busy resort it was around the turn of the last century, when nearby New Harbor was a busy steamboat stop. Pemaquid Beach (207-677-2754), a lovely, town-owned facility, is seldom crowded. Up the road Fort William Henry, a crenellated, 1908 stone re-creation of a 17th-century tower built by the English to ward off the French, draws relatively few visitors; fewer still notice the "Rock of Pemaquid" enshrined within this tower. A century ago, however, this was a hugely popular tourist attraction, billed as the rock settlers alighted on, years before any got to Plymouth. The fort is now part of the Colonial Pemaquid Historic Site (207-677-2423; friendsofcolonialpemaquid.org) and includes a visitors center and museum depicting the layerings of history here. More than 100,000 artifacts unearthed in excavations from the neighboring field document this as a seasonal fishing station, established circa 1610 and evolving into a trading outpost circa 1630–50. Never a fully fledged settlement, the site was forgotten until 19th-century farmers began unearthing its cellar holes and, with the arrival of steamboats, created a tourist attraction. Then the steamboats stopped, numerous big wooden summer hotels closed, and "Maine's Lost City" was forgotten again, until fairly recently.

New Harbor, also right up the road from the lighthouse, is one of the coast's more historic and picturesque harbors. It's filled with lobster boats and serves as the departure point for Hardy Boat Cruises (207-677-2026; hardyboat.com) to Monhegan Island and around Eastern Rock, one of the few Maine islands on which puffins breed. Take off from Shaw's Wharf (207-677-2200), a classic lobster pound in which you select your lobster from the pool below and feed on

Granite Hall Store, Round Harbor — Christina Tree

it upstairs at picnic tables, either inside or out.

The shortest route from Damariscotta to Pemaquid Point is Rt. 130, but if time permits, find your way to Rt. 129 as it winds down the second point on the peninsula. This takes you across the draw-bridge at a busy channel in South Bristol known as "the Gut," and on down to (seasonal) Coveside Restaurant and Marina (207-644-8282) in Christmas Cove.

At the very least drive one way to or from Pemaquid Point on Rt. 32, along the eastern shore of the peninsula, with a stop at Round Pond. There on the public dock Muscongus Bay Lobster (207-529-5528) and Round Pond Lobster (207-529-5725) compete for your business. The weather-proof, famously fine place to eat here is

Lincoln Theater, Damariscotta — Christina Tree

the Anchor Inn (207-529-5584; anchorinnrestaurant.com), open daily in-season for lunch and dinner with a tiered dining room overlooking the harbor. Before leaving Round Pond, stop by the Granite Hall Store, built as a dance hall in the 1880s when this was a busy spot, now a trove of good things from penny candy to Scottish scarves and Maine-made woolens.

Damariscotta is the commercial and cultural heart of this region, its solid Main St. flanked by fine brick buildings constructed after the fire of 1845, studded with shops and restaurants. This is home base for family-owned Renys (207-563-3177; renys.com) with 15 stores scattered around Maine. The original store here sells quality clothing while Renys Underground, across the street, offers everything from tea to bedding, china, toys, a wide assortment of specialty food, boots, and all manner of staples you didn't realize you needed. The antithesis of Walmart, Renys has been the subject of two Maine musicals. Across the way is the vintage Lincoln Theater (207-563-3424; lcct.org) with a renovated, elevator-accessed second floor, a venue for both films and live presentations. At street level the theater is also home to Maine Coast Bookshop & Café (207-563-3207; mainecoastbookshop.com), one of the state's outstanding independent bookstores. Parking in Damariscotta, incidentally, is far easier than it initially looks; there are ample lots behind the buildings on both sides of Main St.

For a sense of beauty of this immediate area, find your way to the Damariscotta River Association (207-563-1393; damariscottariver.org; 110 Belvedere Rd.) headquarters at 115-acre Salt Pond Farm, a quarter mile north of the blinking light on Rt. 1. Its hay fields and salt- and freshwater marshes are laced with walking paths. This is also the site of seasonal Friday farmer's markets; pick up a map to DRA preserves throughout the area. Families intent on warm-water swimming should follow Rt. 32, 9 miles north to Damariscotta Lake State Park (207-549-7600). The beach is long, well tended, and shaded, ideal for a picnic with fixings from the nearby Jefferson Market.

Soda fountain in Renys, Damarsicotta

Christina Tree

Mill Pond Inn

Christina Tree

Checking In

Best places to stay in Damariscotta
and on the Pemaquid Peninsula

The obvious places to stay in Damariscotta are actually just across the bridge in Newcastle. The Newcastle Inn (207-563-5685; newcastleinn.com; 60 River Rd.) offers 14 tasteful and comfortable rooms, some with water view, 8 with gas fireplace; grounds slope to the river overlooking the village of Damariscotta. Just up Rt. 215 in Damariscotta Mills the Mill Pond Inn (207-563-8014; millpondinn.com) is a welcoming vintage-1780 house on a small extension of Lake Damariscotta that's great for swimming and for kay-

aking out into the lake itself. The six rooms, including a two-room suite, are so different from one another that you might want to ask for descriptions, but all are attractive and the same reasonable price. Innkeeper Bobby Weare can be persuaded to take guests down the big lake in his 16-foot restored '50s motorboat, and to arrange fishing trips.

Another hidden gem in nearby Waldoboro is Blue Skye Farm (207-832-0800; blueskyefarm.com; 1708 Friendship Rd.). Original woodwork and fireplaces are part of the charm of a 1775 house restored with care by British innkeepers Peter and Jan Davidson. One hundred acres offer gardens for relaxation, trails for hiking, and a pond for skating. Guests can use the kitchen to make their own dinners or arrange a lobster dinner prepared by the hosts.

Down on the Pemaquid Peninsula the Inn at Round Pond (207-529-2004; theinnatroundpond.com; 1442 Rt. 32) is a delightful B&B with rooms in tasteful colors, furnished with antiques and hung with original art. A third floor and mansard roof were added to this 1830s Colonial around the turn of the last century, when it became the Harbor View Hotel. In New Harbor the family-owned Gosnold Arms (207-677-3727; gosnold.com; 16 Rt. 32) offers 10 simple but comfortable guest rooms and 20 cottage units, 6 of them with decks, smack dab on the entrance to the harbor. The inn is steps from Shaw's Wharf, which means you can walk not just to dinner but also onto an excursion boat for a cruise to Egg Rock or Monhegan; the alternative is parking a way up the road. The turn-of-the-last-century Bradley Inn (207-677-2105; bradleyinn.com; 3063 Pemaquid Point) offers 14 rooms divided between the main house and annexes. It's the only local inn to still offer dinner as well as breakfast; amenities include a spa and clunker bicycles to take you the mile to the lighthouse. Weekly cottage rentals include the Thompson House and Cottages (207-677-2317; thompsoncottages.net), with 21 cottages sleeping up to five people, many facing New Harbor or Back Cove, all with fireplace (wood supplied). In Pemaquid Beach you'll find Ye Olde Forte Cabins (207-677-2661; yeolde fortecabins.com; 28 Old Fort Rd.), a

Ye Olde Forte Cabins, Pemaquid Beach

Christina Tree

Moody's Diner is a Maine must!

Christina Tree

double row of classic 1920s cabins sloping to the shore. Up on Rt. 1 in Waldoboro, Moody's Motel (207-832-5362) is a bargain-priced find for traveling families. Sited up a hill behind their legendary Moody's Diner (see below), the 18 spanking clean units include cottages with screened porches on grounds with lawn games and swings.

Local Flavors

The taste of Damariscotta—local restaurants, cafés, and more

Damariscotta is arguably the best place in the Northeast to eat oysters. For 2,000 years, judging from the famous shell heaps at Glidden Point and along the river, the locals have been eating oysters here. By the 1970s native oyster beds had all but disappeared due to overharvesting, but thanks to the University of Maine's Darling Marine Center on the Damariscotta River, seedlings were reintroduced. The resulting firm, distinctively sweet and salty oysters are served in the world's best restaurants. At the Damariscotta River Grill (207-563-2992; damariscottariver grill.com; 155 Main St.), reserve a table upstairs by the window or sit up at the copper bar. Seasonal Schooner Landing (207-563-7447; Schooner Wharf), waterside on Main St., features an oyster bar. At King Eider's Pub (207-563-6008; kingeiderspub.com; 2 Elm St.) you can make a meal of oysters and the other house specialty, crabcakes, washed down by a wide choice of brews.

Muscongus Bay is a prime lobster source, and seasonal lobster shacks abound on the Pemaquid Peninsula. The busiest is Shaw's Wharf (207-677-200) in New Harbor, which also serves as departure point for Hardy Boat Cruises. Harbor View Restau-

Brussels sprouts and cabbage

Nancy English

rant at the Pemaquid Fisherman's Co-op (207-677-2801), marked from Pemaquid Harbor Rd., is the real deal, as is Broad Cove Marine (207-529-5186), 371 Momak Rd., Bremen. At the town wharf in Round Pond, Muscongus Bay Lobster Company (207-529-5528) and Round Pond Lobster (207-529-5725) compete.

Back up on Business Rt. 1 north of downtown Damariscotta, look for Larson's Lunch Box (207-563-2755; 430 Upper Main St.). Beloved by locals, this roadside snack bar is known for fresh and generous crab and lobster rolls (no credit cards). Don't pass up Round Top Ice Cream (207-563-5307; 526 Main St.), legendary source of the creamiest (15 percent butterfat) house-made ice creams in no less than 60 flavors. North on Rt. 1 in Waldoboro, Moody's Diner (207-832-7785), open early and late, is a genuine gem as well as an icon. Family-run since the 1930s, its specialties remain killer pies and family-style basics like corned beef hash, meat loaf, and stews—at digestible prices.

Rockland Region

INCLUDING THE ISLANDS OF MONHEGAN, VINALHAVEN, NORTH HAVEN, AND MATINICUS

AT ROCKLAND, RT. 1 MEETS PENOBSCOT BAY, beloved by sailors and kayakers for its many safe harbors. Home to the Farnsworth Art Museum and its many offshoot art galleries, shops, and restaurants, Rockland itself retains a busy, working harbor, departure point for car ferries to the islands of Vinalhaven and North Haven. Year-round access to Monhegan, a car-free summer mecca for artists, hikers, and birders, is from Port Clyde on the Georgetown Peninsula, south of Rockland.

Rockland

Check out these great attractions and activities . . .

Rockland's downtown is filled with good restaurants, fine galleries, and shops, thanks in good part to the popularity of its nationally recognized Farnsworth Art Museum (207-596-6457; farnsworthmuseum.org; 16 Museum St.). The museum's permanent exhibit traces Maine landscape painting from Thomas Cole to early-20th-cenutry greats like Rockwell Kent, John Marin, and Marsden Hartley and to their current counterparts. Robert Indiana's *EAT* sign on the outside corner of the building has turned the street into a gallery.

You can tour the neighboring 1850 Farnsworth Homestead to learn about Lucy Farnsworth who, on her death in 1935, left $1.3 million to preserve her house and to build a library and art gallery honoring her father. From the beginning the collection included paintings of Maine by Winslow Homer, George Bellows, and a then little-known local summer resident, Andrew Wyeth. The 3-acre museum campus includes the Wyeth Center, housed in a former church, displaying works by three generations of the Wyeth family: N. C. Wyeth, Andrew, and Jamie.

LEFT: Markley Painting, Monhegan

Nancy English

147

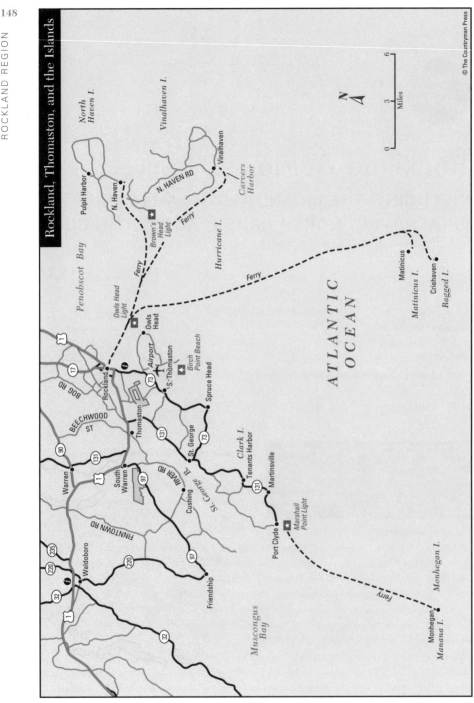

Rockland, Thomaston, and the Islands

© The Countryman Press

Romance of Autumn by George Bellows

Farnsworth Art Museum

Request a map from the museum to the Olsen House, a scenic 15 miles south in Cushing. A National Historic Landmark, the house served as a backdrop to Andrew Wyeth's iconic painting *Christina's World*, and was a frequent work venue for the artist over three decades. It's now administered by the museum and houses 50 of his watercolors of Alvaro and Christina Olsen and the house.

Rockland has repeatedly reinvented itself over the centuries. Initially known for shipbuilding, the city became synonymous with the limestone it quarried, burned, and shipped off to be made into plaster. When wallboard replaced plaster, Rockland switched to catching and processing fish. Today its economic engines are also powered by cultural attractions; waterside packing and industrial plants have been replaced by a harborside park and walkway.

Robert Indiana at the Farnsworth

Nancy English

Main St. is now lined with galleries (see the sidebar), restaurants, and shops. The Strand Theatre (207-594-0070; rocklandstrand.com) has been restored and stages live performances as well as films. Look for Wednesday-evening summer concerts. Using live-streaming mini cams and audio, the Project Puffin Visitor Center (207-596-5566; projectpuffin.org; 311 Main St.) offers a virtual visit with nesting puffins in their burrows; children can crawl into similar burrows to watch puffins feeding their young. The storefront center chronicles the joint venture by Maine Audubon and National Audubon to reintroduce the puffins to Maine islands over the past few decades.

Lighthouse lovers will also want to stop at the Maine Lighthouse Museum (207-594-3301; mainelighthousemuseum.com) at 1 Park Dr. with the Penobscot Bay Regional Chamber of Commerce (207-596-0376; mainedreamvacation.com) visitors center. The museum's many displays include the country's largest collection of Fresnel lenses. Rockland is also home to the American Lighthouse Foundation (207-594-4174; lighthousefoundation.org),a national nonprofit that's headquartered in the former Keepers House at Owls Head Light. Check the website for open hours for both Owls Head and Rockland Breakwater Light, accessible via an uneven but glorious walk out into the harbor along the almost mile-long granite breakwater. The way from Rt. 1 north of town is marked; turn on Waldo St.

To reach Owls Head Light follow Main St. south as it becomes Rt. 73. Turn onto North Shore Dr. and into Owls Head Light State Park. The conical white lighthouse, built on a cliff in 1825, offers an easy climb to a panoramic view of Penobscot Bay, and the Keepers House houses interesting displays as well as a gift shop. The Owls Head General Store (207-596-6038; 2 South Shore Dr.) is an obvious lunch stop here, good for haddock "chowdah" and widely clebrated for its burgers.

Rockland Breakwater Light is a popular walk.   William Davis

Everything at the Owls Head Museum works.

Owls Head Transporation Museum

Back on Rt. 73 don't pass up the Owls Head Transportation Museum (207-594-4418; owlshead.org). It's one of the country's outstanding collections of antique planes and automobiles, and everything works. In the exhibition hall take a 100-year journey through the evolution of transportation, from horse-drawn carriages to World War I fighter planes. Check the website for year-round special events like antique airplane shows and demonstrations of a wide variety of magnificent machines. A ride in a Model T Ford is always on offer.

As you continue south on Rt. 73 keep an eye out for the turnoff for Waterman's beach, site of Waterman's Beach Lobster (207-594-7819; watermansbeach lobster.com) and, a little farther along in Spruce Head, for Miller's Lobster Company (207-594-7406; millerslobsters.com). Both are classic, seasonal lobster pounds (BYOB). Feast on steamed lobster and clams at picnic tables by the water and count on freshly baked pie. In St. George turn south on Rt. 131, following it around scenic inlets on its way to Port Clyde.

The ferry for Monhegan (see below) leaves from the dock here but if you can't jump aboard, consider spending a few hours paddling among the offshore islands with Port Clyde Kayaks (207-372-8100; portclydekayaks.com). Make time for a bite on the wharf at the Port Clyde General Store, or pick up fixings to picnic at the nearby Marshall Point Lighthouse Museum (207-372-6450; marshallpoint.org). It's a small light set in grounds with a sweeping water view; the former keeper's house is now a lively local museum.

Marshall Point Lighthouse   Nancy English

Checking In
Best places to stay in Rockland

Old Granite Inn (207-594-9036; old graniteinn.com; 546 Main St., Rockland) is an 1840s mansion built of local granite, set in a flower garden across from the Maine State Ferry terminal and the Concord Coach Lines stop. It's ideal for people who come without a car and are headed for an island, but innkeepers Edwin and Joan Hantz have added plenty of other reasons to stay here as well. The eight guest rooms include two family suites; common spaces are tastefully, comfortable decorated; and breakfasts are truly exceptional.

The Captain Lindsey House (207-596-7950; lindseyhouse.com; 5 Lindsey St., Rockland) is run by Ellen and Ken Barnes, both previously captains of *Stephen Taber* and now enjoying the solid earth in this 1835 sea captain's house

with nine rooms. Likely a fireplace and certainly a down comforter, big bathroom, and more will indulge you during your stay, when morning will bring a big English breakfast.

Berry Manor Inn (207-596-7696; berrymanorinn.com; 81 Talbot Ave., Rockland) is a luxurious retreat with canopy beds and whirlpool tubs, a deeply upholstered double chaise longue to drift off on in front of a

The Granite Inn, Rockland   Christina Tree

On Board a Windjammer

From late May to early October, Maine's fleet of Windjammers, based in Rockland, Rockport, and Camden, cruise Penobscot Bay and on down east through Eggemoggin Reach into Blue Hill Bay. Passenger-carrying schooners have been a tradition in these waters since 1937, when artist Frank Swift transformed a few former fishing schooners for tours of the islands.

The **Maine Windjammer Association** (800-807-WIND; sailmainecoast.com) represents nine Maine Windjammers, most National Historic Landmarks, and each staffed with experienced, licensed crew. The schooners vary widely in size (carrying between 21 and 40), in comfort, and in ambience. Some accept young children. Most don't. Check the website carefully before picking your vessel. Count on good food, six hours of sailing a day, and relaxation that will revive your love of life. Overnight cruises begin at $230 per person with all meals (lobster included).

Schooner *Stephen Taber*, originally launched in 1871, remains a favorite member of Maine's Windjammer fleet.

P.J. Walters

wood-burning fireplace in Room 1, and a cathedral ceiling with Palladian windows in Carriage House Room 1. The guest pantry is stocked with freshly baked goodies, including pies.

LimeRock Inn (207-594-3762; limerockinn.com; 96 Limerock St., Rockland), a blue turreted Victorian, offers a wide porch with wicker furniture ready for relaxation. A room called North Haven has a cherry sleigh bed, and like every room is fully provided with toiletries and necessities. Whichever room you choose, the shops and restaurants are nearby, as they are for all these Rockland inns.

East Wind Inn (207-372-6366; eastwindinn.com; 21 Mechanic St., Tenants Harbor) offers expansive waterside views and comfort in a small village tucked into a quiet cove on the way to Port Clyde. An inn since the 1920s, when patrons arrived by steamboat, it has been recently renovated, with 19 rooms and suites divided between the main building and Meetinghouse annex. Its Wan-e-set restaurant and Quarry Tavern are open to the public.

Ocean House (207-372-6691; oceanhousehotel.com; 870 Port Clyde Rd.). Built in 1820s as lodging for local mariners, this special lodging place is an extension of Monhegan Island, lovingly restored and maintained by a family with island ties. It's the place to stay if you are headed out for a day trip or month via neighboring Monhegan Boat Line but also the place to capture the special vibes of Port Clyde, itself a destination for artists.

Local Flavors

The taste of Rockland—local restaurants, cafés, and more

Primo (207-596-0770; primorestaurant .com; 2 S. Main St., Rockland) is the first (seasonal) destination for food lovers. Chef Melissa Kelly owns Primo with pastry chef Price Kushner, and together they create dinners in this restored Victorian house that you will remember with pleasure, from the glass of exceptional wine to the house-cured prosciutto, guanciale, and more, made from the business's own Tamworth pigs. On the hill behind the restaurant are gardens burgeoning with tomatoes, lettuces, cauliflower, fava beans, cardoons, squash plants, and far more. Ravioli with herbs, kale, pancetta, and an egg yolk with brown butter Pecorino sauce features it all.

Café Miranda (207-594-2034; cafemiranda.com; 15 Oak St., Rockland) needs reservations, because the endless possibilities on the menu are too intriguing to forget and the locals return over and over again. Friendly and fun, the staff have a jovial quality surely as a result of the boisterous owner Kerry Altiero. At least, he seems boisterous because of that relentless menu. Try the Maine shrimp and mussels in Thai red curry coconut broth.

Suzuki's Sushi Bar (207-596-7447; suzukisushi.com; 419 Main St., Rockland) serves the best sushi on the Midcoast and likely Down East. The owner sources her seafood and shellfish from the freshest possible markets and her own and her staff's fishing expeditions: Mushimono donburi—steamed dishes—include salmon ponzu, and Maine shrimp with bonito dashi silver

Kerry Altiero of Café Miranda   Christina Tree

Atlantic Baking, Rockland

sauce. Noodle bowls might hold local oysters with daikon and scallions in a kelp dashi broth. You will rarely have been fed this well.

Rustica (207-594-0015; 315 Main St., Rockland) is a perfect place for a small or light meal or an herb-roasted chicken dinner. The Italian specialties are competent and the room is comfortable and relaxing. The eggplant Parmesan makes an excellent lunch.

In Thomaston, The Slipway (207-354-4155; maine-slipway.com) is hidden away down at 24 Public Landing. The seasonal restaurant, open 11:30–8:30, is known for owner-chef Scott Yakovenko's bouillabaisse. The extensive menu ranges from hamburgers (all beef) and fried fish baskets to tasty seared fish cakes with mixed greens or the lightly fried local oysters with ginger shallot sauce.

Archer's on the Pier (207-594-2435; 58 Ocean St., Rockland). Overlooking both the harbor and bay, this prime spot is owned by popular local chef Lynn Archer. Rock City Cafe (207-594-4123; rockcitycoffee.com; 316 Main St.), the town meeting place, is a sleek oasis specializing in from-scratch soups and sandwiches served on Borealis bread. Locally roasted coffees are the specialty, but you'll also find chai, wine, and locally brewed beer. Live music, weekends. Atlantic Baking Co. (207-596-0505; atlanticbakingco.com; 351 Main St.). Sited across from the Farnsworth Museum, this busy eatery seduces passersby with the aroma of fresh-baked bread. There's a blackboard sandwich menu and a choice of help-yourself salads in the deli case. The Brass Compass (207-596-5960; 305 Main St.)—Lynn Archer's friendly eatery—is good for seafood stews, overstuffed sandwiches on homemade bread, yummy onion rings and fries, and generous salads. The house special is a lobster club. Beer and wine. Home Kitchen Café (207-596-2449; 650 Main St.), north of the main drag, is a cheery café good for a memorable breakfast that might include huevos rancheros, frittata, or sticky buns. Nearby Claw's (207-975-1230; 743 Main St.) gets top rating for its lobster rolls, served

Rockland Galleries and Shops

Rockland galleries are too numerous to detail; more than 20 host receptions, and the **Farnsworth Museum** is free during seasonal **First Friday Art Walks** (5–8 PM). The oldest is the prestigious **Caldbeck Gallery** (caldbeck.com; 12 Elm St.). Goldsmith Thomas Donovan's **Harbor Square Gallery** (harborsquaregallery.com; 374 Main St.) fills three floors of a former bank building, and the **Dowling Walsh Gallery** (dowlingwalsh.com; 357 Main St.) is another highlight. **Archipelago Fine Arts** (thearchipelago.net; 386 Main St.) represents roughly 300 artists and craftspeople on Maine's "hinged" as well as waterbound islands. **The Museum Store at the Farnsworth Museum** is a trove of quality gifts, including jewelry, books, and toys as well as art books, cards, and prints. **Carver Hill Gallery** (207-594-7745; carverhillgallery.com; 338 Main St.) offers painting, sculpture, fine crafts, and handmade furniture. **Eric Hopkins, Rockland's** most prominent contemporary artist**, welcomes visitors by appointment** (erichopkins .com).

Harbor Square Gallery, Rockland   Christina Tree

The legendary **Maine State Prison Showroom** (207-354-9237; 358 Main St., Thomaston) is worth a stop. The prison has moved but the shop remains, selling wooden furniture and small items made by prisoners.

waterside with Red Claw Ale. South of town on Rt. 1 Dorman's Dairy Dream (207-594-4195; 189 New County Rd., Thomaston) is the local place for house-made ice cream. The Maine Lobster Festival, the first weekend in August, is the world's biggest lobster feed, with some 20,000 pounds served up with all the fixings at the public landing. King Neptune and a Sea Goddess preside over this five-day event, which includes a big parade, colorful contests, and plenty of music.

Dorman's Dream near Rockland   Nancy English

Monhegan Island

Check out these great attractions and activities . . .

Spotting whales and porpoises on a glorious day or hunkering down in rough seas—however you cross the dozen miles to the island of Monhegan, you remember it. By the time the boat curves toward the island dock, sailing between the gray-shingled summer houses of the village and the stony green hulk of Manana Island, you've undergone a passage that's pressed out some of the kinks.

Three ferry companies can take you there. Monhegan Boat Line (207-372-8848; monheganboat.com), the island's primary and only year-round service, sails from Port Clyde. Its *Elizabeth Ann* offers plenty of inside as well as outside seating and takes 50 minutes while the rockier and less comfortable but beloved *Laura B*, a World War II veteran, takes 70. From New Harbor, Hardy Boat Cruises (207-677-2026; hardyboat.com) offers a comfortable, 50-minute crossing aboard *Hardy III*. From Boothbay Harbor, it's a longer ride aboard the Balmy Days II (207-633-2284; balmydaycruises.com).

Early explorers like Captain John Smith and Samuel de Champlain arrived in the 1600s, and European fishermen, pirates, and others soon followed. Artists have sought out the island and its views, its cliffs and cottages since the middle of the 19th century. Robert Henri, Rockwell Kent, Edward Hopper, and three generations of the Wyeth family have all painted here, as have James Fitzgerald and contemporary artist Sonya Sklaroff. Sited just uphill from the ferry dock, The Lupine Gallery (207-594-8131) is the place to pick up island prints, cards, and a sense of

Sunset from the Monhegan ferry dock

Nancy English

Monhegan crafts at Frayed Knot Rope Works   Nancy English

who is currently painting on the island. Jackie Boegel and Bill Boynton represent roughly 100 artists who paint here regularly. From May to Columbus Day more than 20 private studios are open according to posted schedules, and artists can be seen working at easels all over the island.

Monhegan is car-free, with only a few vehicles used for transporting supplies. Bikes are not allowed, and camping is not permitted. It's quiet and peaceful because 80 percent of the island is undeveloped. A total of 480 acres is maintained by the Monhegan Associates (monheganassociates.org), which publishes a hiking map detailing the 17-mile island-wide trail system of amazingly varied trails. Day-trippers are advised to take the Burnt Head Trail (No. 4) to the cliffs and loop back to the village via the Whitehead Trail (No. 7), descending by the lighthouse, or vice versa.

Trail walkers need to prepare themselves for poison ivy and ticks with long pants, for slippery rocks and rough ground with stout walking shoes, and for the likelihood of cold wind with a good windbreaker or fleece jacket. Swimming in the ocean is far too dangerous to attempt on the eastern side of the island, and kayaking should be undertaken only by extremely experienced kayakers. No smoking is allowed outside the village in the extensive woods, and no outdoor fires are allowed. Given the island's inaccessible areas and the scarcity of water, fire is a constant danger to both the woods and the wooden houses.

A must-see is Monhegan Island Light and its keepers' cottages, sited high above the village. Here you'll find the Monhegan Historical & Cultural Museum (monheganmuseum.org; open seasonally). In 1824, when it was first built, the lighthouse burned sperm oil. Today the light is computer-operated by the U.S. Coast Guard with solar power. The Museum Association presents natural history artifacts upstairs; domestic and economic memorabilia and some genuine art treasures on the first floor in the Keeper's House; and annual art shows in the Assistant Keeper's House gallery. Inquire about visiting hours for the Kent-Fitzgerald-Hubert House. Built by Rockwell Kent, it displays the distinctive work of its more recent resident, James Fitzgerald.

An artist at work on Monhegan

Christina Tree

Checking In
Best places to stay on
Monhegan Island

To be sure of a room on your visit, as well as a parking place and a ferry ticket, make reservations. The Island Inn (207-596-0371; islandinnmonh egan.com) stands just above the ferry dock, a long, shingled summer hotel with a proper porch and lawn chairs overlooking the sunset and Manana Island. Old-fashioned and newly renovated, the comfortable dining room is hung with contemporary Monhegan paintings and serves exceptional and sophisticated dinners. A buffet breakfast comes with the rooms, which are divided between the main hotel and a rear annex. Request one with a view.

Shining Sails (207-596-0041; shiningsails.com), open year-round, offers two attractive rooms and five exceptional apartments in a village home, most with decks and water views. A continental breakfast is served seasonally in the living room by the woodstove. Hosts John and Winnie Murdock also offer nightly rentals elsewhere in village, along with some two dozen island cottages, available by the week.

The Monhegan House (207-594-7983; monheganhouse.com) sits at the heart of the village. Its 28 rooms hold antique furniture and offer views of the sea and meadow. Most share the bathrooms on the second floor, but there are half-baths on the third floor and two suites with private bath. A full-service breakfast is included, but it's popular with the whole island so sometimes crowded. Single rooms on the fourth floor are bargain priced, usually reserved by artists. Dinner is served in high season; reservations are a must. The Trailing Yew (207-596-0440; trailingyew.com), on the road to Lobster Cove, invites you to "step back in time"

Fish Beach, Monhegan   Nancy English

in its guest rooms, many lighted by kerosene lamps. Scattered in several cottages and a main building, rooms share baths (with electricity). Rates include breakfast and dinner, where diners are seated at common tables and conversation abounds.

All three of the island's inns welcome dinner guests by reservation (BYOB; wine and beer are available at island stores). Seating is at picnic tables at The Fish House Market on

Fish Beach, the best place to feast on lobster or crabmeat rolls at lunch and on Damariscotta oysters, steamed clams, and seafood stews anytime—but especially as the sun sets on the harbor and the islet of Manana. It's also worth noting that The Novelty, behind Monhegan House, is a source of tasty hiking fuel as you set off up Horn's Hill, prime access to the island's cliff paths. Hand-dipped ice cream and frozen yogurt hit the spot on the way down.

Vinalhaven, North Haven, and Matinicus

Attractions, activities, accommodations, eateries, etc.

From Rockland it's a 75-minute ride on a Maine State Ferry (207-596-5400) to either North Haven or Vinalhaven (vinalhaven.org), but no ferry run serves both islands. Passengers have no problem walking on and bikes are carried at a nominal fee—but be forewarned that getting cars off and on both islands can be tricky in high season.

The North Haven ferry docks in the island's village, steps from the (seasonal and casual) Cooper's Landing restaurant (207-867-2060) and from island shops— the legendary North Haven Gift Shop and Gallery (207-867-4444), operated since 1954 by June Hopkins, mother of Eric (see *Rockland*) and David, who maintains

Birding on Western Penobscot Bay

Birders book the Island Inn on Monhegan Island solid during the late-September and early-October migration season. Among the visitors are groups from Connecticut Audubon, WINGS—a Tucson-based birding tourism company that guides tours around the world—and the Manomet Center for Conservation Sciences, based on Cape Cod.

The charming island 12 miles off the coast of Maine, with its spectacular flocks of birds, as well as passing hawks and falcons, is just one of many places birds love to rest, breed, and winter in Maine. Western Penobscot Bay is rimmed with protected coastal wetlands along with the fine harbors that have given migrating birds refuge from time immemorial.

Belfast Harbor, for instance, holds 8 to 24 of the remaining 250 Barrow's goldeneye, a rare duck with yellow eyes set in its sleek, black-feathered head, from mid-December into March. With white markings and neck, the species attracts birders seeking rare sighting from around the world.

Maine Audubon and the Belfast Bay Watershed Coalition run a Bird Bus that operates in spring in Belfast. The Waldo County YMCA takes reservations and collects fees for the Tuesday trips from mid-March to early June.

"We look for returning waterfowl. My idea of the trips is to capture the progress of spring migration," said Seth Benz, who leads the tours. Benz, a Belfast resident and expert on birding, scouts for warblers up into the nesting season along with shorebirds, other songbirds, and raptors. In February, Benz hosts an event on the pedestrian bridge over Belfast Harbor to celebrate the flock of Barrow's goldeneye. In September he has taken the Bird Bus to Cadillac Mountain for the annual hawk watch. He also leads an Exploritas group, working with Elderhostel, in September to Monhegan.

Benz and mapmaker Margot Carpenter put together the *Belfast Important Birding Locations* brochure, available at the Belfast Chamber of Commerce.

Sears Island is one of the best places for birders during spring and fall migration, Benz said. In late fall and winter waterfowl frequent Fort Point Cove, Stockton Springs, accessible in and around the Fort Point Park. And at the mouth of the Ducktrap River near Lincolnville Beach in late autumn and winter, birders can encounter red-necked grebes, loons, mergansers, and several species of sea ducks.

For fine birding places here and all over the Maine coast, *The Maine Birding Trail*, written by Bob Duchesne, is available at Maine Audubon in Gisland Farm, Falmouth, and online at Down East Books. You can download a free shorter brochure at mainebirdingtrail.com/Brochure.pdf.

the neighboring Hopkins Wharf Gallery. It's also an quick walk to gracious Nebo Lodge (207-867-2007; nebolodge.com), a vintage-1912 inn tastefully revamped with nine crisp bedrooms and delightful common space, including a dining room and a locally sourced menu that changes nightly. Recently renovated Calderwood Hall offers the island's best pizza.

Carver's Harbor, Vinalhaven   Christina Tree

Swimmers test the waters in a Vinalhaven quarry.   Christina Tree

Beyond the village a 10-mile loop beckons bicyclists through rolling, open fields, spotted with idyllic farmhouses. North Haven's year-round population is just 350 but its summer colony ranks among the country's wealthiest. The former general store at the dock is now Waterman's Community Center (207-867-2100; watermans.org) with a state-of-the-art theater, the venue for summer lectures, concerts, and plays.

Vinalhaven is Maine's largest island and—with 1,200 year-round residents—represents its largest island community. There's a bustle to Carver's Harbor, the island's village and home to one of the world's largest lobster fleets.

Gearys Beach, Vinalhaven, is an island beach.

Christina Tree

Grab a waterside table at the Harbor Gawker (207-863-9365) and order the island crabmeat and veggie wrap and then browse your way along Main St. Artist Elaine Crossman's New Era Gallery (207-863-9351; Main St.) displays serious painters, sculptors, and photographers, a clue to the quantity and quality of artists salted away on the island. That striking Victorian lodge at the center of the village is Robert Indiana's home and studio.

The Vinalhaven Historical Society Museum (207-863-4410; vinalhaven historicalsociety.org) is a short walk up High St. and worth the climb. Displays feature the island's 19th-century boom years, during which more than 40 quarries supplied granite for many of the country's most imposing monuments and buildings.

Two quarries are now delightful public swimming holes, easily accessible by bike from Carver's Harbor. Allow another couple of hours for the pleasant walk from Main St. out along the harbor to Lane's Island, the most accessible and one of the most rewarding of 20 preserves maintained by the Vinalhaven Land Trust.

Basic bikes, cars, and kayaks are available from Phil Crossman at the Tidewater Motel and Gathering Place (207-863-4618; tidewatermotel.com) in Carver's Harbor. The author of *Away Happens*, a genuinely funny description of island life, Phil also offers visitors physical access to much of this island's beauty—places like The Basin, a large, tidal saltwater inlet that once used to hold as many as 150,000 lobsters until the price peaked. Now it's an ideal place to kayak, sometimes surrounded by seals.

The Tidewater itself spans the tidal stream connecting the harbor and Carver's Pond. It's evolved over decades from motel to a complex that includes some remarkable rooms and suites with decks overlooking a harbor full of lobster boats. At sunset this view is so spellbinding that you don't want to move. The other lodging option is Libby House (207-863-3696; libbyhouse1869.com; open April through November 1). Longtime host Philip Roberts offers spotless, old-fashioned

Fort Knox, the Penobscot Observatory, and Bucksport

Whoosh and the elevator sets you 43 stories above the Penobscot River, atop one of the two obelisk-like pylons anchoring the Waldo–Hancock bridge. This is the **Penobscot Narrows Observatory** (207-469-6553; maine.gov/observatory; open daily May through October 9–5, until 6 in July, August). Far below, Bucksport is a toy town, and from another window Penobscot Bay sweeps away to the horizon. This is the only bridge with an observatory in the country.

West of the bridge a traffic light on Rt. 1 eases access to the Fort Knox grounds, site of the elevator up to the observatory. Access is limited to 49 visitors at any one time, so at the parking-lot gate you receive a ticket stamped with a "go time." In July and August expect a wait. You can picnic at one of the tables overlooking the river and explore the fort.

Fort Knox (fortknox.maineguide.com) tours are available Memorial Day through Labor Day, then weekends. In the visitors center interpretive panels tell the story: Built in 1844 of granite cut from nearby Mount Waldo, the fort includes barracks, storehouses, a labyrinth of passageways, and picnic facilities. The fort was to be a defense against Canada during the Aroostook War with New Brunswick. It's a venue for reenactments and a wide variety of events, sponsored by Friends of Fort Knox.

The best view of both fort and bridge is from the mile-long walkway and park (with restrooms), across the mouth of the Penobscot River in Bucksport. A workaday river town, Bucksport is a great way stop. There's the **Harbor View Grille** (207-486-3396; 96 Main St.), **Wahl's Dairy Port** (79 Main St.), and **Book Stacks** (71 Main St.), a full-service bookstore with a cyber café. **The Bucksport Historical Society Museum** (207-469-3284) is housed in the former Main Central Railroad Station, and the **Alamo Theater** (85 Main St.), home to **Northeast Historic Film** (207-469-0924; oldfilm.org), sells vintage films from its store. If it's dinner you need, **MacLeod's** (207-469-3963; macleodsrestaurant.com; 63 Main St.) is a dependably satisfying restaurant.

Penobscot Narrows Bridge   Nancy English

July 4 is big on Vinalhaven.

Christina Tree

rooms, a two-room apartment, and comfortable common space on the edge of the village, handy to Lane's Island Preserve.

The island's newest noteworthy addition is SALT Restaurant (207-863-4444; saltvh.com; 64 E. Main St.). Upscale and as locally sourced as possible, it gets rave reviews. Open daily in-season, weekends year-round.

Matinicus, Maine's outermost island, lies beyond the outer edge of Penobscot Bay, 23 miles at sea. It's a year-round home to fewer than 40 hardy souls, just 200 in summer. There are walking trails through meadows and along the shore and two sand beaches, one at each end. The 750-acre island is a haven for birds, with 650 species identified, and Matinicus Rock offshore is a protected nesting site for puffins.

At Tuckanuck Lodge (207-366-3820; tuckanuck.com), Nantucket Island native Bill Hoadley offers five rooms, some with water views and all with breakfast and kitchen privileges; dinner is also served (BYOB). From Knox County Regional Airport you can fly there in 15 minutes with Penobscot Island Air (207-596-7500; penobscotislandair.net), weather permitting (there's a frequent fog factor). By water taxi (207-691-9030; matinicusexcursions.com) it's—at best—a 70-minute ride from Rockland. The Maine State Ferry takes more than two hours and comes several times a month in summer, less frequently off-season.

Camden to Bucksport

INCLUDING ROCKPORT, BELFAST, SEARSPORT, AND ISLEBORO

NORTH OF ROCKLAND, Rt. 1 shadows Penobscot Bay for 50 miles, along the way threading towns with fine brick 19th-century centers and proudly built clapboard homes, constructed with money earned in the shipping trade. Each community is tantalizingly different from the next. Camden and Rockport both enjoy gorgeous harbors, and just inland from that pretty coast are the Camden Hills, 6,500 acres of which are wrapped up in Camden Hills State Park. With their picturesque ports and backdrop of hikable hills, the towns have an old resort feel.

Skiffs lined up at Rockport Harbor.

These towns, inhabited year-round by writers, retired intelligence officers, and plain old wealthy people, have art, crafts, galleries, and concerts galore, and even the Great Recession has not, so far, made a difference in that rich array. Just behind the busy sidewalks of Camden is a lovely park beside its harbor, and between that park and the handsome library is a tranquil, shaded amphitheater. Maine's Windjammer fleet of more than a dozen independently owned schooners stands ready to carry passengers out into the bay and its more remote harbors.

Past Lincolnville Beach is Belfast, a place with a wonderful downtown and a remarkable vitality, drawing shoppers and diners. Searsport is home to The Penobscot Marine Museum, showcasing the area's seafaring past.

LEFT: The setting sun lights up Rockport Harbor   Nancy English

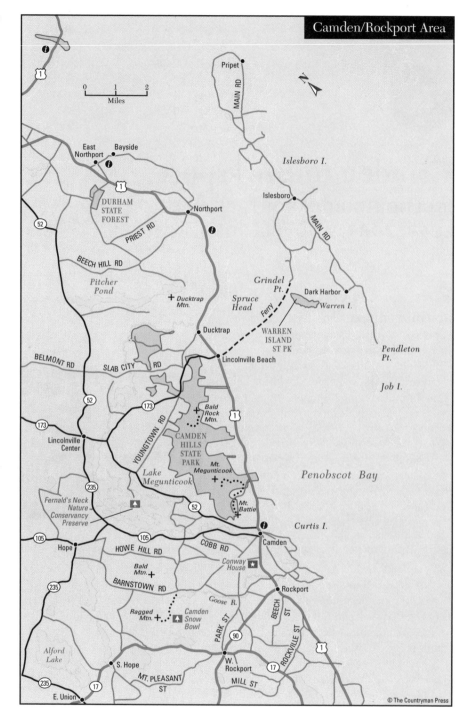

Camden/Rockport Area

Camden and Lincolnville

Check out these great attractions and activities . . .

Camden Hills State Park (207-236-3109; 280 Belfast Rd., Rt. 1) features hiking trails, camping sites, and a shore picnic area. Maiden Cliff Trail offers views from on top of 800-foot cliffs across Lake Megunticook, and connects with the Ridge Trail to the top of Mount Megunticook, the highest point on the Midcoast. Merryspring Nature Center (207-236-2239; merryspring.org; just south of the village off Rt. 1) is open year-round with walking trails and herb, daylily, and demonstration gardens. The Beech Hill Preserve (207-236-7091; coastalmountains.org; Beech Hill Rd., Rockport) is a prime spot for birding and for blueberrying, though you can't pick the berries unless it's one of the annual free picking days. The berry harvest is sold to support the preserve.

The Center for Maine Contemporary Art (207-236-2875; cmcanow .org; 162 Russell Ave., Rockport) offers exhibitions into the early winter. Maine Media Workshops (207-236-8581; mainemedia.edu; 18 Central St., Rockport) draw students of photography, filmmaking, and more to Rockport every summer for one of more than 200 programs for every skill level. The Center for Furniture Craftsmanship (207-594-5611; woodschool.com; 25 Mill St., Rockport) offers another kind of class, with hands-on workshops for novice, intermediate, and advanced woodworkers. The Messler Gallery on the campus of the center shows off some of the finest examples of wood craftsmanship during five annual exhibitions.

Windsor Chairmakers (207-789-5188; windsorchair.com; Rt. 1, Lincolnville Beach) produces Windsor chairs, tables, bed frames, and more, as you can see for yourself on a self-guided tour of the workshop next door.

The view of Camden Harbor from the amphitheater

The Owl and Turtle Book Shop (207-230-7335; 33 Bayview St., Camden), with author events and the best coffee in town, locally roasted to prefection, and Sherman's Books (207-236-2223; shermans.com; 14 Main St., Camden), with a huge toy selection, feed a population hungry for reading matter.

Bay Chamber Concerts (207-236-2823; baychamberconcerts.org; 18 Central St., Rockport) presents concerts through fall, winter, and spring and sponsors a

Windsor Chairmakers workshop

Nancy English

music festival in summer. Thursday-evening chamber music concerts are held in the Rockport Opera House.

In Northport, Swan's Island Blankets (207-338-9691; swansislandblankets .com; 231 Atlantic Hwy., Rt. 1) is looking for well-heeled customers, but everyone will wish to own one of these exquisite, handwoven blankets.

Checking In

Best places to stay in Camden and Lincolnville

Hawthorn Inn (207-236-8842; camden hawthorn.com; 9 High St., Camden) has been carefully restored; under new owners Ted and Lisa Weiss the hospitality meets high standards. The Camden Maine Stay (207-236-9636; camdenmainestay.com; 22 High St.) is just down the street, and holds the same kind of well-cared-for, handsome rooms furnished with taste and kept to a high polish.

A Little Dream (207-236-8742; littledream.com; 60 High St., Camden) farther up Rt. 1 and with comfortable

chairs and beds, enjoys some water views from the hillside it sits on, so that the annual Parade of Sails can be enjoyed from a few rooms. Treetops has a private deck, and the view is especially lovely when the full moon rises over Camden harbor.

Cedarholm Garden Bay Inn (207-236-3886; cedarholm.com; Rt. 1, Lincolnville Beach) offers a water view and private waterside cabins, so away-from-it-all you'll wonder if you just drive here from crowded Camden. A lush garden is the first symptom of the lavish care at this spot with four per-fect, upscale cabins or cottages, two of them just steps from the sea.

Inn at Ocean's Edge (207-236-0945; innatoceansedge.com; Lincoln-ville Beach) is a luxurious modern hotel with two buildings, and the one called Hilltop holds rooms with balconies. The Spa building has two luxury suites and a heated infinity-edge pool. A full breakfast and a weekly cocktail party are included.

The High Tide Inn (207-236-3724; hightideinn.com; 505 Belfast Rd., Rt. 1, Camden), with ocean views and its own 250-foot private beach a short drive from Camden, holds a variety of accommodations that start below $100 even in high season. The fine knack for hospitality of its innkeeper Jo Freilich shows in the delectable popovers and muffins she serves her guests in the screened porch of the main inn. Motel rooms with connecting rooms work for families at the top of the property. Within hearing of the waves lower on the hill are commodious rooms with ocean views, while some of the charming cabins and three of the inn rooms overlook Penobscot Bay.

Local Flavors

Local restaurants and cafés in Camden and Lincolnville

Francine Bistro (207-230-0083; francinebistro.com; 55 Chestnut St., Camden). *Flavor* is the byword here, from dry-aged steak that tastes better than any beef you've ever had to incredibly fresh fish. Count on straightforward meals that are somehow better than seems possible, plus crusty fresh bread and good wine. The owner opened Shepherd's Pie (207-236-8500; 18 Main St., Rockport) in 2010. Chicken liver toast, fresh oysters, shepherd's pie made with lamb shanks braised with Madeira, organic hamburgers, barbecued ribs—you read the menu item and you want it, it's that

High Tide Inn, Camden

Nancy English

Produce from Beth's Farm in Warren is served at Francine Bistro, Camden. Nancy English

simple. Owner Brian Hill's food follows the late Nora Ephron's rule that every calorie be worth eating. Seabright Pizza (207-230-1214; www.seabright camden.com; 7 Public Landing, Camden), open Wednesday to Sunday, maintains the rule with fig jam, Gorgonzola, and prosciutto pizza; another features roasted cauliflower, along with the incomparable classic mozzarella and tomato sauce with basil.

Long Grain (207-236-9001; 31 Elm St., Camden) serves the best lunch and many think the best dinner in town—but make sure to time your visit for Tuesday to Saturday. Asian food is rarely made to high standards, but that is starting to change along the coast and Long Grain is one Thai place leading the change. Noodle dishes, steamed mussels, Panang curry, and bean cakes receive raves.

Atlantica (207-236-6011; atlantica restaurant.com; 9 Bayview Landing, Camden) has stood the test of time— unlike so many places that vanish in one season. The deck on the water is a fabulous spot for a good meal, which is what you will find here.

40 Paper (207-230-0111; www .40Paper.com; 40 Washington St., Camden) has won praise for many of its more-than-40 cocktails; carbonara made with bucatini and whatever local vegetables are in season may be starring on a changing menu with an Italian focus.

Natalie's (207-236-7008; natalies restaurant.com; 83 Bayview St., Camden) serves elaborate meals in a stunning, modern dining room with red chairs and hanging lamps; expensive.

The Lobster Pound and Andy's Brew Pub (207-789-5550; lobster poundmaine.com; 2521 Atlantic Hwy., Lincolnville). Started in 1992, when craft beers were new and strange, Andrew's Brewery ales and porters

Isleboro

Visitors to Islesboro, reached by ferry from Lincolnville Beach, won't find anyplace to stay at all these days, so a visit either is a day trip or involves a rented cottage (islesboro.com/rentVac.htm). A car is almost a necessity on this long, rural island. **Artisan Books and Bindery** (207-734-6852; artisanbooksandbindery.com; 111 Derby Rd.) is a fine small bookstore, with coffee, that holds 20,000 volumes and is open year-round; call for hours. You can find ice cream and sandwiches from Memorial Day to Labor Day at **The Dark Harbor Shop** (207-734-8878), but call first to make sure it's open.

established themselves quickly as the best in the area. You can find them on tap inside The Lobster Pound in Lincolnville Beach in a partnership that should flourish, given the perfect pairing of lobster and beer. Decide for yourself whether Red Ale, Scottish Ale, Golden Ale, or another is the best of all.

Whale's Tooth Pub (207-789-5200; 2531 Atlantic Hwy., Rt. 1, Lincolnville) presents the sea from outside and inside tables, serving battered fried fish and seafood Mornay. Huge logs are burned in the fireplace when it's cold, and beer from Andrew's Brewery is on tap.

Dot's (207-706-7922; 2457 Atlantic Hwy., Lincolnville), aside from offering a high standard for coffee (both hot and iced) and fine baked goods, grills lamb burgers on Friday

Dinner is under way and the open kitchen at Shepherd's Pie is moving fast.   Nancy English

Wines and Spirits

Cellardoor Vineyard (207-763-4478; mainewine.com; 367 Youngtown Rd., Lincolnville) and **Cellardoor Winery at the Villa** (Rts. 90 and 1, Rockport) both offer free wine tastings. A replanting of the vineyard with grape hybrids suitable to the Maine climate led to a 2012 harvest of grapes destined for sparkling wine. Other wines are made with purchased grapes, and some are award recipients. **Breakwater Vineyards** (207-594-1721; breakwatervineyards.com; 35 Ash Point Dr., Owls Head) opened in 2010 for wine tasting from late May to mid-October. Sea Smoke, a dry red, is made with the vineyards' own Marquette grapes; it's related to Pinot Noir.

Cellardoor Winery at the Villa, Rockport

Nancy English

Inland in Union, **Savage Oakes** (207-785-2828; savageoakes.com; 174 Barrett Hill Rd.) planted grapevines in 2002; all its wines are made with 100 percent Maine grapes or blueberries, and Nor'easter is Maine's only grape port. Free tastings. **Sweetgrass Farm Winery & Distillery** (207-785-3024; sweetgrasswinery.com; 347 Carroll Rd., Union) distills fragrant Three Crow Rum, vermouth, and an excellent apple brandy that rivals Calvados, as well as producing blueberry, apple, and peach wines. Free tastings mid-May to December.

Sweetgrass Winery also has a tasting room in Portland.

Nancy English

and roasts chickens for meals ready to bring home all week long. There's wine, cheese, fancy-schmancy stuff,

and a perfect custardy lobster pie— which you can scarf up at a table inside for an extraordinary breakfast.

Belfast and Searsport
Attractions, activities, accommodations, eateries, etc.

Penobscot Marine Museum (207-548-2529; penobscotmarinemuseum.org; 5 Church St., Searsport) holds a fantastic archive of historical photographs, many on display. View ships' models and marine fine art, attend events—contra dancing, historic photography lectures, and lighthouse model making were offered in 2012—and brace yourself against the raging storm winds of historic wealth and historic ruin on the Maine shipbuilding coast.

Penobscot Marine Museum in Searsport
Courtesy of Penobscot Marine Museum

Fortunately life is quieter now in Searsport, with most of the shipbuilding consisting of putting together model kits at BlueJacket Shipcrafters (207-548-9974; bluejacketinc.com; 160 E. Main St., Searsport). The Captain A. V. Nickels Inn (207-548-1104; captainnickelsinn.com; 127 E. Main St., Rt. 1) reopened in

Belfast street sculpture

Nancy English

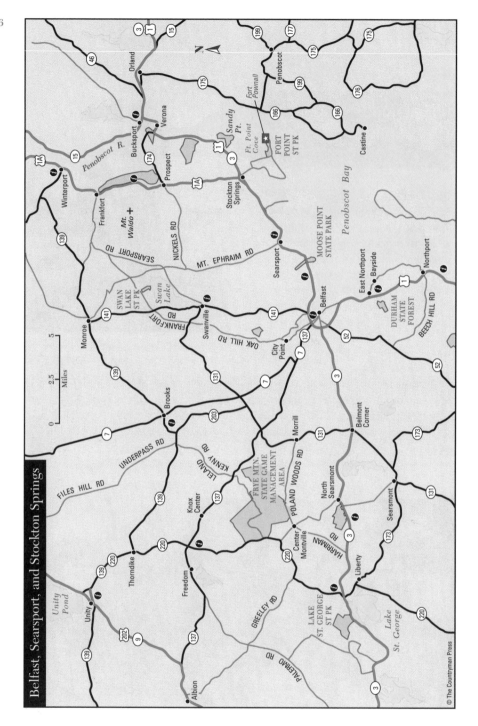

Belfast, Searsport, and Stockton Springs

© The Countryman Press

Shipbuilding and rail created prosperity in 19th-century Belfast, with the architectural evidence visible along its streets.

Nancy English

late 2011 after a complete renovation: The rooms are well appointed, the linens fresh, and the place sparkling. The Captain's Table Restaurant and Port of Call Wine and Tapas Bar complete the hospitality, with views of the bay.

Searsport is also well known for its flea markets, like The Hobby Horse Antiques Flea Market, on Rt. 1.

Just south in Belfast, Belfast Bay Inn (207-338-5600; belfastbayinn.com; 72 Main St.) is right in the middle of town, and its crystal chandeliers light up the lobby. The rooms and suites are over the top with luxurious appointments;

Enjoying the creative public seating in downtown Belfast

Nancy English

Breakfast is served in this room and, in good weather, on the deck at the Captain A. V. Nickels Inn.

Nancy English

some have a view of the harbor and a fireplace. Breakfast included.

Belfast galleries show off local talents and crafts like the tree trunk faces sculpted by Ron Cowan. Waterfall Arts (207-338-2222; waterfallarts .org; 256 High St.) has both classes and exhibits.

Count on Belfast for good meals. Chase's Daily (207-338-0555; 96 Main St.) makes thin-crust Margherita pizza with heirloom tomatoes (in-season); the huevos rancheros employs a smoky and voluptuous ranchero sauce, but the daily omelet enfolds the garden stuff for sale in the back. Call for hours.

For more incredible sustenance, Eat More Cheese (207-358-9701; eatmorecheese.me; 94 Main St.) next door has just the thing, from delicious salami to creamy French triple crèmes. Around the corner at 92 Main St. is Northwoods Gourmet Girl (207-930-2050; www.northwoodsgourmetgirl .com), bringing impeccable jams,

Hobby Horse Antiques Flea Market

Nancy English

Eggplant and squash at Chase's Daily in Belfast

Nancy English

ketchups, and other condiments made in Greenville to the coast, perfect hostess gifts or souvenirs that you can sample before purchasing.

Three Tides Waterfront Bar & Marshall Wharf Brewing Co. (207-338-1707; 3tides.com; 2 Pinchy Lane, Belfast) lies at the bottom of Main St. to the left, with a second-floor covered deck that overlooks the glittering blue water of Belfast Bay filled by the Passagassawakeag River. When you order the Pemaquid oysters on the half shell, you will be honoring the first residents of this area, indigenous members of the Wabenaki Nation, and later the early Europeans, who made oysters and clams joyful summer soul food. David and Sarah Carlson opened this place in 2003 and feature on tap some of the more than a dozen brews made in their next-door craft brewery, Marshall Wharf Brewing, like Wrecking Ball Baltic Porter and Sexy Chaos.

Young's Lobster Pound (207-338-1160; 2 Fairview St., Belfast) sells cooked lobster and mussels, steamers, and lobster and crab rolls. The business is open year-round as a retail and wholesale seafood market, but takes off in the warm weather when its cavernous upper floor and a deck outside overlooking the water fill with hundreds of people ripping up their lobsters. Look no farther if you have a hankering for Maine's first citizen of the sea, but bring your own tablecloth and bottle of wine if you prefer to dine with more sophistication.

The Gothic (207-338-4684; 108 Main St., Belfast) serves vegetarian, sophisticated fare under 16-foot-tall ceilings festooned with ornamentation in the former Belfast National Bank Building, designed in high Gothic style in 1878. Matthew Kenney, who has roamed the country during his many-chaptered cooking career, serves Aroostook potatoes or perhaps roasted chanterelles with polenta, depending on the season and what was just foraged in the local woods.

East Penobscot Bay

INCLUDING THE BLUE HILL PENINSULA, DEER ISLE, AND ISLE AU HAUT

THE SERIES OF PENINSULAS AND ISLANDS defining the eastern rim of Penobscot Bay, an intermingling of land and water along bays and tidal rivers, is a landscape that's exceptional, even in Maine. One finger of land, with Castine at its tip, points down along the Penobscot River toward the bay, but the bulk of the Blue Hill Peninsula wanders away southeast. It's divided from Deer Isle by the 10-mile-long Eggemoggin Reach, a busy shortcut between Penobscot and Jericho Bays. The reach is spanned by a vintage-1939, improbably narrow, soaring suspension bridge to Little Deer Isle, which in turn is a stepping-stone linked by a causeway to Deer Isle proper. Stonington at its southern tip is the departure point for Isle au Haut. Technically Stonington is just 36 miles south of Rt. 1, but the drive takes an hour—and if you stop in Blue Hill, as you must, and find your way to Brooklin or Brooksville, as you should, it can take several satisfying days.

State of Maine at the Castine Town Dock

Christina Tree

The entire area is webbed with narrow roads threading numerous land fingers, leading to studios of local craftspeople and artists. What you remember afterward

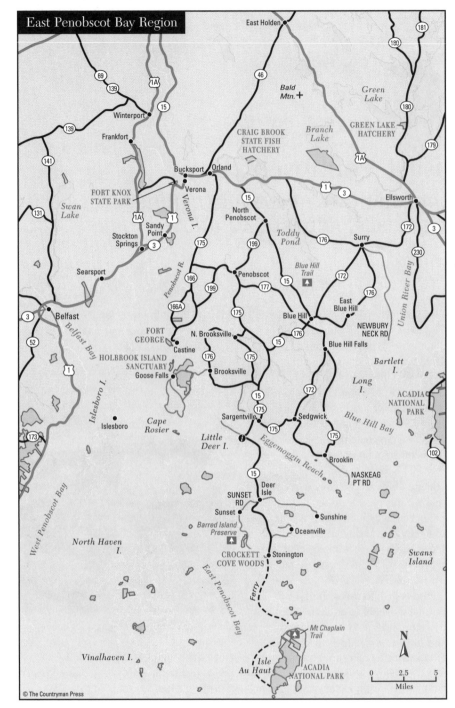

East Penobscot Bay Region

East Holden

181

180

69 139 1A

46

Bald Mtn. +

Green Lake

180

15

Winterport

Frankfort

CRAIG BROOK STATE FISH HATCHERY

Branch Lake

GREEN LAKE HATCHERY

179

141

139

Bucksport Orland

Verona

1A

Ellsworth

3

FORT KNOX STATE PARK

Swan Lake

131

Stockton Springs

Sandy Point

1A 1

North Penobscot

15

Toddy Pond

176 Surry

172 3

230

Searsport

199

Penobscot

Blue Hill Trail

172

166

199 177

15

East Blue Hill

176

Belfast

166A

175

Blue Hill

176

NEWBURY NECK RD

52

FORT GEORGE

N. Brooksville

176

15

Blue Hill Falls

1

HOLBROOK ISLAND SANCTUARY

Castine

176 175

Brooksville

Bartlett I.

Goose Falls

15

172

Long I.

ACADIA NATIONAL PARK

Islesboro I.

Cape Rosier

Sargentville

175

Sedgwick

Blue Hill Bay

102

Islesboro

Little Deer I.

175

Brooklin

173

West Penobscot Bay

15

NASKEAG PT RD

Deer Isle

SUNSET RD

Sunset

Sunshine

Barred Island Preserve

Oceanville

North Haven I.

CROCKETT COVE WOODS

Stonington

Swans Island

Vinalhaven I.

East Penobscot Bay

Ferry

Mt Chaplain Trail

Isle Au Haut

ACADIA NATIONAL PARK

N

0 2.5 5

Miles

© The Countryman Press

Eggemoggin Reach Bridge

Christina Tree

is the beauty of clouds over fields and quiet coves, some amazing things that have been woven, painted, or potted, and conversations with the people who created them.

Blue Hill Peninsula

Check out these great attractions and activities . . .

The first Rt. 1 turnoff for the Blue Hill Peninsula (bluehillpeninsula.org) is Rt. 175, the way to Rt. 166 and Castine (castine.me.us). Occupying a mini peninsula at the confluence of the Penobscot and Bagaduce Rivers, this town still looms larger on nautical than road maps and remains a popular yachting port. It is also home to the Maine Maritime Academy and its training vessel, *State of Maine*, which is open to visitors for tours mid-July through mid-August.

Castine is one of Maine's most photogenic towns, its streets lined with handsome 19th-century clapboard homes and buildings, all uncannily well preserved. Even the elm trees that arch high above its sloping Main St. escaped the general blight. Most of the hotels built here during the steamboat era are gone, but descendants of the families who arrived by steam or sail still return each summer.

According to the historical markers that pepper its tranquil streets, this town has been claimed by four different countries since its early-17th-century founding

Main Street, Blue Hill

Christina Tree

The Castine Historical Society tells an amazing story.

Christina Tree

Merrill & Hinckley is Blue Hill's genteel general store.

Christina Tree

as Fort Pentagoet. All of downtown Castine is on the National Register of Historic Places. Pick up the free pamphlet *A Walking Tour of Castine*, available at local shops. Begin at the town dock, with its welcoming picnic tables, parking, and restrooms. Amble uphill past antiques shops or down along Perkins St. to the Wilson Museum (207-326-8545; wilsonmuseum.org), with historical and changing art exhibits. The Castine Historical Society (207-326-4118; castinehistorical society.org), housed in the Abbott School Building on the town common, is well worth a visit to see its multimedia presentation about the infamous defeat of the colonial navy here by the British during the Revolution (see "Sense of Place"). Up on Battle Ave. you can also inspect Fort George, the unimpressive earthenworks fortification the British built and then occupied during the War of 1812 as well as the Revolution.

Blue Hill, we should clarify, here refers to this entire peninsula (bluehill peninsula.org) and also to a specific hill and town. Turn off Rt. 1 onto Rt. 15 and follow it a dozen miles south to find the town of Blue Hill (bluehillme.gov), cradled between its namesake hill and bay. At the walkable center you'll see a pillared town hall, a handsome WPA library (207-374-5515; 5 Parker Rd.), and Federal-era historic houses, like the Jonathan Fisher House (jonathanfisher house.org). The summer season here roughly coincides with the Kneisel Hall Chamber Music Festival (207-374-2811; kneisel.org), one of the oldest chamber music festivals in the country, with a series of Sunday-afternoon and Friday concerts, June through August.

Blue Hill's shops and galleries showcase the best of the peninsula's artists

and artisans, among others. Handworks Gallery (207-374-5613;
handworksgallery.org; 48 Main St.)
is filled with stunning handwoven
clothing, jewelry, furniture, rugs,
blown glass, and art by Maine artists and artisans. North Country
Textiles (207-374-2715; north
countrytextiles.com), corner of
Main and Union Sts., specializes
in custom rag rugs, pottery, handcrafted woodwork, and weaving.
The Jud Hartmann Gallery (207-
374-9917; judhartmanngallery.com;
79 Main St.) exhibits Hartmann's
nationally known realistic bronze
sculptures of northeastern Native
Americans as well as the work of
other prominent local artists.
Also check out the Randy Eckard
Gallery (207-374-2510; randy
eckardpaintings.com; 29 Pleasant
St.), across from Blue Hill Books
(207-374-5632; bluehillbooks.com),
a long-established, independent,
full-service bookstore with frequent
author readings. At the northern
end of town on Rt. 172, Rackliffe

Handworks Gallery, Blue Hill   Christina Tree

Pottery (207-374-2297; rackliffepottery.com) produces distinctive small pieces,
featuring local clays and their own glazes. Visitors are welcome to watch. Pick up
a copy of the free *Arts Guide*, available in most shops and galleries, highlighting
studios throughout the peninsula.

Over the entrance of the Bagaduce Music Lending Library (207-374-5454;
bagaducemusic.org) on Rt. 172 a mural depicts the area as the center of con-
centric creative circles. Back-to-the-earth pioneers Helen and Scott Nearing,
searching for a new place to live "the Good Life" in the 1950s, swung a dowsing
pendulum over a map of coastal Maine. It came to rest on Cape Rosier, a mini
peninsula protruding westward. For many decades the small town of Brooklin
was a familiar byline in *The New Yorker* thanks to E. B. White, who also wrote
Charlotte's Web and *Stuart Little* here at about the same time millions of children began to read about Blueberry Hill in Robert McCloskey's *Blueberries for
Sal* and about Condon's Garage in South Brooksville in his 1940s classic *One
Morning in Maine*. Energy lines or not, this peninsula is exceptionally beautiful,
with views to the east across Blue Hill Bay toward Mount Desert as well as back
across Penobscot Bay.

There is no single best way south from the town of Blue Hill. Whichever
road you choose, you strike gold but miss another sterling route. The most direct
road to Deer Isle is Rt. 15, which runs down the center of the peninsula, cresting

at Caterpillar Hill where—whatever else you do—be sure to stop at the pullout to take in the spectacular panorama west across Penobscot Bay to Camden Hills.

If time permits, detour onto Rt. 176 and stop before the fast-moving, reversing Bagaduce Falls at Bagaduce Lunch (see *Local Flavors*) to savor both exceptional views and seafood. Continue on Rt. 176 as it winds down along the bay to South Brooksville. You can pick up a sandwich or wine and cheese at Buck's Harbor Market and picnic by this yacht-filled harbor.

Hikers and birders might want to extend this detour—allow at least an extra hour—to explore Cape Rosier, the most remote part of the peninsula, much of it a wildlife sanctuary. Roughly 2 miles north of Bucks Harbor turn left off Rt. 176 onto Cape Rosier Rd. and follow it through the woods, forking left at the grange to finally reach the shore at Weir Cove. Chances are you will want to explore the rocks and beach. Across the way the Good Life Center (207-326-8211; goodlife .org), Helen and Scott Nearing's Forest Farm, is now open to the public in July and August. Organic gardening guru Eliot Coleman, who came here to work with the Nearings on the late '60s, operates Four Season Farm (609 Weir Cove Rd.; fourseasonfarm.com) down the road. Continue on to the village of Harborside and on across Goose Falls to Holbrook Island Sanctuary State Park. One way or the other, return through the woods to Rt. 176.

Another way south from Blue Hill takes you along Blue Hill Bay to Brooklin. Begin on Rt. 172/175, then turn left at 2.5 miles onto Rt. 175 and head over the bridge across reversing Blue Hill Falls, a favorite spot with kayakers pitting their skill against the white water. Continue 9.5 miles south along the bay to the Brooklin

Bucks Harbor

Christina Tree

General Store and down Naskeag Rd. to the WoodenBoat School (207-359-4651; woodenboat.com). A spin-off from *WoodenBoat* magazine, this nationally famous seafaring institute offers courses that range from building your own sailboat or kayak to navigation. The store is a shopping destination in its own right.

On the way back to the village center, note the colorful selection at Maine Hooked Rugs (6 Naskeag Rd.). As you turn west on Reach Rd. (Rt. 175), don't speed up. Betsy's Sunflower (12 Reach Rd.) is a true trove of gadgets, gifts, book, toys, and much more; Handmade Papers (113 Reach Rd.) features Gigi Sarsfield's exquisite lamp shades and other creations from fiber, including tufts of cattail and bits of lichen. The road winds along Eggemoggin Reach and over the Benjamin River into Sedgwick. Farther along, the Eggemoggin Textile Studio (497 Reach Rd.) features wraps and pills that Chris Leith weaves with yarns she also spins and dyes. Reach Rd. joins Rt. 15 just north of the Deer Island Bridge.

Checking In

Best places to stay on the Blue Hill Peninsula

Blue Hill Inn (207-374-2844; blue hillinn.com; 40 Union St., Blue Hill), a classic 1830s inn on a quiet village street, offers comfortable elegance in 11 guest rooms, along with two suites in the neighboring Cape House cottage that are open year-round. Guests gather in the parlor or garden in the evening, and rates include a full breakfast, served in a large, sunny dining room that's open to the public (see *Local Flavors*).

In Castine the Pentagöet Inn (207-326-8616; pentagoet.com; 26 Main St.) is a lovingly restored, turreted Queen Anne–style survivor from the steamboat era. Guest rooms in the inn itself are unusually shaped, and all 16 (including the neighboring annex) are imaginatively furnished with comfortable antiques. Innkeeper Jack Burke presides in the exotically decorated Passports Pub, an inviting gathering sport, along with the wicker-furnished and flowery veranda. The dining room is ranked among Maine's best. Up at the end of Battle Ave., The

Manor Inn (207-326-4861; manor-inn .com) also has plenty of appeal. An expansive 1890s stone-and-shingle summer mansion set above lawns bordering conservation land, its 14 rooms vary (as do the rates) from huge to snug. The Castine Inn (207-326-4365; castineinn.com; 33 Main St.) is an 1890s summer hotel with 19 second- and third-floor rooms and suites, 10 with harbor views. No dinner but breakfast is open to the public.

The remaining best places to stay on the peninsula are widely scattered. Sited near the tip of Newbury Neck in Surry, Wave Walker Bed & Breakfast (207-667-5767; watersidehideaways .com; 28 Wavewalker Lane), open year-round, offers spectacular views across the bay to Mount Desert Island. The Brooklin Inn (207-359-2777; brooklininn.com; 22 Reach Rd.) is a casual, friendly, year-round haven that's also best known as a restaurant. The four moderately priced, pleasant upstairs bedrooms cater to yachtsmen (innkeeper Chip Angell picks up at nearby moorings). On Cape Rosier, well off the beaten track, Hiram Blake Camp (207-326-4951; hiramblake.com) has been operated by the same family since 1916, explaining the great value as well as peace this family-geared

Pentagöet Inn, Castine

Christina Tree

compound offers. This is the kind of place where you come to stay put. All cottages (5 one-bedroom, 6 two-room, 3 three-bedroom) are within 200 feet of the shore, with views of Penobscot Bay. Each has a living room with a wood-burning stove; some have a fireplace as well. In shoulder seasons guests cook for themselves, but in July and August everyone gathers for breakfast and dinner in the dining room—which doubles as a library, because thousands of books are filed away by category in shelves ingeniously hung from the ceiling. Many guests bring kayaks, and there are rowboats at the dock.

Cottage Rentals

Peninsula Property Rentals (207-374-2428; peninsulapropertyrentals.com),

Main St., Blue Hill, features a range of area rentals.

Two former full-service resorts offer cottages in superb settings. Oakland House (207-359-8521; 435 Herrick Rd.) in Brooksville offers 10 one- and two-room cottages scattered through the woods and along the shorefront, which includes a beach, at the entrance of Eggemoggin Reach. Its exquisite site can only come from being in the same family since 1889. The same goes for the seven cottages at The Lookout (207-359-2188; the lookoutinn.biz; 455 Flye Point Rd.) in Brooklin. Here the extensive property faces across Blue Hill Bay toward Mount Desert. The seriously old-fashioned old hotel functions primarily as a restaurant. It's a popular place for weddings.

Local Flavors

The taste of the Blue Hill Peninsula—local restaurants, cafés, and more

Arborvine (207-374-2119; arborvine .com; Main St., Rt. 172, just south of Blue Hill Village) is one of the most widely acclaimed restaurants in Maine; dinner reservations may be necessary a couple of days in advance. Chef-owner John Hikade and his wife, Beth, restored this handsome 1820s Hinckley homestead, retaining its original Dutchman's pipe vine above the door. The several open-beamed dining rooms with fireplaces, once the parlors, are simple and elegant. The menu presents local produce in memorable ways, maybe Bagaduce River oysters on the half shell with a frozen sake mignotte, or broiled Stonington halibut with grilled polenta, lemon butter crumb crust, and orange-miso sauce. The adjacent DeepWater Brew Pub (207-374-2441; no reservations) features its own brew and a pub menu. A shingled mansion, Barncastle (207-374-2300; barn-castle.com; 125 South St.), open daily year-round from 3 PM, is the unlikely but delightful venue for the area's best pizza. The ambience is upscale, the oven is wood-fired, and the pie comes with a choice of 30 toppings. The reasonably priced menu ranges from spanakopita to St. Louis ribs.

Elsewhere on the peninsula Buck's Restaurant (207-326-8688) is hidden gem in the village of South Brooksville, behind the Buck's Harbor Market. Chef-owner Johnathan Chase has an enthusiastic following, and his informal dining room, decorated with work by local sculptors and artists, is known for turning local ingredients into memorable meals. The Brooklin Inn (see Checking In), open year-round, religiously serves only wild fish and produce that's local and organic; the menu changes nightly. The setting is a pleasant dining room and sunporch in this venerable village inn. Elsewhere in Brooklin, The Lookout Inn & Restaurant (see Checking In) is a bit of a local secret, with consistently good dining on a many-windowed sunporch overlooking meadows that slope to the bay.

In Castine the Pentagöet Inn (see Checking In) is a popular dining destination. Chef-owner Julie Vandegraaf makes memorable use of local ingredients; the signature dish is lobster bouillabaisse. Dine in an airy, candlelit dining room with well-spaced tables, on the porch, or in exotic Passports Pub.

At The Manor Inn (see Checking In), open year-round, co-owner Nancy Watson is the chef and the crabcakes are a family recipe. The formal dining room overlooks a sweeping lawn. The Pine Cone Pub here offers a lighter menu. For casual lunch or dinner in Castine, Dennett's Wharf (207-326-9045), near the town dock, occupies an open-framed harborside structure said to have been built as a bowling alley after the Civil War. It features homebrew and a huge all-day menu. When the summer sun shines, The Breeze is also a great place for fried clams and soft ice cream, right on the town dock. Along with Castine Variety (207-326-9920) at the foot of Main St., it's owned by Hawaii-born and -trained chef Snow Logan; daily specials at both places might include Hawaiian "Lokomoko," miso soup, and combinations like crabmeat and avocado.

If you're looking for a quick bite in Blue Hill there are several local secrets. At the north end of the village near the junction of Rts. 172 and 176 north, the Blue Hill Food Co-op &

For Blue Hill's best lobster roll or an entire shore dinner, the Fish Net is worth the line.

Christina Tree

Boatyard Grill, Blue Hill, is in a working boatyard.

William A. Davis

Café (207-374-2165) is an oasis for vegetarians, while the neighboring Fish Net (207-374-5240; 162 Main St.) serves the best lobster and crab rolls in town; its picnic tables are also a good spot to feast on lobster and steamers (there's inside seating as well). Just up Rt. 176 in a working boatyard, The Boatyard Grill (207-374-3533; 13 E. Bluehill Rd.) is a seasonal seafood venue, sited in an actual boatyard, with water views and a kid-friendly pirate ship. Marlintini's Grill (207-374-2500), south on Rt. 15/176, is a combination

Bagaduce Lunch, South Penobscot

Christina Tree

sports bar and family restaurant, open for lunch and dinner.

Don't leave town without sampling the truffles at Black Dinah Chocolatiers (207-374-5621; blackdinahchoco latiers.com; 5 Main St.), hidden away in the Fairwinds Florist building. Founded on Isle au Haut, these creations, handcrafted from Peruvian and Venzuelan chocolate and local butter, have won national acclaim. The café, open daily year-round, also serves espresso, chocolate drinks, and more.

If it's a sunny day, a steady stream of traffic heads south on Rt. 15, then turns onto Rt. 176 north and follows it west a mile or to Bagaduce Lunch (open daily 11–7, closing at 3 on Wednesday), a family-owned takeout since 1946. Here the fishburgers are

enormous, crispy-fried fresh fillets and the clam baskets are legendary. Tables are scattered on a waterside slope with the coveted seats by Bagaduce Falls, a prime spot to watch swift-moving reversing tides and the seabirds that feed there. Also well worth finding: Millbrook Company Bakery and Restaurant (207-326-4197; millbrook company.com; 160 Snow's Cove Rd., Sedgewick). Open year-round (but check days and hours), this attractive dining spot features its breads, focaccias, and "local chef's salad" with or without marinated chicken or fish, daily specials.

On Rt. 15 in Sargentville, El El Frijoles (207-359-2486; elelfrijoles .com; 41 Caterpillar Rd.) is a great seasonal lunch, dinner, or takeout spot for authentic Cal/Mex—but with local ingredients. The house special is spicy lobster.

The area's best classic lobster shack is at the totally opposite end of the peninsula in the town of Surry, with picnic tables on a wharf, overlooking Mount Desert. Perry's Lobster Shack (207-667-1955; 1076 Newbury Neck Rd.) serves up the freshest crab and lobster with sweet corn on the cob and homemade ice cream sandwiches (BYOB). Call before coming to make sure they are open.

Blue Hill's big event of the year is The Blue Hill Fair (immortalized in *Charlotte's Web*), celebrated all Labor Day weekend, culminating with fireworks best viewed from the top of nearby Blue Hill (as in *Blueberries for Sal*).

Deer Isle, Stonington, and Isle au Haut

Check out these great attractions and activities . . .

Deer Isle is characterized by the kind of coves and lupine-fringed inlets equated with "the real Maine." It's divided between the towns of Deer Isle and Stonington, and there are vestiges of onetime communities like Sunset southwest of the small but very real village of Deer Isle, and Sunshine, home to the nationally respected Haystack Mountain School of Crafts. Galleries display outstanding work by dozens of artists and craftspeople who live, or at least summer, in town.

The village of Stonington at the southern tip of the island remains a working

Stonington Harbor

Christina Tree

fishing harbor, home to one of Maine's largest fishing/lobstering fleets. Most of its buildings, scattered on smooth rocks around the harbor, date from the 1880s to the World War I boom years, during which Deer Isle's pink granite was shipped off to face buildings such as Rockefeller Center and Boston's Museum of Fine Arts. The Deer Isle Granite Museum (207-367-6331; Main St.) depicts Stonington at the height of the granite boom with a population of 5,000; the present combined year-round population of Deer Isle and Stonington is 2,400.

The summer season is short but busy, with a number of seasonal shops and galleries along waterside Main St. However, the Opera House (207-367-2788; operahouse.org) stages live presentations and films year-round. While property values have soared in recent years, the number of nature preserves has multiplied, including a dozen maintained by the Island Heritage Trust (207-348-2455; island heritagetrust.org). Six miles offshore, the southern half of Isle au Haut is part of Acadia National Park (nps.gov/acad).

Crossing the half-mile, soaring Deer Isle Bridge is an adventure in itself, especially on a foggy night when you seem suspended inside a cloud. Of all Maine's "hinged" islands, this is the only one with a bridge long and dramatic enough to reinforce your feel of leaving the mainland behind.

The seasonal, volunteer-staffed Information Building (with facilities), maintained by the Deer Isle–Stonington Chamber of Commerce (207-348-6124; deerisle.com), is just beyond. Even if it's closed you can usually pick up the chamber's current map/guide outside; if it's open be sure to snag leaflet guides to island walking trails. Nearby Scotts Landing, for instance, is a 24-acre preserve on Eggemoggin Reach that includes a sandy beach. There's also parking along the causeway to Deer Isle.

It's just 5 miles down Rt. 15 to Deer Isle Village, but half a dozen rewarding detours to studio/galleries beckon. Down Reach Rd., for instance, the Greene-Ziner Gallery (207-348-2601; melissagreene.com) is a barn, surrounded by meadows, filled with Eric Ziner's ornate and whimsical metal sculpture and Melissa Greene's thrown earthenware pieces. Be sure to stop just north of the village at the Turtle Gallery (207-348-9977; turtlegallery.com), showcasing exceptional jewelry as well as biweekly changing shows of contemporary crafts.

Deer Isle Village is sited at the island's narrow waist, with water on both sides of its short main street (Rt. 15A). Here Red Dot Gallery (207-348-2733; reddotgallery.net; 3 Main St.) is a cooperative showing the work of established local artists in mixed media, painting, fiber, jewelry, and clay; and Deer Isle Artists Association (207-348-2330; deerisleartists.com; 15 Main St.) is a 150-member cooperative with frequently changing exhibits. Don't miss The Periwinkle, a tiny shop with a vintage-1910 cash register, crammed with books and carefully selected gifts and cards.

Rt. 15 snakes south to Stonington but, again, there are enticing detours. The Sunshine Rd. branches off and winds 7 miles to Haystack Mountain School of Crafts (207-348-2306; haystack-mtn.org). Studios are generally closed aside from a weekly tour and scheduled events, but the campus itself is a work of art, a series of spare, shingled buildings, all weathered the color of the surrounding rocks and fitted between trees, connected by steps and terraced decks, floated above lichens and wildflowers on land sloping steeply to Jericho Bay. Keep an eye out on the way to and from for studio/galleries. There's no missing Nervous Nellie's Jams and

Eric Ziner displays his whimsical creations and potter Melissa Greene, her handsome pottery, at Yellow Birch Farm, Deer Isle.

Christina Tree

Jellies (207-348-6182; nervousnellies .com; 98 Sunshine Rd.) with its whimsical life-sized sculptures, including a red lobster playing checkers as a 7-foot alligator looks on. Tea, coffee, and scones are served here, along with wild blueberry preserves, blackberry-peach conserve, and hot tomato chutney.

Half a dozen miles farther down Rt. 15 the Oceanville Rd. presents another tempting detour. The big attraction here is defunct Settlement Quarry, now a trail-webbed nature preserve with a view off across Webb Cove. Not far beyond is Old Quarry Ocean Adventures (207-367-8977; old quarry.com; 130 Settlement Rd.), the

Stonington Co-op by Jill Hoy

departure point for Captain Bill Baker's seasonal excursions to Isle au Haut as well as a variety of other cruises. This is also the area's prime source for guided kayaking and kayak rentals. The waters off Stonington are studded with islands, ideal for kayakers. Old Quarry also offers platform tent sites and a camp store.

The village of Stonington is the iconic Maine coastal village. Its mansard-

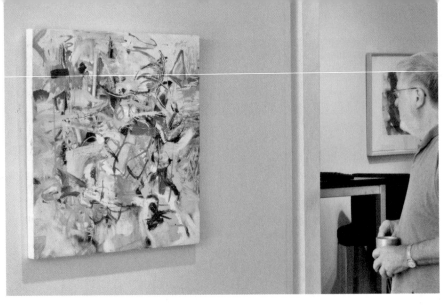

gWatson Gallery, Stonington

Christina Tree

roofed houses are perched where rocks permit, and the harbor is filled by afternoon with fishing boats; for Windjammers this is a weekly port. Narrow Main St. is now home for a dozen or so seasonal art galleries, with receptions on first Fridays, July through October (stoningtongalleries.com). At the east end of Main St., bold, bright landscapes by Jill Hoy (207-367-2368; jillhoy.com) are housed in a big white barn. The gWatson Gallery (207-367-2900; gwatsongallery.com; 68 Main St.) shows contemporary painting and sculpture featuring prominent East Coast artists, and Isalos Fine Art (207-367-2700; isalosfineart.com; 26 Main St.) shows painting, sculpture, photography, and mixed media art by more than a dozen local artists.

Dockside Books & Gifts, Stonington

Christina Tree

Among the special shops here, don't miss Dockside Books & Gifts (207-367-2652; 62 W. Main St.) at the far end of the village. Al Webber's waterside bookstore has an exceptional selection of Maine books and gifts, sweaters by local knitters, and a great harbor view from the deck. Virginia Burnett's landmark Prints & Reprints (207-367-5821; 31 Main St.) features framed arts and antiquarian books, and The Dry Dock (207-367-5528) at the center of Main St. stocks tempting women's clothing and crafts.

The hilly island visible from downtown Stonington is Isle au Haut (pronounced *eye-la-HO*), named "high island" in 1605 by Samuel de Champlain. This is a substantial island, 6 miles long and 3 miles wide, home to some 80 year-round residents, including best-selling author Linda Greenlaw, who has depicted island life in *The Lobster Chronicles*. From Stonington the Isle au Haut Ferry Service (207-367-5193; isleauhaut.com) makes the 45-minute crossing frequently in-season, stopping twice daily in warmer months at Duck Harbor in the Acadia National Park section of the island. There are no reservations on the ferry, but those with camping reservations are given priority.

Most visitors come to hike the 20-mile network of trails around Dark Harbor and along the cliffy southern tip. On a beautiful July or August day, though, it's enough of an excursion to take the ferry to the town dock and walk to Black Dinah Chocolatiers (207-335-5010; blackdinahchocolatiers.com), a café with WiFi, serving breakfast, lunch, and Sunday brunch as well as their amazing chocolates. Of course, to really enjoy the island without pressure of catching a boat, you need to spend a couple of days.

Checking In

Best places to stay in Deer Isle and Stonington

At the Inn on the Harbor (207-367-2420; innontheharbor.com; 45 Main St., Stonington; open year-round) guest rooms come with binoculars, the better to focus on lobster boats and regularly on the schooners in the Maine Windjammer fleet, for which each of the 14 comfortable rooms is named. The inn backs on Stonington's bustling Main St., but most rooms, some with decks, face the harbor. Our favorites are the *Stephen Taber* (a former barbershop), and the *American Eagle* suite with two bedrooms, an open kitchen, a dining area, and a living room. A flowery ground-floor deck is shared by all.

The gracious, four-story, hip-roofed Pilgrim's Inn (207-348-6615; pilgrimsinn.com; open mid-May to mid-October) stands in the middle of Deer Isle Village but both fronts and backs on water. Built as a private home in 1793, it has big front parlors and guest rooms of varying sizes, some with gas log fireplaces. There are also three nicely decorated, two-bedroom cottages. The inn's popular dining room, The Whale's Rib, is open by to the public (reservations advised).

Off by itself in a northern corner of Deer Isle, The Inn at Ferry Landing (207-348-7760; ferrylanding.com; 77 Old Ferry Rd.) overlooks Eggemoggin Reach. Open year-round, this 1840s seaside farmhouse offers water views, spacious rooms, and a common room with huge windows and two grand pianos. The six guest rooms include a master suite with a woodstove and skylights. There's also an adjacent two-story, two-bedroom, fully equipped housekeeping weekly rental.

In Stonington, Pres du Port (207-367-5007; presduport.com; W. Main and Highland Ave.) is a cheery, comfortable B&B in an 1849 home with a light- and flower-filled sunporch overlooking the harbor. Charlotte Casgrain is a warm hostess who enjoys speaking French and offers three imaginatively furnished guest rooms, one with a loft and kitchenette. The generous buffet breakfast—perhaps crustless crabmeat-and-Parmesan quiche—is served on the sunporch. Also in Stonington, Boyce's Motel (207-367-2421; boycesmotel.com; 44 Main St.; open year-round) is a bit of a local secret, far larger than it looks from the street. Most of the 11 reasonably priced units, including several with cooking facil-

ities, line a quiet lane that angles off from Main St.

The best selection of rentals on Deer Isle and Isle au Haut is through Island Vacation Rentals (207-367-5095; islandvacationrentals.biz; 50 Main St., Stonington).

Local Flavors

The taste of Deer Isle and Stonington—local restaurants, cafés, and more

In Deer Isle the Whale's Rib Tavern in Pilgrim's Inn (see *Checking In*), housed in a many-windowed old barn with white-clothed tables, is our top pick. The frequently changing dinner menu might range from fish-and-chips to lobster and shrimp risotto.

In Stonington, Aragosta (207-367-550, aragostamaine.com; 27 Main St.) offers fine dining. At lunch a large deck extends the dining area but the restaurant is smallish, so reserve for dinner. Dine on local oysters and Stonington lobster ravioli with house-made pasta and farm greens. The Factory Tavern (207-367-2600; thefactorytavern.com; 25 Seabreeze Ave.) has a great two-story harborside location with a mix-it-up lunch and dinner menu.

The Cockatoo Restaurant at Goose Cove in Sunset (207-348-2600;

Pilgrim's Inn, Deer Island Village

Christina Tree

View from Harbor Café, Stonington   Christina Tree

goosecovelodgemaine.com), open daily in-season for lunch and dinner, is named for chef Suzen Carter's pet cockatoos. The dining room in this classic old lodge overlooks the water, and there's dining on the deck. The menu features Azorean dishes.

In the middle of Stonington the Harbor Café (207-367-5099) is a dependable oasis, open year-round from 6 AM until closing, spanking clean and friendly with booths, great for seafood every way from rolls to the all-you-can-eat Friday fish fry (reserve). Next to the quarryman statue on the dock there is also The Fisherman's Friend (207-367-2442; 5 Atlantic Ave.), open year-round for lunch and dinner. It's a vast barn of a place in which you can always find a seat, good for a wide choice of fried and broiled fish, chowders and stews, burgers, and more.

Acadia Area

MOUNT DESERT AND THE SCHOODIC PENINSULA

Including Ellsworth, Bar Harbor, Hancock, the Cranberry Islands, Swan's Island, and Frenchboro

THE LODESTONE OF THE MAINE COAST and likely of the whole state is Acadia National Park, the first national park east of the Mississippi River, which occupies almost half of the land of Mount Desert Island as well as other landmasses nearby. Hanging off the coast of Maine like an enormous lobster claw, Mount Desert Island or MDI is laced with lakes and almost cut up through the middle by Somes Sound, the closest thing to a fjord on the East Coast. The island's terrain is mountainous, and those mountains, so dramatic when seen by sea, are built of bare pink granite, the source of its name—bestowed by Samuel de Champlain in 1604—l'Isle des Monts-déserts (pronounced with the accent on the second syllable).

Sand Beach   Nancy English

Hudson River School artists who painted the Mount Desert landscape in the 1800s infused their signature numinous light into the surroundings—or was it vice versa? Bar Harbor was then called Eden and considered a paradise, at least in summer. Wealthy inhabitants of Mount Desert Island had arrived seeking the vision on the artists' canvases. They had built enormous "cottages" and grown to treasure their surroundings when other

LEFT: A young boy crowns the 17th-century Italian fountain in the Bar Harbor village green.

Nancy English

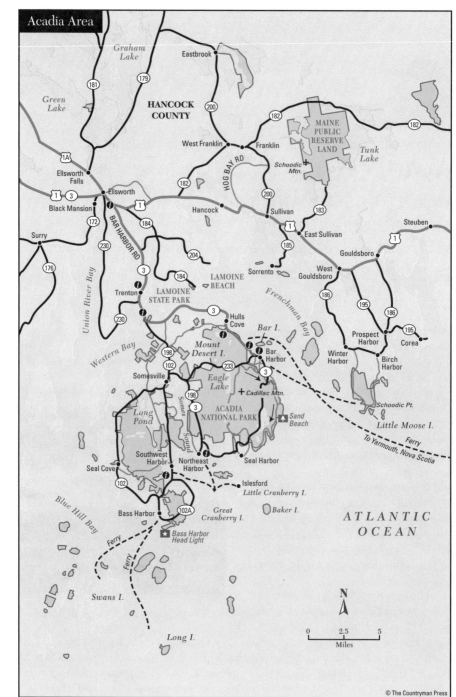

Acadia Area

© The Countryman Press

Paddleboarding near the waterfront in Bar Harbor

Nancy English

kinds of development pressures began to compete with the scenery by the end of the 19th century.

Luckily for their contemporaries and for the more than two million visitors who arrive annually today, the resources of those wealthy summer residents, including thousands of acres of land, were pooled into the first 11,000 acres accepted by the federal government as a park in 1919. Boston textile heir George Dorr began the campaign to amass acreage in 1901, finding a ready response among many, including Harvard University president Charles W. Eliot.

Appalled at the noisy invasion of early automobiles, John D. Rockefeller donated 45 miles of carriage roads and erected 17 stone bridges, each unique and elegantly arched over the crushed-stone roads now limited to bikes, walkers, cross-country skiers, and of course carriage rides and horses. But whether you visit Acadia by sitting inside a car touring the 27-mile Park Loop Road, or by climbing up the rungs of the iron ladders set into granite cliffs on the hardest trails, you will encounter its beauty many times over.

Other sections of this chapter describe the towns and islands that surround the park, from Bar Harbor with its sidewalks crowded into the evening to Swan's Island, as peaceful as whatever weather is in charge. Most visitors travel here by car from Ellsworth down Rt. 3 past many quirky and engaging tourist businesses, but a meal in Cleonice, a visit to an elegant gallery in Ellsworth, and a devotedly French dinner at Le Domaine in Hancock are all excursions or detours more than worth your while.

Driving beyond Bar Harbor or bypassing its village entirely down the west side of the island brings you to many small, tranquil communities, some still infused by the traditions of wealthy summer visitors and others as quiet as any Maine town. Northeast Harbor and Southwest Harbor both contain fine shops, and at both towns' harbors you can embark on a ferry for the Cranberry Islands. Along the southwest edge of the island, in Bass Harbor, you can catch a ferry to Swan's Island and to Frenchboro's Long Island.

Ellsworth
Attractions, activities, accommodations, eateries, etc.

Ellsworth's brick-lined Main St. is part of Rt. 1 for a brief moment before you turn right onto Rts. 3 and 1, where travelers who opted to use the highway are heading south to MDI. But consider slowing to a stop in Ellsworth to enjoy art at the Courthouse Gallery (207-667-6611; courthousegallery.com; 6 Court St.), just up the hill from the stop sign south of Ellsworth village. The 1834 building is listed on the National Register of Historic Places and has been devotedly restored. Your eyes will be forgiven if they stray from the gleaming old floors and newly painted tin ceilings to the vibrant art on the walls. An affection for exuberant paintings and brilliant color mark the artwork exhibited here, like the moments revealed in John Neville's work, about dory fishermen off the coast of Nova Scotia, and Stephen Pace's galloping horses.

Around the corner from Courthouse Gallery, just down Rt. 172 in the direction of Surry, is Woodlawn Museum, Gardens and Park (207-667-8671; woodlawn museum.com; 19 Black House Dr., Rt. 172), where the Captain Black House museum (closed in winter) is filled with 19th-century furniture, the gardens holds a tournament-sized croquet court for visitors to play on for a fee, and 2 miles of trails are open during daylight year-round. High tea is served on Wednesday at 3 in-season; reservations required. Telephone Museum (207-667-9491; thetelephone museum.org; 166 Winkumpaugh Rd., off Rt. 1A north of Ellsworth) celebrates telephone technology with hands-on exhibits. Place a call to someone you know from a switchboard in the museum.

Kisma Preserve (207-667-3244; kismapreserve.org; Rt. 3, Trenton) is on the road to MDI, and you might pass it by thinking it's a hokey tourist trap. Instead, if you stop here you will encounter many species of nondomestic animals from a wide variety of backgrounds who have found a permanent home. Among the changing population you may encounter bears, primates, reptiles, birds, and wolves in residence. Adults can arrange to encounter some of the animals up close for a fee, by reservation only and subject to availability. Rules are strict to maintain the tranquility that this preserve guarantees its animal residents.

The Grand Auditorium (207-667-9500; grandonline.org; Main St., Ellsworth) offers live performances and movies in its renovated and glorious interior. Much of Ellsworth was rebuilt during the worst of the Depression, a seeming miracle offering inspiration to nearby Bar Harbor's campaign to revive its own theater.

A seasonal roundtrip train ride from Ellsworth, Downeast Scenic Rail (207-667-7819; downeastscenicrail.org), brings riders into the countryside. Volunteers have devoted themselves to bringing this excursion into being, work well worth enjoying.

By now you're hungry. If it's lunch or dinnertime, your best bets are either Union River Lobster Pot (207-667-5077; lobsterpot.com; 9 South St.)—where you can enjoy a steamed lobster and all the fixings or superior fried seafood in a lovely setting on Union River (but call for hours)—or Cleonice (207-664-7554; cleonice

.com; 112 Main St.). Cleonice is open year-round with changing hours, and its offerings whet the appetite anytime of year, with an emphasis on Mediterranean tapas, like terrific grilled baby octopus and a perfect calamari salad (not fried and delicate and delicious) and finely prepared, wholesomely sourced ingredients including local grass-fed beef and fresh fish. The wine list is good, and desserts worth the indulgence. Karen's Café (207-412-0102; 100 Main St.) makes an excellent pesto chicken sandwich for a satisfying lunch.

With all this going for it, Ellsworth is an option for an overnight stay made simple by the owners of Twilite Motel (207-667-8165; twilitemotel.com; Rt. 1), just south of the village. Inexpensive motel rooms, which are well maintained, come with a continental breakfast of muffins and coffee and with friendly owners who can guide your next steps on the coast. Small pets are welcome, for a fee.

Campers looking for other sites than the often booked campgrounds on Mount Desert Island can enjoy an ocean view and beach at Lamoine State Park (207-667-4778; campwithme.com; Rt. 184).

Acadia National Park

Check out these great attractions and activities . . .

First, of course, at the Hulls Cove Visitor Center, the park campgrounds, or the information center next to the Bar Harbor Town Green and other locations, pick up a week's pass ($20 with a car, $5 without) and receive a little introduction to the majestic sprawling realm of Acadia National Park (207-288-3338; nps.gov/acad; off Rt. 3 just north of Bar Harbor).

A marsh near Bass Harbor   Nancy English

Most park visitors get themselves to the top of Cadillac Mountain and around some or all of the Park Loop Road, most of it one-way. Built over the years between 1922 and the 1950s, the Park Loop Road offers good places to stop, hike, photograph, and contemplate the landscape of ocean, wood, and stone. The Island Explorer buses (207-667-5796; exploreacadia.com) are free, and its Number 4 Loop Road bus can take you around the sites, dropping off and picking up all day through Columbus Day. Stop at Wildwood Stables (877-276-3622; carriagesof acadia.com) and you can enjoy an hour carriage ride on the carriage roads for $20 (in 2014). If you are lucky enough to be able to bring your own horse, that horse can board at the stables ready for your daily rides, but there are no horse rentals.

Back on the bus, Number 3 Sand Beach takes passengers to Sand Beach and to Blackwoods Campground (207-288-3274; reservations required May through October at 877-444-6777 or recreation.gov), one of two campgrounds in the park. The other is Seawall near Southwest Harbor, or a ride on Number 7—with less frequent service come fall.

From parking areas all over the island, most accessible by bus, the trailheads beckon. Precipice Trail features iron rungs set into the nearly vertical route up Champlain Mountain, an attraction for the intrepid, but closed during peregrine falcon nesting. The Precipice Trailhead is on the Park Loop Road south of the Sieurs de Monts entrance off Rt. 3, south of Bar Harbor. Gentle, nearly flat Wonderland is a trail that stretches out over a point of land at the southern end of the island, off Rt. 102A between Seawall and Bass Harbor.

But altogether the park counts dozens of trails. Over the last 15 years, an additional 12 miles of trails have been rebuilt with hundreds of hours of labor after years of neglect; ask at the visitors centers about one, Homan's Path, with its many granite steps. Swimming, while forbidden on many of the lakes skirted by carriage roads, is offered at Echo Lake, with access off Rt. 102 south of Somesville and at a little beach on Long Pond on Pretty Marsh Rd. Sand Beach, off the Park Loop Road south of Bar Harbor, gives you the Maine ocean in its frigid glory, with water that stays 55 degrees and colder.

Echo Lake   Nancy English

Just a little farther on the Park Loop Road is Thunder Hole, where the formation of the cliffs at the edge of the water amplifies the fury of the surf's roar—but beware the dangerous allure of big surf in a storm. During Hurricane Earl's visit in 2010, park officials closed the area off entirely. Rt. 3 at Seal Harbor is often inundated with waves during big storms at high tide, and it's another good watch point for surf and waves.

Park rangers lead myriad activities

The tall stand of spruce and fir in the Acadia National Park Pretty Marsh picnic area on western MDI

Nancy English

at Acadia, and guest educators are another bonus. Abenaki storytelling at the Abbe Museum at Sieur de Monts and stargazing at Sand Beach were offered in 2014, for example, and ranger-led canoe trips, nature walks, and junior and senior ranger programs are given all summer, with a monthly program schedule to be found at the park information centers.

During The Acadia Night Sky Festival (acadianightskyfestival.com), park employees show off the stargazing that Acadia, unpolluted with lights, presents every gaudy night of the year.

All season long, the fresh popovers at Jordan Pond House (207-276-3316; jordanpond.com; Park Loop Road near Seal Harbor) provide a respite on a tour of the park, whether by carriage, on foot, or by bicycle or car—but please remember your park pass. The free Island Explorer bus takes you there from the Hull's Cove Visitor Center (and offers a 10 percent discount card); in the busy season you will save time and avoid the headache of waiting for a parking spot. With lawn seating overlooking the pond or indoor tables in a vast, handsome building, the restaurant, owned by the park, offers lunch, tea, dinner—and its specialty at all times, crisp, light, and airy popovers with butter and jam. Call for a reservation to assure your own.

Bar Harbor, Town Hill, and Hull's Cove

Check out these great attractions and activities . . .

So much of Bar Harbor burned during the Great Fire of 1947 that the village as it once stood can barely be imagined. Photographs of the Bar Harbor in its glory can be viewed at the Bar Harbor Historical Society (207-288-0000; bar harborhistoricalsociety.org; 33 Ledgelawn Ave.), where you can also learn more about the devastating conflagration.

The fire also mowed down stands of spruce and balsam firs that had ringed

Twin Rodman/Dahlgren cannons on the waterfront were originally part of the Central Defense Battery on Egg Rock in 1898.   Nancy English

Bar Harbor's marina   Nancy English

the town and clung to the bits of soil left among the granite outcroppings across the island, leaving hardwood seedlings with the chance to grow tall for the first time in, perhaps, centuries.

Today the logging that goes on maintains the woods instead of reaping them.

The birds are grateful. The Acadia Birding Festival (acadiabirdingfestival .com) of late May gathers guides and experts who offer tours, lectures, slide shows, and walks that could bring you up short near peregrine falcons or warblers on their summer visit to Maine. Michael B. Good (207-288-8128; downeastnature tours.com) leads Downeast Nature Tours throughout the year, with trips to special bird-watching sites like Three Pines Bird Sanctuary.

But during summer the main migrants to MDI are always found crowding the sidewalks of Bar Harbor, night and day. Shops, restaurants, and ice cream offer them diversions, but you get the impression that the vastness of the park might have driven them together after hikes and tours to take comfort from their own kind.

The July 4 Independence Day Celebration includes music played on the town green and fireworks set off by the town pier a short walk away. The lobsters that race—or crawl, or dally, or retreat—down seawater-filled Plexiglas tracks at the athletic fields are the high point, with $1 bets adding to the drawn-out drama.

Inside Acadia National Park is the old Abbe Museum at Sieur de Monts Spring, accessible though the Wild Gardens of Acadia with more than 300

The Abbe Museum at Sieur de Monts Spring is open in summer; downtown Abbe Museum is open year-round.

Nancy English

species of indigenous plants. Park founder George B. Dorr had his hand in this establishment, having bought up the natural spring to prevent its becoming a springwater business. But Dr. Robert Abbe was the genius of the original museum, building the structure in the late 1920s to protect his own and others' valuable collections of Native American artifacts. The temple-like building has a soul and poetry about it that appeal to any romantic of history—and when a door blew shut in 2001, we could have sworn Dr. Abbe himself had just taken his leave. The Bar Harbor branch of the Abbe (207-288-3519; abbemuseum.org; 26 Mount Desert St.) in downtown Bar Harbor presents extensive collections acquired in the years since the museum's founding, including centuries-old basketry and crafts made by original inhabitants of Maine and the Maritimes from the Passamaquoddy, Maliseet, Penobscot, and Micmac Nations now collectively known as the Wabenaki.

The early-July Native American Festival and Basket Makers Market on the grounds of the College of the Atlantic gives visitors a chance to meet Wabenaki craftsmen and -women, listen to traditional music, and buy what is surely the best souvenir imaginable, a basket or other craft made with a history of tradition beyond memory.

And at the same place, The George B. Dorr Museum of Natural History (207-288-5395; coa.edu; Rt. 3, just north of Bar Harbor) brings you up close to wild animals and birds you might not otherwise get a chance to glimpse alive. At The Oceanarium (207-288-5005; theoceanarium.com; 1351 Rt. 3) the creatures under the waves are close at hand, and visitors can take a marsh walk or view a lobster hatchery.

Of course, sometimes tourist traps are just the ($8.95 adult) ticket. Pirate's Cove (piratescove.net/bar-harbor; 268 Rt. 3, Bar Harbor), "The Original Adventure Golf," offers tee times 9 AM–10:30 PM in-season. When you drive by, the spot's illuminated waterfalls and emerald putting greens appear like a vision out of the darkness. Watch out for the pirate's roar inside that cave!

Bar Harbor is a center for biking, with two big, full-service bike rental and sales shops and the wonderful Island Explorer Bicycle Express, a van with a bike trailer that chauffeurs bikers from the village green to the carriage road entrance of Acadia National Park on Eagle Lake. The graceful Carriage Roads, built with design insight from Frederick Law Olmsted Jr., offer walking and biking that is peaceful and serene. Kayakers can rely on the rental businesses themselves for a ride to a lake, and all of them offer guided kayaking tours. Sailors can find the Margaret Todd with her distinctive four masts and red sails on the waterfront at Bar Harbor, along with whale-watching ships and tour boats. Readers flock to Sherman's Books and Stationery (207-288-3161; shermans.com; 56 Main St.) to stock up on good reads for beach visits and early evenings; the business started here in 1886 and now has five Maine locations.

The Maine Crafts Guild Show (mainecraftsguild.com) in Bar Harbor in August presents some of the best craftswork done in the state.

Abbe Museum at Sieur de Monts Spring

Nancy English

Checking In

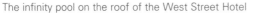

Ullikana Bed & Breakfast (207-288-9552; ullikana.com; 16 The Field) has been our favorite bed & breakfast for years, and so long as innkeepers Helene Harton and her husband, Roy Kasindorf, stay at the helm, it will probably remain so. Their gracious hospitality sets you at ease from the get-go, and the stuffed baked pancakes at breakfast, on the lawn with the sea in the distance, are superb. Everything in the rooms is solid and well maintained, from the tiled floors to the exuberant decorative painting on the walls.

The Bass Cottage Inn (207-288-1234; basscottage.com; 14 The Field) is right next door, and has been decorated with elegance and style. Gas fireplaces, whirlpool tubs, and TVs are in all rooms, which are utterly comfortable, like the pillowtop beds. Count on a fine breakfast in the glassed-in porch

and the friendly guidance of hosts Teri and Jeffrey Anderholm.

Somewhat less expensive, Primrose Inn (207-288-4031; primroseinn .com; 73 Mount Desert St.) was purchased in 2012 by local innkeeper Melissa Collier DeVos, who maintains this inn's high standards and serves a generous breakfast and afternoon tea, perhaps with apple or blueberry pie. The inn has an outstanding reputation.

The Saltair Inn (207-288-2882; thesaltairinn.com; 121 West St.) has a waterfront location in the historic district, three blocks from the middle of town. Suites and rooms, eight in total, offer gas fireplaces and some balconies overlooking the water.

Three big places for tourists who prefer them are Bar Harbor Inn (207-288-3351; barharborinn.com; Newport Dr.), Harborside Hotel and Marina (207-288-5033; theharborsidehotel .com; 55 West St.), and West Street Hotel (207-288-0825; theweststreet hotel.com; 50 West St.). The first two perch over the harbor. Bar Harbor

The infinity pool on the roof of the West Street Hotel   Nancy English

Burning Tree

Matt McInnis

Inn is more old school, handsome and restrained, although new additions are fully outfitted and all rooms have what anyone would expect from a fine hotel. The Harborside is a little glitzier, and more expensive. West Street Hotel, with rooms that can be noisy, is across the street from the harbor, is aimed at adults, limiting its heated, vanishing-edge roof pool to guests 18 and older. A $25 daily resort fee is charged here and at sister property Harborside Hotel, where children from both places can use the pool.

Local Flavors

The taste of Bar Harbor—local restaurants, cafés, and more

Burning Tree (207-288-9331; Rt. 3, Otter Creek) is at the top of its long-played game, serving fresh vegetables out of its own gardens and imaginative vegetarian and seafood dinners, like gray sole with sautéed radicchio and a Dijon cream sauce. Cantaloupe salad with chorizo was one special salad, and a purple basil mojito made a delicious cocktail.

Mache Bistro (207-288-0447; machebistro.com; 321 Main St.). Kyle Yarborough makes hanger steak with smoked blue cheese butter and salmon with tapenade. Pain perdu will tempt you beyond your capacity, so don't say you weren't warned.

McKay's Public House (207-288-2002; mckayspublichouse.com; 231 Main St.) was every local's recommendation. A good wine list and friendly atmosphere combine with excellence in the kitchen to make McKay's, open year-round, a favorite for the tourists, too. Fish-and-chips, crabcakes, and roasted beet salad comprise the "elevated pub fare"—or just call it pub fare the way it should be, much of it sourced locally.

Fathom (207-288-9664; fathom

Breakfast at Café This Way

barharbor.com; 6 Summer St.) is a standout among the dinner spots, dishing up spicy drunken shrimp and goat-cheese-stuffed zucchini blossoms to start and great grilled lamb, or lobster with gnocchi. Local fishermen supply the stars of the changing menu.

Café This Way (207-288-4483; cafethisway.com; 14½ Mount Desert St.) makes dinner, for which you should get a reservation, and breakfast, which can be equally crowded. The Ann, an omelet with goat cheese, basil, and tomatoes, hit the spot one day, but The Smokey with smoked trout needed a little more finesse. Dinner veers south with Brazilian shrimp, scallops and mussels, or a pork flatiron steak with mango chimichurri.

Havana (207-288-2822; havana maine.com; 318 Main St.) was observing its 10th anniversary in 2012 by wowing customers with its ever-fabulous mojitos and pisco sours,

paella, smoked pork, and lobster moqueca in coconut broth.

Side Street Café (207-801-2591; sidestreetbarharbor.com; 49 Rodick St.) makes a fantastic lobster roll, filled with the meat of a lobster and a half; lobster stew, a lobster quesadilla, and lobster mac and cheese round out the first priority of a visitor to Maine. Other sandwiches, burgers, and salads (add lobster!) are on the long menu. Lompoc Café (207-288-9392; www .lompoccafe.com; 36 Rodick St.) is nearby. With a bocce court and an outdoor patio, it is a beloved Bar Harbor hangout offering good falafel burgers, and mussels in a Dijon cream sauce.

Reel Pizza Cinema (207-288-3811; reelpizza.net; 33 Kennebec Place) combines first-run movies with excellent pizza, all named for favorite movies. "Godzilla" is topped with sweet or hot sausage, pepperoni, onion, green pepper, mushroom, and tomato, while

"Moonstruck" is all white, with ricotta, mozzarella, Parmesan, and Monterey Jack.

Sometime or other, either after the bike ride or following the movie, Mount Desert Island Ice Cream (207-460-5515; mdiic.com; 7 Firefly Lane and also 325 Main St.) is a prime stop. Nutella, Vietnamese coffee, and sea salt caramel ice cream are some of the lures owner Linda Parker and her staff think up.

Across the top of MDI is Town Hill, where Town Hill Bistro (207-288-1011; townhillbistro.com), a beloved restaurant in search of a location, planned to make a comeback in 2015; check for news on the website.

Northeast Harbor, Otter Creek, and Seal Cove

Attractions, activities, accommodations, eateries, etc.

Northeast Harbor lies across the mouth of Somes Sound from Southeast Harbor, and the two small towns share a quiet tranquility far from the hustle of Bar Harbor, but Brooke Astor used to shop on the Main St.—and Martha Stewart still does. Inside Magraths (207-276-5548; 131 Main St., Northeast Harbor) you can find a copy of the Red Book, published annually, which lists summer residents and their winter addresses, new and old, along with advertising, for $8. The gelato for sale augments the newspapers, children's books, and coffee to make this a dependable pitstop.

Even if none of the Red Book names mean much to you, the tony shops show off expensive goods with a certain confidence that someone will come along with the wherewithal to buy them. Peter England sweaters for $520, thick, silky, and fabulous, fill a back table at The Kimball Shop & Boutique (207-276-3300; kimball shop.com; Main St., Northeast Harbor—kitchen and housewares are next door to the clothes shop). The rest of us need not fear—the basement room is stuffed with clothes on clearance and sale that are fabulous deals, if you don't mind that they are perhaps a season old, and make it easy to shrug off the sense that you're help being gifted with the cast-offs. Meanwhile, upstairs, a summer resident from Texas is selecting her entire year's wardrobe and having the staff pack it up to be shipped off.

Naturalist's Notebook (207-801-2777; thenaturalistsnotebook.com; 16 Main St., Seal Harbor, and also 115 Main St., Northeast Harbor; 207-276-4120) open late June to mid-October, is both a curiosity shop and an event center, "For anyone who's even a little bit curious about the last 13.7 billion years." With specimens (some are birds hit by cars and taxidermied, courtesy of College of the Atlantic), prints, books, and workshops in identifying wildlife and plants held during the summer, it is a must-stop for human specimens of all ages. Island Artisans (207-288-4214; 119 Main St., Northeast Harbor, and also 99 Main St., Bar Harbor) sells fine crafts, including stunning basketry.

Instead of Lord and Taylor's Bird's Cage, Northeast Harbor has The Colonel's Restaurant & Bakery to retreat to for a cup of tea. The front seating area was empty one summer afternoon, perfect for that tea and a late-afternoon perusal of the *New York Times*.

Harbourside Inn (207-276-3272; harboursideinn.com; Rt. 198, Northeast Harbor) is a shingle-style "cottage" set on 2 acres, open mid-June to mid-

September. The trees obscure the harbor views, but the 14 rooms and suites have their own engaging pleasures, from fine 19th-century furniture, to fresh flowers, to the organic blueberry muffins, fruit, and coffee served with breakfast on the sunporch. A working inn since 1888, the property is close to many trails and in walking distance of the famous gardens and of town.

The Asticou Inn (207-276-3344; asticou.com; Rt. 3, Northeast Harbor). With its beautiful location, heated pool, and multiple accommodations from a tiny single room to a house, the historic inn certainly has a lot going for it. It's perfect for weddings, but can be noisy for paying guests. Continental breakfast is included, and in good weather you'll enjoy it on the deck overlooking the harbor. Dinner at the Asticou's restaurant is made up of Maine restaurant standards like rack of lamb, seared sea scallops, and filet mignon.

Kimball Terrace Inn (207-276-3383; kimballterraceinn.com; 10 Huntington Rd., Northeast Harbor) is the place for inexpensive rooms with tennis and a pool—off-season deals are likely.

Asticou Inn   Nancy English

On Rt. 198/3 north of Northeast Harbor, Abels Lobster Pound (207-276-5827; www.abelslobsterpound.com) offers the shade of tall evergreen trees set above the frigid blue of Somes Sound. Lobster dinners at its picnic tables are some visitors' favorite meals; there are tables inside too.

Southwest Harbor, Manset, and Bernard

Attractions, activities, accommodations, eateries, etc.

Ringing the southwestern coast of MDI, in a west-to-east direction, are Southwest Harbor, Manset, Bass Harbor, and Bernard, each with reasons to visit. Southwest Harbor is the largest community, and The Wendell Gilley Museum (207-244-7555; wendellgilleymuseum.org; Rt. 102) is one of its highlights. An amateur who became a master bird decoy carver, Gilley shaped more than 10,000 birds in his lifetime, beginning in the 1930s. Workshops in decoy carving could give you your own start at craftsmanship.

Another beacon of craftswork is inside Aylen & Son Fine Jewelers (207-244-7369; peteraylen.com; 332 Main St., Southwest Harbor), where Peter and Judy Aylen turn semiprecious and precious stones into exceptional jewelry.

Two croquet courts host summer tournaments at the Claremont Hotel. Nancy English

Antique Wicker (207-244-3983; antiquewicker.com; 270 Main St., Southwest Harbor), sells wicker from every school and style ever made, enough stock to furnish your own new oceanside cottage; much of it in storage, so be sure to ask.

The Claremont Hotel (207-244-5036; theclaremonthotel.com; 22 Claremont Rd., at the end of Clark Point Rd. in Southeast Harbor) is the oldest hotel on the island, but keen management sustains the beautiful accommodations, from inn rooms and suites to cottages. A great chef, Daniel Sweimler, has been keeping the kitchen skill levels high and dinner at The Xanthus beyond appetizing. In July and August lunch and cocktails are served at the Boathouse, on the water's edge. The croquet court lies below the porch and the dining room windows, ready for the Croquet Classic in August and all the hours of practicing that lead up to it. Clay tennis courts, bikes for tooling around the village, badminton, and a little beach are included in the rates, along with breakfast. You might want to pay for the rooms with a wonderful ocean view. A 15 percent gratuity is added to the bill.

Lindonwood Inn (207-244-5335; lindonwoodinn.com; 118 Clark Point Rd., Southwest Harbor) rents 15 rooms April to November 1, and with a fire burning in the breakfast room the charm survives the cold. Some rooms have a fireplace of their own and a balcony overlooking the water. The pool, hot tub, and honor system bar are the right amenities for guests at the end of a hot day.

Red Sky (207-244-0476; redskyrestaurant.com; 114 Clark Point Rd., Southwest Harbor) wins loyalty and praise year in and year out, for a salad of duck breast with sun-dried cherries and tomatoes, for example, and slow-braised ribs. A cheese course for dessert and a fine wine list make an evening here alluring.

And just down the road for another evening is XYZ Restaurant (207-244-

5221; xyzmaine.com; off Seawall Rd., Manset), with food that tastes straight from Mexico. Familiar to the owners because they spend their winters there, Mexican food shows up on these Maine plates the way it was first imagined far south. Start out with the freshly squeezed lime juice drinks, either a margarita or a limeade, then dive into the colorful and tasty meals. Chiles rellenos—ancho chilis stuffed with corn and cheese—holds an almost meaty rich flavor. Count on a variety of chilis and tender pork, short rib and chicken dishes that will linger in memory all next winter.

Beyond Bass Harbor and its ferry boats lies Bernard, where Thurston's Lobster Pound (207-244-7600; thurstonslobster.com; Steamboat Wharf Rd., Bernard) held the mantle of best MDI lobster pound for years; it remains one of the most scenic spots around, with a big deck situated on Bernard's working harbor.

Linda Fernandez Handknits (207-244-7224; 41 Bernard Rd., Bernard) sells sweaters and Christmas socks. In our last encounter she was busy knitting her 2,278th Christmas stocking—for the pet of the couple whose stockings she'd just finished, as a wedding present.

The Cranberry Islands
Attractions, activities, accommodations, eateries, etc.

Reached by ferries and cruises that depart from both Northeast Harbor and Southwest Harbor, the Cranberry Islands make a fine day trip in the summer season. Little Cranberry, also

Bernard

Nancy English

known as Islesford, has the particular attraction of a wonderful restaurant open for lunch and dinner called The Islesford Dock Restaurant (207-244-7494; islesforddock.com). Cynthia and Dan Lief, owners, chefs, and managers, manage to stay smiling through the ebb and flow of crowds off tour boats, whose passengers clamor for the delicious burgers or maybe hanker after salt cod sliders, typical of the invention on the dinner menu. Do not worry if you'd rather have a plate of ribs or something else equally familiar and loved.

Longtime summer resident and potter Marian Baker is often at work at her shop, Islesford Pottery (207-244-5686), on the dock near the restaurant.

The Islesford Historical Museum (207-244-9224) is a private collection of artifacts now maintained by Acadia National Park. It offers intriguing seasonal exhibits.

Great Cranberry has a larger year-round population of lobstermen—perhaps 40 brave souls. With a general store for sandwiches, a historical society, and a café for meals and ice cream, the island is its own attractive destination away from it all.

Swan's Island and Frenchboro

Attractions, activities, accommodations, eateries, etc.

Island Cruises (207-244-5785; bass harborcruises.com; Little Island Marine, Bass Harbor) offers narrated trips including one to Frenchboro, with 50 year-rounders, on the lookout for birds and sea creatures. Captain Kim Strauss's family bought the Philip Moore House, where Ruth Moore, a well-known author, was born—it was a general store and boardinghouse, too. A lot of Ruth Moore's writings are about the comings and goings of people, Strauss said, and her take on summer people was a little bitter. "Islands are very different from the mainland. There's a tension on islands." Year-round island communities have mostly disappeared off the coast of Maine with the advent of railroads and the end of oceangoing schooners, and Strauss can tell you this history.

The Maine State Ferry (207-244-3254) serves Frenchboro's Long Island, with its seasonal dockside deli and Frenchboro Historical Society.

Also reached by that ferry from Bass Harbor, Swan's Island requires either a car of your own or indefatigable legs and a bicycle. The high point of the year for many of its inhabitants is The Sweet Chariot Festival (sweetchariotmusicfestival .com), when folksingers and performers gather on the island to sing chantey concerts in the afternoon, perform nightly concerts, and carouse at parties. In 2012 Geoff Kaufman, Lisa Redfern and Randall Williams, Denny Williams, and Moira Smiley were just a few of the performers whose most distinctive moment came with the three-part harmony serenades of the schooners visiting just for this, sung from rowboats and kayaks in Burntcoat Harbor 4 miles from the ferry dock. Count on dancing, if not clogging, and impromptu music sessions. Carrying Place Market and Take-out (207-526-4043; 40 North Rd.) serves takeout pizza, seafood, and sandwiches.

Hancock and the Schoodic Area

Check out these great attractions, activities, and eateries

Nowhere in Maine does the coast change as abruptly as along the eastern rim of Frenchman Bay. On the western side is Mount Desert Island with Bar Harbor and Acadia National Park, a magnet for everyone from everywhere. The northern and eastern shores are, in contrast, a quiet, curving stretch of coves, tidal bays, and peninsulas, all with views of Acadia's high, rounded mountains.

These views continue all the way down the western shore of the Gouldsboro Peninsula. The 2,100-acre headland at its tip, a land finger known as the Schoodic Peninsula (acadia-schoodic.org), is part of Acadia National Park (nps.gov/acad/plan yourvisit/upload/schoodic.pdf). It's directly accessible late June through August by ferry from Bar Harbor (207-288-2984; barharborferry.com), with connecting bus service to trailheads and points of interest via the Island Explorer (207-288-4573; exploreacadia.com).

This is one place along the coast, however, where we suggest land over water. The drive around the bay is so glorious that it's been nationally recognized as the 29-mile Schoodic Scenic Byway (schoodicbyway.org). It begins on Rt. 1 at the Hancock/Sullivan bridge and follows Rt. 186 down along the western shore of the Gouldsboro Peninsula, then loops around Schoodic.

Biking Schoodic   Christina Tree

Weaver Susanne Grosjean at Hog Bay Pottery, Franklin   Christina Tree

From Sullivan the Schoodic Scenic Byway shadows the bay, offering spectacular views. The only detours we suggest here are for crafts studios, particularly thick right at the beginning, marked from the Sullivan Common. The Barter Family Gallery (207-422-3190; bartergallery.com), 2.5 miles down Taunton Bay Rd. from Rt. 1, is foremost among these. Philip Barter is nationally known for his bright, bold, and distinctive landscapes, sculpture, and furniture. The shop also features wife Priscilla's braided rugs, family-made jewelry, and cards. Lunaform (207-422-0932; lunaform.com), just off Taunton Rd., is also worth a stop to see

View of Frenchman's Bay from a pullout on the Schoodic Scenic Byway   Christina Tree

the distinctive garden urns (some huge); also pots and planters shaped in a former granite quarry. Farther east on Rt. 1, a quarter-mile detour up Rt. 200 brings you to Spring Woods Gallery (207-442-3007; springwoodsgallery.com), set in gardens. A visit to Hog Bay Pottery (207-565-2282; hogbay.com) is worth the extra 3 miles for Charles Crosjean's one-of-a-kind pieces and his wife Susanne's multicolored, hand-dyed and -woven rugs.

On Rt. 1 itself be sure to stop in Hancock's Sullivan Harbor Salmon (sullivan harborfarm.com) for a taste of the area's best smoked salmon, and in Sullivan at the scenic turnout just before Dunbar's Store for a spectacular view back across

Frenchman's Bay. Views continue as you follow Rt. 186 south, stopping at the Lee Glass Studio (207-963-7280), 3 miles south of Rt. 1. The former South Gouldsboro post office showcases Wayne Taylor's distinctive fused-glass tableware.

To find Winter Harbor turn right at the point Rt. 186 meets the bay. Until recently the village was home to a U.S. naval base that sent and intercepted coded messages from ships and submarines; it has also served a longtime summer community on neighboring Grindstone Neck. At the heart of the village the Winter Harbor 5 & 10 (winterharbor5and10.com) is the genuine article, filling multiple needs. Across the way J. M. Gerrish (207-963-7300) is the town gathering spot. Better known as "Gerrish's," open daily 8–5, the seasonal café serves up breakfast, lunch, and snacks, especially ice cream.

Farther along Main St., Works of Hand & Winter Harbor Antiques (207-963-7900) is set back behind a flowery, visitor-friendly garden. The two-story gallery showcases work by 50 of the area's quality craftspeople in a wide range of media.

Heading up Rt. 186 in the opposite direction, Littlefield Gallery (207-838-2156; 145 Main St.), is an exceptional contemporary gallery, with a mix of paintings and pieces by

Barter Family Gallery in Sullivan   Christina Tree

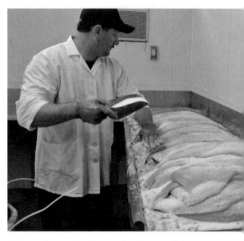

Salmon is smoked, sampled, and sold at Sullivan Harbor Salmon's Route 1 shop.

Christina Tree

prominent sculptors. Village food options include the chef-owned Fisherman's Inn Restaurant (207-963-5585; 7 Newman St.), and Chase's Restaurant (207-963-7171; 193 Main St.), open year-round for all three meals.

Allow anywhere from an hour to a day for the stunning shore road that loops around Schoodic Peninsula, mostly one-way. Frazier Point (restrooms) is a your first stop, the place to unload bikes if you want to tour on two wheels; ample picnic tables offer water views. A little more than 2.5 miles along the unmarked, unpaved road up to Schoodic Head may or may not be open. Visitors are encouraged to accesss the views from this rocky 400-foot high summit via hiking trails. Bear right at the intersection for Schoodic Point (this portion of the road is one-way). You can pick up a map and hiking advice at the Schoodic Education and Research Center (sercinstitute.org), occupying the navy's former 100-acre campus. Now a nonprofit

Schoodic section of Acadia National Park

learning center, SERC is geared to groups but open to the public for frequent lectures and special events. Rockefeller Hall, the staffed visitors center, includes displays on the park's history, its ecology, and the cryptologic operations carried on here between 1935 and 2002. Schoodic Point at the outer tip of the peninsula thrusts into the Atlantic, and on a sunny day tidal pools invite clambering. This

a popular spot to watch storms whip spray as high as 40 feet—but the surf can be deadly. A mile or so farther along, the Blueberry Hill Parking Area accesses most of the park's hiking trails.

Winter Harbor 5 & 10

The shore road continues northeast past Birch Harbor. Turn east on Rt. 186 to Prospect Harbor, a quiet fishing village from which Rt. 195 wanders off into the even quieter village of Corea. During the Schoodic Arts Festival (schoodicarts.com), the first two weeks of August, this entire area comes alive with dozens of arts and crafts workshops as well as performances. The festival underscores the abundance of local talent; check acadia-schoodic.org for details the many studios and galleries as well as lodging and dining. Following Rt. 186 north along the eastern side of the Gouldsboro peninsula, be sure to stop at U.S. Bells and Watering Cove Pottery (207-963-7284). Richard Fisher designs and casts bells that form musical sculptures, and Liza Fisher creates wood-fired stoneware and porcelain.

Back on Rt. 1 east, take the short signposted detour to Bartlett Winery and Spirits of Maine (207-546-2408; bartlettwinery.com). Open for tastings June through October, Tuesday through Saturday 1–5, this is Maine's oldest winery, nationally recognized for its fruit wines and brandies.

Checking In

Best places to stay in Hancock and the Schoodic area

A good base for forays to both Mount Desert Island and Schoodic, Ironbound (207-422-3395; ironboundinn.com; 1513 Rt. 1) offers five attractive rooms and suites on the quiet backside of the inn, overlooking tall pines. For many decades this was Le Domaine, known for its restaurant's genuine French fare. Now named for an island in Frenchman Bay, it's an informal bistro featuring local seafood, produce, brews, and spirits.

Crocker House Inn (207-422-6806; crockerhouse.com) is a genuine country inn at the center of an 1880s summer colony at Hancock Point. The 11 rooms are furnished with American antiques and quilts, and there's a comfortable living room as well as a den with TV (adjoining a room with

Crocker House offers lodging at the heart of an 1890s summer colony, Hancock Point.

Christina Tree

a hot tub). The dining room, open to the public, is known for steak, duck with Grand Marnier ginger sauce, and scallops in lemon and wine sauce. The inn is set in gardens, but water is a short walk in most directions.

On Rt. 1 in Sullivan the Island View Inn (207-422-3031; islandview innmaine.com) is a spacious, gracious 1880s summer mansion set well back from Rt. 1 with splendid views of Frenchman Bay and the mountains on Mount Desert. Farther along Rt. 1 in Gouldsboro, Acadia View Bed & Breakfast (866-963-7457; acadia view.com) is a contemporary mansion designed and built specifically as a B&B, with guest rooms facing Frenchman Bay. Three miles south of Rt. 1, Bluff House Inn (207-963-7805; bluff inn.com) off Rt. 186 in South Gouldsboro is a modern lodge with reasonably priced rooms, including a two-room efficiency, and common space overlooking the water. The beach below is good for launching kayaks.

View from breakfast at Oceanside Meadows Inn   Christina Tree

In Prospect Harbor, Elsa's Inn on the Harbor (207-963-7571; elsasinn.com; 179 Main St.) is a gabled, mid-1800s family homestead that Megan Moshier and her husband, Glenn, have totally renovated. The six bright guest rooms with handmade quilts have water views, as do the spacious living room and veranda. Lobster bakes can be arranged for in-house guests.

Beyond Prospect Harbor the hospitable Oceanside Meadows Inn (207-963-5557; oceaninn.com) is set in 200 acres webbed with trails leading to a salt marsh; wildlife includes moose and eagles. Sonja Sundaram and Ben Walter are passionate conservationists who offer trail guides to the guests checking in to their inn's 15 rooms, divided between an 1860s sea captain's home and a neighboring 1820s farmhouse, both overlooking Sand Cove. Breakfast is a multicourse event, featuring local ingredients. Check the website for details about the Oceanside Meadows Institute for the Arts and Sciences series of lectures and concerts.

Way Down East

WASHINGTON COUNTY
AND CAMPOBELLO ISLAND

Including Milbridge, Cherryfield, Machias, Eastport, and Lubec

BEYOND GOULDSBORO you enter Washington County, a ruggedly beautiful and lonely land unto itself. Its 700-mile coast harbors some of the most dramatic cliffs and deepest coves—certainly the highest tides—on the eastern U.S. seaboard, but relatively few tourists. Created in 1789 by order of the General Court of Massachusetts, Washington County is as large as the states of Delaware and Rhode Island combined. Yet it's home to less than 33,000 people, widely scattered among fishing villages, logging outposts, Native American reservations, and saltwater farms. Many people (not just some) survive here by raking blueberries in August, making balsam wreaths in winter, and lobstering, clamming, digging sea worms, harvesting sea cucumbers, and diving for sea urchins.

View from Lubec   Christina Tree

What happened along this particular coastline in prehistoric times has recently taken on new interest to scientists studying global warming. Apparently the ice sheet stalled here some 15,300 years ago, evidenced by the region's extensive barrens and number of bogs, eskers, and moraines.

The most recent development to affect travel to this area is, unfortunately, the

LEFT: Puffins on Machias Seal Island   Christina Tree

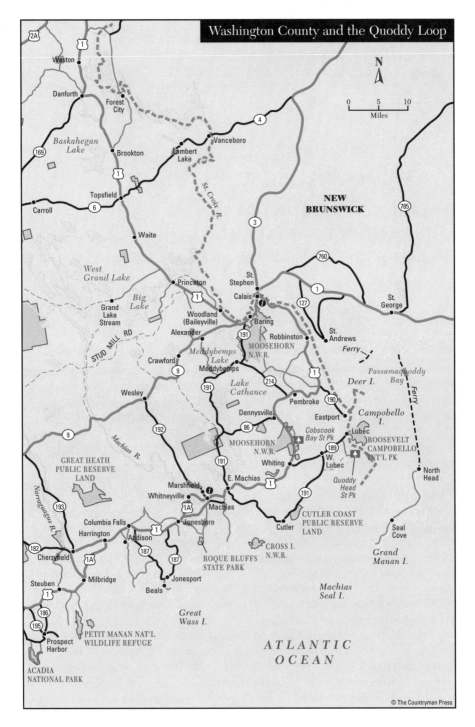

Washington County and the Quoddy Loop

requirement of passports or passport cards (see getyouhome.gov) to visit Roosevelt Campobello International Park (506-752-2922; fdr.net) just across the bridge from Lubec but technically in New Brunswick, Canada, from which it's separated by Passamaquoddy Bay.

We have divided Washington County into two sections: The Bold Coast; and Eastport, Cobscook, and Passamaquoddy Bays.

Cherryfield is a center for antiques shopping.
Christina Tree

The Bold Coast: Milbridge to Lubec

Check out these great attractions and activities . . .

Washington County produces 90 percent of the nation's blueberries and is the world's largest source of wild, lowbush berries, the kind that grow best on the undulating "barrens" that you see as you continue to drive east. These literally turn blue by August when they're harvested, then red in the fall. As you enter Milbridge note the JASPER WYMAN AND SONS sign on a vintage, white-clapboard building, offices for one of the oldest and largest blueberry processors. Beyond Milbridge, Rt. 1 threads the blueberry barrens for much of the next 30 miles. Before setting off through this bleakly beautiful landscape, you might want to stop here at 44 Degrees North (207-546-4440; 44-degrees-north.com; 17 Main St.), or at atmospheric Fisherman's Wife Café (207-546-7004; 11 School St.) hidden around the corner at the junction of Rt. 1 and 1A (BYOB). Millbrook House Restaurant (207-546-4454; 20 Main St.) is the place for breakfast, and Vazquez Mexican Takeout (207-598-8141; 38 Main St.) is the real thing.

Cherryfield General Store
Christina Tree

April Adams of Columbia Falls Pottery

Christina Tree

Ruggles House in Columbia Falls

Christina Tree

Blueberry Lane, Rt. 1, Columbia Falls

Christina Tree

The Milbridge Historical Society Museum (207-546-4471; milbridgehistorical society.org) has changing exhibits as well as displays on the town's vanished ship-yards and canneries.

From Milbridge, Rt. 1A is the shortest way east, but that way you miss Cherryfield, which styles itself "blueberry capital of the world" and is a growing antiques center with several shops clustered at the center of town by the Narra-guagus River. Be sure to make the quarter-mile detour off Rt. 1 into the village of Columbia Falls. At its center is the Ruggles House (207-483-4637; ruggleshouse

Sign at the Cherryfield General Store

Christina Tree

.org; open June to mid-October, Monday through Saturday for guided tours). This is a glorious Federal-style mansion built in 1818 with an exquisite flying staircase. Next door at Columbia Falls Pottery (207-483-4075; columbia fallspottery.com; 150 Main St.) April Adams makes striking, useful pottery as well as custom Delft-style tiles.

Jonesport (jonesport.com), 12 miles down Rt. 187 from Rt. 1, faces Moosabec Reach, which is, in turn, spanned by a bridge leading to Beals Island. Both communities are all about fishing and together boast eastern Maine's largest lobstering fleet. The bridge is a viewing stand for the annual July 4 lobster-boat races, and Beals is known for the distinctive design of its lobster boats. At the southern end of Beals, Great Wass Island offers 1,579 acres with trails maintained by The Nature Conservancy. On the eastern edge of Jonesport the Maine Coast Sardine History Museum (207-497-2962; 34 Mason Bay Rd.) is worth a stop.

Machias (207-255-4402; machiaschamber.org), 20 miles northeast of Jonesport, is the seat of Washington County, also home to a branch of the University of Maine. A center of colonial resistance during the Revolution, it was repeatedly burned—but somehow the 1770s Burnham Tavern (207-255-6930; burnham tavern.com) survived. It's just off Rt. 1 on Rt. 192, after you cross the bridge over Little Bad Falls. Downtown Machias comes alive during the Wild Blueberry Festival (third week of August), but otherwise it's a far cry from its early-19th-century days as a major shipbuilding and lumber port. Most motorists stop here to fill their tank and their stomachs. Sadly, Helen's Restaurant (helensrestaurant

Jonesport

Christina Tree

Never know what you'll find on the Dyke, Machias.   Christina Tree

Capt. Andy of the Bold Coast Charter
Company heading for Machias Seal Island

Christina Tree

machias.com), the town's landmark restaurant, burned to the ground in 2014, though plans call for it to reopen in 2015; check the website. Options include Blue Bird Ranch (207-255-3351; 78 Main St.), a capacious family restaurant with a large menu and portions and fried seafood.

East of Machias, Rt. 1 is a straight, heavily wooded road. It's 10 miles to Rt. 189 and another 11 to Lubec. Birders and hikers may want to turn off Rt. 1 in East Machias onto Rt. 191 to Cutler, departure point for Andrew Patterson's Bold Coast Charter Company (207-259-4484; boldcoast.com) tours to Machias Seal Island to see puffins (see the *Puffin-Watching* sidebar in "Basics"). Machias Seal is the only place you can actually view puffins on land; five-hour tours are offered, weather permitting, May to early August.

Captain Andy was the first to popularize the name *Bold Coast*, which is now used to promote a far larger area but originally applied just to the 20 miles of dramatically high cliffs between Cutler and West Quoddy Head. An extensive trail network along these cliffs is maintained by the Maine Bureau of Parks and Lands (207-287-4920; maine.gov/doc/parks); look for the CUTLER COAST UNIT TRAILS sign 4 miles east of town on Rt. 192. Other preserves maintained by the Quoddy Regional Land Trust (207-733-5509; qrlt.org) are spaced along the coast here. Rt. 191 turns inland at South Trescott to rejoin Rt. 1, but we usually continue

West Quoddy Light

Christina Tree

along the coast on Boot Cove Rd. for another half a dozen miles through open bar-rens to Quoddy Head State Park (207-733-0911; maine.gov/doc/parks).

Despite its name, the red candy-striped West Quoddy Head Light marks the easternmost tip of the United States. There are benches for those who come to be among the first in the country to see the sunrise (fog permitting), and there's a beautiful 2-mile Coastal Trail along the cliffs to Carrying Place Cove. The Keepers House (207-733-2180; westquoddy.com) doubles as the area visitors center (open Memorial Day to mid-October) and a museum, with displays that tell the story of the lighthouse, built in 1858.

McCurdy's Smokehouse, Lubec

Christina Tree

Northern Tides is one of several shopping finds in Lubec

Christina Tree

Lubec is half a dozen miles north of the lighthouse, linked by a short bridge to Campobello Island. Water St. here is transitioning from sardine cannery row to a lively lineup of shops and eateries. McCurdy's Smokehouse (207-733-2197; mccurdyssmokehouse. org; 50 Water St.) has been restored by Lubec Landmarks to evoke the era of smokehouses and canneries.

An unlikely catalyst for the town's current upswing is SummerKeys (summerkeys.com), a series of weeklong programs for a variety of instruments, begun in 1992 and still orchestrated by piano teacher Bruce Potterton. With no prerequisite skills, students fill local lodging places, and there are weekly concerts in local venues. Hundreds of musicians have discovered Lubec this way and passed the word along about the town with a wandering, 97-mile coast, reasonably priced real estate, and an end-of-the-world feel.

From Lubec it's an easy walk across Roosevelt Campobello International Bridge into New Brunswick, but this was an easier stroll before recent passport requirements. Don't try it these days without a passport or a passport card; still, there's rarely more than a few minutes' wait at either inspection station. In sum-

Roosevelt Cottage, Campobello Island

Christina Tree

mer, however, you lose an entire hour, given the fact that new Brunswick is on Atlantic Time, one hour ahead of Maine's Eastern Time.

If Campobello Island (campobello.com) were in the United States—as it would be except for an 1840s treaty badly negotiated by Daniel Webster—it would undoubtedly be far more crowded and less enjoyable. In 1881 much of the 9-mile-long island was sold to Boston and New York developers who built three large, now long-gone hotels. As happened from Kennebunkport to Bar Harbor, some wealthy families who patronized the hotels, the Roosevelts among them, built their own expansive summer "cottages." Franklin spent every summer here from 1883 (he was a year old) until 1921, when he was stricken with polio. He returned several times during his subsequent stints as governor and president, and Eleanor returned throughout her life.

The 2,800-acre Roosevelt Campobello International Park (877-851-6663; fdr.net; open daily, Memorial Day weekend through Columbus Day weekend), administered by a park commission composed of both Canadian and American members, was dedicated in 1964. The Visitors Centre here shows a 15-minute film dramatizing FDR's relationship to the island, and the exhibits focus not just on Roosevelt but also on his times. The neighboring 34-room Roosevelt Cottage is sensitively maintained as the family left it, charged with the spirit of a dynamic man and his equally dynamic wife, Eleanor. Inquire about afternoon "Tea with Eleanor," served in neighboring Hubbard Cottage. Beyond this immediate compound the park includes 8 miles of trails and 15.4 miles of park drives, modified from the network of carriage drives that the wealthy "cottagers" maintained.

The Hubbard Cottage is the setting for "Tea with Eleanor."   Christina Tree

There's more to Campobello than the park. Follow Rt. 174 north for Herring Cove Provincial Park (506-752-2449) with its nine-hole golf course, restaurant, pebble beach, and 76 campsites, 40 with electrical hookups (reservations: 506-752-7010). The big attraction at the end of this road is the striking East Quoddy Head Lighthouse (lighthousefriends.com), known locally as Head Harbour Light. Built in 1829 and recently restored by a dedicated local group of "Friends," it is accessible only at low tide and with care; the tide surges in quickly through the narrow channel that separates it from the headland—where a small park offers a great view not just of the lighthouse but frequently of whales, too. Local whale-watching cruises depart from Head Harbour Wharf, a couple of miles back down Rt. 174.

Checking In

Best places to stay along the Bold Coast

Given the distances covered in this section, we are listing our lodging choices as they appear geographically, from west to east. The Englishman's Bed and Breakfast (207-546-2337; english mansbandb.com; 122 Main St.), north of Milbridge in Cherryfield, is a beautifully restored four-square 1793 Federal-style mansion set above the Narraguagus River, with a wide back deck and screened gazebo. Kathy and Peter Winham offer two guest rooms in the house itself and a delightful "guesthouse" unit with a fridge and hot plate. A full breakfast is served by the 18th-century hearth

Hiking along the Bold Coast   Christina Tree

in the dining room. Cream teas are a specialty.

In Addison, south of Rt. 1, Pleasant Bay Bed & Breakfast (207-483-4490; pleasantbay.com) is a find, a spacious, contemporary house with many windows and a deck overlooking the tidal Pleasant River. Joan Yeaton grew up in the area and returned after raising six children, clearing this land and building the house with her husband, Leon. It's a working llama farm, and guests can meander the wooded trails down to the bay with or without the animals. The four reasonably priced upstairs rooms with water views include one family-sized room with private bath and a lovely two-room suite with a living room, kitchenette, and deck overlooking the water. There are moorings for guests arriving by water.

Micmac Farm Guesthouses and Gardner House (207-255-3008;

micmacfarm.com), off Rt. 92 in Machiasport, is a classic Cape, built by Ebenezer Gardner above the Machias River in 1776; it's also the oldest house in Machias and a real treasure. In summer guests are treated to a large, very private downstairs bedroom furnished in family antiques, with a deck overlooking the river. There are also three comfortable, well-designed housekeeping cabins, each with two double beds and river views.

The core of Riverside Inn (888-255-4344; riversideinn-maine.com) on Rt. 1, East Machias, dates from an 1805 house, but its heart—the first thing guests see—is a professional kitchen. Innkeepers Ellen McLaughlin and Rocky Rakoczy offer fine dining as well as two suites in the Coach House, with decks overlooking the river. There are also two nicely decorated upstairs guest rooms with private bath in the house.

West Quoddy Station (877-535-7414; quoddyvacation.com), the former U.S. Coast Guard station within walking distance of Quoddy Head State Park in South Lubec, has been transformed into six attractive units, nicely furnished with antiques, fitted with

Private guest area at Micmac Farm   Christina Tree

phones and TV; upstairs units offer sea views.

In Lubec, Peacock House (207-733-2403; peacockhouse.com; 27 Summer St.), a gracious 1860s house on a quiet side street, was home to four generations of the owners of the major local cannery; the three guest rooms and four suites, one handicapped accessible, are carefully, comfortably furnished. Up the hill Home Port Inn and Restaurant (207-733-2077; home portinn.com; 45 Main St.), another vintage mansion, offers seven tastefully decorated guest rooms and fine dining. Inn at the Wharf (207-733-4400; wharfrentals.com; 69 Johnson St.) was the town's last surviving sardine cannery, recently transformed into spacious suites and two-bedroom, two-

bath apartments, all right on the water. This is also the source of bicycle and kayak rentals.

Across the international bridge, The Owen House (506-752-2977; owenhouse.ca) is reason enough to come to Campobello. Built in 1835 by Admiral William Fitzwilliam Owen, son of the British captain to whom the island was granted in 1769, this is probably the most historic house on the island, and it's a beauty, set on a head-land overlooking Passamaquoddy Bay. Joyce Morrell, a watercolor artist who maintains a gallery here, has furnished the nine guest rooms (seven with private bath) with friendly antiques, handmade quilts, and good art. The ferry (see the sidebar on page 243) leaves from the neighboring beach.

Owen House, Campobello

Local Flavors

The taste of the Bold Coast—
local restaurants, cafés, and more

Dining-out options are few and far between along this lonely stretch of coast, so reservations are a must at Riverside Inn (see *Checking In*) in East Machias, open for dinner year-round. Specialties include lobster and scallops in champagne butter sauce, and fresh salmon stuffed with shrimp and crabmeat.

Lubec's Water Street Tavern (207-733-2477) has great views, atmosphere, and a menu studded with seafood and pasta. Neighboring Frank's Dockside (207-733-4484) is open for lunch as well as dinner with a deck, specializing in the evening in Italian veal and vegetarian classics as well as seafood, from fried clam baskets to crab-stuffed haddock. Fisherman's Wharf Restaurant (207-733-4400; 69 Johnston St.) is another prime spot for lobster, steamers, and local seafood, an attractive dining room walled in windows overlooking the water, part of the former sardine processing plant that's now the Inn on the Wharf. On Campobello Island the Fireside Restaurant (406-752-2922; 439 Rt. 774) is housed in the vintage 1916 log lodge built by Roosevelt cousins. Formerly Lupine Lodge, it has been renovated and is now owned/managed by the International Park and a good bet for dinner.

Head Harbour Light, Campobello Island
Christina Tree

In Lubec, Fisherman's Wharf is a former sardine cannery now offering waterfront lodging and dining.   Christina Tree

As they appear geographically, we have noted 44 Degrees North, Fisherman's Wife Café, Millbridge House Restaurant, and Vazquez Mexican Takeout in Milbridge, as well as Helen's Restaurant and Bluebird Ranch in Machias.

Eastport, Cobscook, and Passamaquoddy Bays

Check out these great attractions and activities . . .

Eastport (eastportchamber.net) is just 3 miles north of Lubec by boat but 43 miles by land around Cobscook Bay. *Cobscook* is said to mean "boiling water" in the Passamaquoddy tongue, and tremendous tides—a tidal range of more than 25 feet—seemingly boil

Fisherman statue in Eastport   Christina Tree

Music at Peavey Library, Eastport   Christina Tree

in, sloshing up deep inlets divided by ragged land fingers along the north and south shores.

Cobscook is itself an inlet of larger Passamaquoddy Bay on Eastport's eastern and northern shores. Here the surge of the tide is so powerful that in the 1930s President Roosevelt backed a proposal to harness its energy to electrify much of the northeastern coast. Recently turbines have been submerged off Eastport, a more modest experiment. Old Sow, a whirlpool between Eastport and Deer Island said to be 230 feet in diameter, is reportedly the largest in the Western Hemisphere.

Never know what you'll find at the 45th Parallel gift shop, Route 1 east of Eastport.
Christina Tree

Eastport consists entirely of islands, principally Moose Island, which is connected to Rt. 1 by Rt. 190 via a series of causeways (actually, tidal dams built in the 1930s for the failed tidal power project), linking other islands. It runs through the center of Sipayik, the Pleasant Point Indian Reservation home to some 700 members of the Passamaquoddy Indian tribe. It hosts the Waponahki Museum (207-853-2600; wabanaki .com) and three-day Indian Ceremonial Days in early August.

Eastport's wealth of Federal and Greek Revival architecture is a reminder that by the War of 1812 this was an important enough port for the British to capture and occupy; their former officers' quarters, now the Barracks Museum (74 Washington St.), houses the town historical collection. Sardine canning in Maine began in Eastport in 1875 and a boom era quickly followed, evoked in the hand-

Eastport Gallery   Christina Tree

Passamaquoddy sweetgrass baskets at The
Shop at the Commons, Eastport   Christina Tree

some brick commercial buildings along
Water St. Welcoming you to town at
the point Rt. 190 becomes Washington
St., Raye's Mustard Mill (207-853-
4451; rayesmustard.com) is another
holdover from that era, the country's
last remaining stone-ground-mustard
mill. The company has been in business since 1900 and today its mustard is Eastport's biggest export, sold
throughout the country.

The current population of this
island "city" is less than half what it
what was in 1900. Still, it remains a
"city" and a working deepwater port,
the deepest on the U.S. East Coast.
There are many gaps in the old waterfront, now riprapped in pink granite to
form a seawall. With its flat, haunting

Hugh French at the Tides Institute and
Museum of Art, Eastport   Christina Tree

light, Eastport has an end-of-the-world feel and suggests an Edward Hopper painting. It's a landscape that draws artists, and there are galleries along Water St. The
Commons (thecommonseastport.com; 51 Water St.) displays the works of more
than 90 Passamaquoddy Bay artists and artisans, including fabric art, carved burl
bowls, pottery, and the best selection of Passamaquoddy sweetgrass baskets. Also

check out The Eastport Gallery (207-853-4166; eastportgallery.com; 74 Water St.). The Tides Institute Museum of Art (207-853-4047; tidesinstitue.org; 43 Water St.) fills an 1880s bank building with a collection of amazing art and archival photographs focusing on Passamaquoddy Bay, as well as changing exhibits. The Eastport Arts Center (207-853-5803; eastportartscenter.com), housed in the vintage-1837 Washington Street Baptist Church, is home to half a dozen arts organizations and a venue for films, concerts, and live performances.

As much as anywhere in Maine, the thing to do here is to get out on the water. Passamaquoddy is a broad, delightful, island-spotted bay. You can explore it on the Ada C. Lore (207-853-2500; eastportwindjammers.com), a 118-foot Chesapeake Bay oyster schooner; aboard the Eastport Ferry (208-853-2635; eastportferry.com); or via the ferry to Deer Island (see the *Quoddy Loop* sidebar).

Checking In
Best places to stay in Eastport

Kilby House Inn (207-853-0989; kilbyhouseinn.com; 122 Water St.) is a Queen Anne–style house on the quiet end of the waterfront with an attractive double parlor that invites you to sit down and read. Innkeeper Gregg Noyes's passions include playing the organ and refinishing antiques. There are five pleasant upstairs guest rooms, including the sunny master with its four-poster canopy bed and water view, and two antiques-furnished rooms with private bath. Reasonable rates includes a very full breakfast. Upstairs at The Commons (207-853-4123; thecommon seastport.com) two second-floor, two-bedroom units overlooking the harbor are available by the week.

Local Flavors
The taste of Eastport—local restaurants, cafés, and more

Eastport Chowder House (207-853-4700; 167 Water St.), open seasonally for lunch through dinner, is on the bay, said to be the site of the country's first fish and sardine cannery. It's a good bet for lunch, from sandwiches to fish stews and lobster. It's possible to get takeout (and thus park in line) for the ferry that departs from the adjacent beach.

Quoddy Bay Lobster Co. (207-853-6640; 7 Sea St.) is hidden back behind the Tides Institute but well worth finding for its fabulous lobster

Seating at the Quoddy Bay Lobster Co., Eastport   Christina Tree

rolls drizzled with butter, fried clam rolls so thick you have to eat them with a fork, and great fish chowder. Order and eat overlooking the water at picnic tables.

The Quoddy Loop

Beyond Eastport you don't drop off the end of the world. On a sunny summer day when the car ferries are running, the crossing on Passamaquoddy Bay to New Brunswick is among the most scenic and satisfying in the East. **East Coast Ferries Ltd.** (877-747-2159; eastcoastferries.nb.ca), based on Deer Island, serves both Campobello Island (30 minutes) and Eastport (20 minutes). The ferries are modified tugs with long, hydraulically operated arms linked to barges. Passengers

The Algonquin is the region's grandest hotel.

Christina Tree

and bikes, cars, and even buses board on ramps lowered to the beach. Back in deep water the steel arm turns the barge, reversing direction. Service to Deer Isle is frequent and reasonably priced; most passengers continue on across the island and board the larger **New Brunswick Department of Transportation ferries** (506-453-3939). These make the 20-minute run, usually every half hour, to L'Etete, NB, handy to St. Andrews, New Brunswick's Bar Harbor, with great shopping, dining, and more lodging options than all of Washington County combined. The Algonquin Resort, a vintage-1890s grand hotel with a famous golf course and more than 230 rooms, recently reopened after sevral years' closure for total renovation. Most visitors stay at least a night in St. Andrews and, depending on the weather, drive or ferry back across the bay. This circuit has come to be called the **Quoddy Loop** (quoddyloop.com).

The New Friendly Restaurant (207-853-6610; Rt. 1, Perry), just beyond the turnoff for Eastport, is a homey restaurant with booths and food that's known as the best around: fish stews and chowders, basics like liver and onions, not-so-basics like an elegant crab salad and the most lobster in a lobster sandwich. Beer and wine served.

WaCo Diner (207-853-9226, 47 Water St.) is Eastport's landmark eatery, with a water view and much improved under new ownership.

Raye's Mustard Mill and Pantry (207-853-3351; Rt. 190). Sample the many varieties of mustard in the Pantry, where soup and sandwiches are also served. Tours of the mustard mill are offered year-round, daily on the hour (except the lunch hour).

Index